Cross-cultural perspectives on educational research

Conducting educational research

Series Editor: Harry Torrance, Manchester Metropolitan University

This series is aimed at research students in education and those undertaking related professional, vocational and social research, It takes current methodological debates seriously and offers well-informed advice to students on how to respond to such debates. Books in the series review and engage with current methodological issues, while relating such issues to the sorts of decisions that research students have to make when designing, conducting and writing up research. Thus the series both contributes to methodological debate and has practical orientation by providing students with advice on how to engage with such debate and use particular methods in their work. Series authors are experienced researchers and supervisors. Each book provides students with insights into a different form of educational research while also providing them with the critical tools and knowledge necessary to make informed judgements about the strengths and weaknesses of different approaches.

Cross-cultural perspectives on educational research

Anna Robinson-Pant

Open University Press

Open University Press
McGraw-Hill Education
McGraw-Hill House
Shoppenhangers Road
Maidenhead
Berkshire
SL6 2QL

e-mail: enquiries@openup.co.uk
world wide web: www.openup.co.uk

and Two Penn Plaza, New York, NY 10121-2289, USA

First Published 2005

A catalogue record of this book is available from the British Library

ISBN-13   978 0335 21456 3 (pb)   978 0335 21457 0 (hb)
ISBN- 10   0 335 21456 8 (pb)   0 335 21457 6 (hb)

Library of Congress Cataloging-in-Publication Data
CIP data applied for

Typeset by RefineCatch Ltd, Bungay, Suffolk
Printed in Poland by OZ Graf. S.A. www.polskabook.pl

Contents

Acknowledgements

As soon as you start reading this book, you will see the influence of the research community in CARE from whom I have learnt so much over the past four years. I would like to thank the following people who have contributed to the writing of this book – indirectly, through our weekly research methods seminars or supervision meetings, and directly, through written reflections, interviews and comments on the first draft of this book: Azhar bin Md. Adnan, Dekheel Al-Bahadel, Yousef Al-Maini, Ayedh Al-Motairi, Huda Al-Yousef, Judith Castaneda-Mayo, Hasani Dali, Hisham Dzakiria, Marta Einarsdottir, John Elliott, Tekleab Elos, Steve Fairbrass, Chris Karakoidas, Zuber Hassan, Othman Lebar, Ted Liu, Manal Madini, Howida Mahmoud, Dominic Mensah, Halim Abdul Mohammed, Scholastica Mokake, Noralf Mork, Terry Phillips, Asmahan Abd. Razak, Alan Rogers, Karim Sadeghi, Anna Sallnow, Ken Takaira, Steve Thacker, Tesfay Tsegay, Rob Walker.

For the past decade or so, the 'cross-cultural' has been a big part of my everyday life and conversations with my husband, Mahesh Pant, and children, Ben and Anita, as we have moved between cultures in Nepal and the UK. Mahesh's insights and comments on the book – both as a former international student and providing a more critical perspective on our shared experiences in Nepal – have added a greater complexity to my analysis. My interest in this area also originates in my own experience as a research student at the University of Sussex where my supervisor, Brian Street, engaged us in a continuous process of reflection on our academic literacy practices. Brian's research in the area of academic literacies has continued to influence my learning – but even more so, his approach to teaching, as I model my current practice on his role as supervisor. Almost too late in this particular journey, I met Anna Magyar, whose ideas on the first draft and her own work on the 'cross cultural' in educational research sent me off in exciting new directions.

Finally, I would like to thank Maggie MacLure for the idea of turning my weekly PhD seminar reports into a book, even though it wasn't quite as easy as she suggested ('just put them between two covers'). As commissioning editor, Harry Torrance has helped shape that process, from the proposal to the finished book.

Anna Robinson-Pant
February 2005

In memory of Terry Phillips

List of acronyms and abbreviations

CARE	Centre for Applied Research in Education
CLT	communicative language teaching
EALP	English for Academic Legal Purposes
ELT	English Language Teaching
ICT	Information and Communications Technology
ISs	international students
IT	information technology
MSRT	Ministry of Research, Science and Technology (Iran)
OHP	overhead projector
OME	Organization for the Measurement of Education (Iran)
PGCE	Postgraduate Certificate in Education (UK)
TEFL	Teaching of English as a Foreign Language
TESL	Teaching of English as a Second Language
TESOL	Teaching of English to Speakers of Other Languages
UEA	University of East Anglia

Introducing a cross-cultural perspective on the PhD research process

Introduction

How critical is critical?

Should I write two theses or one? My employer might not like the kind of thesis my supervisor encourages me to write.

Saying 'I' in my home culture might be seen as being self-centred.

Questions and issues such as these raised by international students[1] in research methods seminars have led me to write this book. As a PhD supervisor and examiner in a UK university, I have become increasingly aware of my underlying assumptions about what makes 'good' educational research through discussions with students who hold differing values and practices. All too often, however, these contrasting perspectives come to the fore only when a student is defending their thesis at a viva, trying to find a response to the examiner who says their work is 'too descriptive' or 'too prescriptive' and 'not critical enough'. As an examiner, I have had to guard against my tendency at that stage to focus on the text, the PhD thesis as the end-product, as opposed to finding other ways of assessing the PhD as a process of learning how to do research. In the context of educational research, it is particularly important to explore how the thesis may be shaped not just by the students' assumptions about the nature of knowledge and research, but also by their own experiences of education. Relationships between the teacher and student before and during a PhD course may influence whether a student feels he or she can 'be critical' and also what 'being critical' might mean in a new cultural context.

Over the past decade, the research student population of many higher education institutions has expanded to include students from a wider range of cultural and educational backgrounds. However, training courses on research methods and many texts on research methodologies are still directed at the traditional UK student population, assuming an initial shared understanding around key issues in the research process, such as ethics or the need to be critical. International students in particular often begin a PhD course in education without realizing the adjustment they will be expected to make. As well as learning to use different registers of written and spoken English, they will constantly have to re-examine their beliefs and practices, questioning what learning and what research should look like in this new context. From the supervisor's perspective, such students may appear frustratingly slow to adjust to the research process – expecting to be 'spoon-fed', writing stiff, depersonalized, formalized accounts of their projects or even plagiarizing published work.

In this book, I explore some of the methodological differences arising between supervisors and their students from contrasting cultural backgrounds. Drawing on discussions between research students, as well as their written reflections, the book traces not just the adjustment that international students (and to a similar extent, 'non-conventional' home students) begin to make, but also raises new issues around the research process that bring into question the assumptions of all those engaged in educational research. By participating in this dialogue between research students and their supervisors, I hope that you as reader will be encouraged to reflect critically on your own research practices and to question the boundaries of what is considered to be 'good' academic research.

For those readers less familiar with qualitative research (particularly ethnographic case study), I should explain that my account is not intended to be representative of other UK higher educational contexts, nor even of the University of East Anglia where I am employed. As will soon become apparent, my specific context as a lecturer in the Centre for Applied Research in Education (CARE) at the University of East Anglia has influenced how I approached the task of writing this book, as well as being reflected in the material (both theoretical and empirical) on which I base my analysis. CARE's unique and often controversial history of experimentation with qualitative research methodologies, encompassing action research, democratic evaluation and discourse analysis, therefore forms the backdrop to this book. Some readers may find this problematic, as my analysis of the 'culture clash' between international students and CARE could be seen to parallel that between CARE and UK policy makers or conventional educational researchers at the time when Stenhouse established this Centre.[2]

Origins of this book

My own interest in 'cross-cultural perspectives on educational research' pre-dates my current role as lecturer and researcher in CARE. I have spent much of my professional life in Nepal, learning about different approaches to research and education as part of my work with international and local development organizations. Like the international students with whom I now work in the UK, I was constantly aware of the need to adapt my practices to a differing context and at times to question values that I had taken for granted. In particular, what I considered to be good research (in the development project context, the term 'research' was used often synonymously with 'evaluation') was not necessarily shared by my colleagues. On a practical level, I was struggling to communicate in a second language (Nepali), learning to switch between registers as I worked with communities in the rural areas or with government officials in Kathmandu.

There was, however, an important difference between my experience in Nepal and that of international students in the UK: my higher status as an 'ex-pat'. As a development worker with various aid agencies, I was frequently regarded as an expert transferring Western approaches that could be used in place of local indigenous practices – whether new ideas about health practices or even an ideology of equal gender relations. For me, this was probably the hardest challenge of living and working in another culture: how to resist imposing your views, yet also not to be reluctant to state your values ('not to suspend your moral code'; Devereux and Hoddinott 1992a: 19). In some cases, this was a dilemma common to many researchers: whether to stop being a passive observer and intervene on 'moral' grounds when, for example, a teacher beat a young child for not listening (a common practice in Nepali schools, defended by some as a 'cultural' difference). The more ambiguous cases, however, were around our differing assumptions about the purpose of research: trying to explain that the reason why I could not give someone 'a case study' for the aid agency's annual report was that the 'cases' that I had collected were not chosen to illustrate good practice but to analyse critical issues that I observed. At times, I failed to understand the differences in our approach to evaluation. For example, when I commented negatively on a teacher's performance on a supervisor's form, I was told that I should have given these suggestions verbally and filled in the form with descriptive details (such as how many students had pencils). When I look back at these instances, I realize how difficult it must be for international students to learn the subtleties of how to be critical in another culture or to understand what might be different about their way of conducting research. I am also aware that many of the misunderstandings that arose about our differing expectations of the research process and text could also be related to the interface between academic and policy-oriented research 'cultures'.

As a novice teacher and researcher going to work in Nepal for the first time in 1985 (with the British volunteer agency, Voluntary Service Overseas), I was helped to make these transitions by the provision of training courses in cultural adaptation, when many of the rules about differing behaviour were made explicit. This advice was usually at the level of 'do's and don'ts' (such as not to point the soles of your feet at someone, as this is insulting), but sometimes also included the reasons for differing beliefs (such as why certain foods were eaten for certain illnesses). As a researcher later in my career, I was also able to draw on an extensive literature produced originally by anthropologists going to work in 'alien' lands in the form of fieldwork diaries (see, for instance, Rabinow 1977). In an attempt to demystify the fieldwork process (which was often seen as a rite of passage), anthropologists later began to produce manuals introducing and explaining the research methods they used in developing country contexts (e.g. Ellen 1984). More recently, researchers have written reflectively about wider issues that arise when conducting research in differing cultures – taking into account the difficulties of communicating in another language and adopting a more culturally sensitive approach (see Vulliamy *et al.* 1990; Devereux and Hoddinott 1992b). All these texts were written with the 'ex-pat' researcher in mind, with the emphasis on how to adapt your methods and your identity to fit the new cultural context in the 'field'. Although a chapter by an Iranian researcher conducting fieldwork in Iran is included in Devereux and Hoddinott's volume, Razavi (1992) points out that as a middle-class urban woman, she is also partly regarded as an outsider in the village context.

International students in UK higher education: a research perspective

Relating my experiences as a newcomer in Nepal to those of international students starting a PhD in the UK, I am struck by the relative lack of literature relating to their perspective as 'outsiders' in an unfamiliar educational system. In the Australian context, there is a longer established body of research about international students (see www.canberra.edu.au/QPR). The few UK studies that did focus on international students in the past tended to take a deficit approach, seeing them as a group with special needs and writing primarily for an audience of British academics. Commenting on the common viewpoint in the literature that 'students were in need of and dependent on the knowledge and education that we in Britain could provide', Elsey and Kinnell (1990: 2), for instance, describe how their research project started in this context. Though they 'couldn't avoid a problem-centred focus', their research explored how students' needs could be met through 'problem solving approaches to teaching, learning, inter-cultural communication and effective policies of infrastructure support' (p. 6). Several years on, McNamara and Harris (1997: 3), discussing the 'ever growing body of literature on research and teaching in higher education', point out that there is 'little mention of overseas students and the special problems that they present when studying in the UK environment'. Though their book includes collaborative pieces written by international students with their supervisors comparing their differing educational practices (Chan and Drover 1997; Cortazzi and Jin 1997), it is surprising that the dominant academic discourse on international students has barely changed over the decades.

Even the acknowledgement that international students are valuable clients (and so deserve an improved service) has not challenged the practice of writing about this group of people for an audience of UK (or Australian) professionals, rather than for students themselves [Ballard and Clanchy's (1984) *Study Abroad* is an exception]. However, the contrasting perspectives put forward by international students, for example on the difference between repetitive learning and rote learning, can provide lecturers with greater insight into differing ways of interpreting students' attitudes towards education: 'So while Westerners may correctly see Asian students as being preoccupied with a high degree of repetitive work, they may be wrong in seeing that activity as rote learning and as a surface learning strategy' (Chan and Drover 1997: 55). Biggs (2003: 127) deconstructs these cultural stereotypes as 'myths' (such as 'they are passive, they won't talk in class' or 'they don't understand what plagiarism means'), and gives an alternative 'slant' on so-called 'cultural' learning-based problems. He distinguishes three perspectives on teaching across cultures: teaching as assimilation (level 1), teaching as accommodation (level 2) and teaching as educating (level 3). Referring to the first two levels as 'deficit approaches', and level 3 as a 'contextual approach' (p. 138), he points to the importance of 'focusing on getting students to learn' (p. 124) and seeing 'cultural' differences in the widest context, including the cultural gap between university and school. In their analysis of the transition from the 'conserving' attitudes to knowledge in the Anglo-Australian primary school to the 'extending' attitudes at university, Ballard and Clanchy (1997: 12) present a model of the 'influence of cultural attitudes to knowledge on teaching and learning strategies' that emphasizes the parallel experiences learning about new cultures of learning of both international students and home students. Their book, *Teaching International Students*, starts from the premise that 'many of the difficulties international students experience in their study derive not from "poor English" . . . but from a clash of educational cultures' (p. viii).

Ballard and Clanchy's (1997) book marks a shift within the literature towards seeing the problems encountered by international students and teaching staff 'as a basis for positive change' (p. ix). Recent action research conducted by teachers in higher education (see articles in Ryan and Zuber-Skerritt 1999; Ryan 2000; Wisker 2000) has emphasized the importance of being 'prepared to explore ways of changing your teaching and learning practices' in order to value and respond to the differing cultural practices of students in the classroom (Ryan 2000: 3).[3] Despite the attention to differences in learning styles in the literature, little is mentioned about creating knowledge and how research (or teaching) is evaluated.

Comparing this small body of work on overseas or international students to recent literature on 'academic literacies' (see Candlin and Hyland 1999; Lea and Stierer 2000; Lea and Street 2000), I am aware of the very different research approach and tone adopted. The reflective articles on the experiences of newcomers to the Academy (whether mature students or new undergraduates) are written not just with tutors or supervisors in mind, but with and for the students themselves. Rather than adopting a 'how to fix it' approach for either students or teachers, the authors attempt to juxtapose these differing perspectives and raise critical questions about how the learning process could be more effective for both parties. Written as a dialogue between the two viewpoints of adult learner and researcher of academic literacies, Ivanic and Weldon's (1999) chapter, for instance, raises issues about power and ownership of text, both in its content and form as a collaborative piece of writing. Academic literacies researchers take as their starting point the idea that: 'writing in higher education is a social practice which is embedded in the values, relationships and institutional discourses constituting the culture of academic disciplines in higher education' (Lea and Stierer 2000: 2). Adopting this stance has pedagogical implications, suggesting 'a wider institutional approach to student writing, rather than merely locating problems with individual students' (Lea and Street 2000: 31). This approach recognizes, above all, that cross-cultural communication ('culture' in its widest sense) is an integral part of learning and teaching and higher education. As Ballard and Clanchy (1988: 8) observed: 'most student "illiteracy" is the result of a misreading of the culture'.

My purpose in discussing the academic literacies researchers' focus on how students learn what counts as 'good' academic work is to highlight the ways in which a similarly explicit ideological stance could enhance the research on international students' experiences. This might involve analysing how 'good research' is constructed within the discourse of the UK academy, in a similar way to that of 'good academic literacy'. Implicit in this account would be the inevitable power dimensions of that relationship between tutor and student, UK and overseas institutions – which in most accounts have remained unexamined. It is worth noting that the body of research on academic literacy, though emphasizing the hierarchical relationships between professional and academic discourses (for instance) or lay person/academic literacy practices, has rarely focused on the inequalities around culture identified most closely with post-colonial research. As I will discuss later, by defining 'culture' in broader terms than the literature on international students does (which often focuses on 'differences in ethnicity between home and university cultures'; Biggs 2003: 121), academic literacy researchers sometimes appear to have overlooked the differences implicit, for example, between a higher educational institution in the UK and one in Tanzania. Ivanic and colleagues' (2000) study of writing courses in these two contexts, for instance, makes little distinction between them – only in institutional terms, rather than an analysis taking into account any differing ideological values.

The origins of this book lie, therefore, in an attempt to start a more equal debate about research methodologies and processes from the perspective of international students in the UK. I intend to draw on the philosophy and methods of the academic literacies approach. This is partly because of my background in this area of literacy research, but also because I see this as a way of making visible the hierarchical institutional relationships that have shaped discourses around international research students. In the next section, I explore some of the differences between my approach and that of academic literacy researchers. As I mentioned earlier, these relate in particular to the concepts of 'cross-cultural' and the consideration of PhD research as a wider social practice encompassing more than academic literacy practices.

Unpacking 'cross-cultural'

> The 'other' is never outside or beyond us: it emerges forcefully within cultural discourse when we *think* we speak more intimately and indigenously 'between ourselves'.
>
> (Bhabha 1990: 4)

I will begin by looking more closely at the term 'cross-cultural' as I am aware that in the context of international students, there can be a tendency to essentialize the 'culture' of the students involved (whether 'Chinese', 'Kenyan' or 'Indian' culture). As Magyar (1996: 16) warns in the parallel context of comparative educational research, 'by and large, an ethnocentric view of "cross-cultural" has been promoted'. Rather than using the term 'cross-cultural' to polarize the relationship between 'us' and 'the other', I want to explore the more complex interplay of identities implicit in any educational setting (as suggested by Bhabha's comment above). The literature on international students reveals this tension between the desire to fix cultural identity (for example, analysing the specific learning styles of Chinese students), as well as the recognition that there is diversity within cultures or that differences between the UK and overseas contexts may be 'generational' rather than 'cultural'. For example, Dudley-Evans and Swales (1980), analysing the study modes of students from the Middle East, note the similarities with English students of twenty years before, when they ask: 'Is it a difference in social, moral, ideological codes or little more than a generation gap?' (p. 92). Another chapter in the same book points to the possibility that the students who come to the UK are atypical (as compared to other people in their home context), in that they wish to develop other learning styles: 'the student who comes from an "exotic culture" may not reflect the values of that culture' (James 1980: 14).

Defining 'cross-cultural' in the UK higher educational context

As the home student population has diversified to include a wider cross-section of UK society, the apparently differing educational needs of international students have been brought into question. Todd (1997: 178) warns against the tendency to assume that the needs of home and 'overseas' students differ, suggesting that this is 'to ignore the cultural complexities of the UK and the fact that we can find evidence of the whole range of attitude-to-knowledge continuum in our own country, within institutions and between institutions and disciplines'. We can see that the term 'cross-cultural' here could refer to several different aspects of the international student's experience as a researcher, entering new 'cultures' within higher educational institutions and within diferent academic disciplines. As I mentioned earlier, research on academic literacies has revealed the extent to which academics in higher education too readily assume that new students (both international and 'home') will be familiar with the academic discourse of that institution.

Within this book, I am particularly concerned to analyse the international student's experience in this wider context of becoming part of a new 'community of practice' (Lave and Wenger 1991) in higher education. As Candlin and Hyland (1999: 15) comment in the Australian context, 'A substantial part of the writing competence of a "professional" or legitimate member of such a community is held to involve familiarity with its conventional discursive forms and the ability to exploit these effectively in his or her writing'. From the angle of the research student, adopting a cross-cultural perspective involves analysis of research as a social practice within the culture of higher educational institutions. While the literature on international students has discussed the cultural differences between the UK academy and, for instance, Chinese higher education (see Cortazzi and Jin 1997), there is also a corresponding recognition of the diversity of 'cultures' within higher education in each country context. In relation to the 'academic socialization approach' to student writing, Lea and Street (2000: 35) critique the notion of the Academy as a 'relatively homogeneous culture, whose norms and practices have simply to be learnt to provide access to the whole institution'. Academic practices may differ greatly within any one individual institution: 'disciplines are like cultures in that their members have shared, taken for granted beliefs' (Myers in Candlin and Hyland 1999: 12).

As well as cultural differences between disciplines, there are also often differences within disciplines – particularly in education, which attracts such a wide range of practitioners (including, for instance, health professionals) with quite contrasting research approaches and assumptions. As academic literacy researchers emphasize, there is a need for students to be addressed as 'novice members' of the academic community (Lea and Street 1999: 64), to begin to explicate the cultural norms and practices specific to an institution and even to a particular course. Sandeman-Gay (1999: 46) notes these pedagogical implications in relation to her research with Iranian students: 'The notion that academic discourse is context-specific and is ideologically and culturally constructed . . . poses a number of linguistic, cognitive and ethical issues for supervisors'.

Whose culture dominates?

Taking a cross-cultural perspective on postgraduate research implies a similar continuous movement between being an outsider and insider (of a 'culture'), as I have just discussed in relation to academic literacy practices. Lea and Stierer (2000: 5) refer to this task of documenting the 'texture of everyday practices of academic literacies' as 'contributing to the collective enterprise of creating an "ethnography of the disciplines"'. In the context of doctoral research, I am aware that it can be easier to focus on the insider/outsider issues around the writing process (whether 'writing up' or writing fieldnotes; see Sanjek 1990) than to begin to analyse the 'doing' of research as a cultural practice. This could be related to observations that international students' difficulties in communication are often said (by tutors and students) to be around 'language problems' (Hawkey and Nakornchai 1980), disguising the fact that the issue may be more to do with differences in academic practices or assumptions about research processes. As an Italian postgraduate commented, 'We used language as an alibi. There were other difficulties of communication, but we blamed language' (Barker 1997: 117). Analysing PhD fieldwork as a social practice might expand the usual debate about English language difficulties to involve consideration of how students choose to prioritize spoken and written accounts within their research as a whole. In the UK context of ethnographic research on interaction in a psychiatric hospital, Barrett (1999: 246) identifies the 'common assumption [by staff] that seeing was primary and writing up was a secondary reflection of that primary reality'. This assumption contrasts with the privileging of written texts in academic discourse and could help us to analyse how fieldwork interactions are shaped by the end goal of the thesis. As I discuss later in this book, new international students in my own department faced the challenge of how to bring together their immersion in an unfamiliar research culture (in CARE) with their formal learning about new methods through written texts.

The 'clash' that Stierer (2000) identifies between professional and academic cultures – and the privileging of academic practices within research on professional areas – has been particularly evident in the field of educational research. Stierer describes how teachers enrolling on an MA course 'to enhance their effectiveness and/or status within the professional culture of school teaching' discover that 'the discursive practices of the academy position them as novice academics' (p. 193). He explains the 'clash between the professional culture of school teaching and the (higher status) professional culture of the academy' in terms of the 'way that institutions of higher education use language to sustain and legitimate an epistemological hegemony' (ibid.). The contrasting cultural perspectives of UK teachers and higher education teachers in his account highlight the power dimensions, which sometimes remain only in the background of discussions about how international students engage with UK academic institutions.

Rather than regarding 'cross-cultural' perspectives as simply a question of diversity, we need to recognize the hierarchical relationships that determine who decides which research practices are legitimate within a doctoral course of study. Research like that of Stierer (2000), which looks at the interface between professional and academic discourses, provides a useful starting point for my exploration into differing values and viewpoints on the PhD process. It is not just about improving 'cross-cultural' communication (a common emphasis within writing on international students' experience in higher education; see Trahar 2003), but also about acknowledging that differing professional and academic cultures may emphasize and value quite contrasting research practices.

The cross-cultural in relation to 'international' educational research and researchers

I began this section with an exploration of 'cross-cultural' in relation to the UK higher education 'non-conventional' home student population, in order to move away from the concept of 'culture' as a fixed entity and the idea that international students face only one kind of cultural adjustment. Taking an analogy with Gee's (1990) analysis of 'Discourses' as compared to 'discourses',[4] Culture with a big 'C' is what first comes to mind when we talk about international students. But, as I hope to explore in this book, culture with a small 'c' comes into play in this context too, as international students encounter both new and familiar cultures within UK higher education. We can tend to assume that everything is 'new' and different in the UK system, thus overlooking opportunities for building on international students' previous experience. Many students, however, come from countries whose education systems may have originally been modelled on that of their colonizers – so some elements may be familiar, whereas other aspects have evolved in a different way. A British Council study highlights this experience of moving between two academic cultures: 'how overseas students mediate the two academic cultures they experience – the culture in which they have learned how to succeed and the one in which they hope to succeed' (James 1980: 11).

Street (1999a: 55) distinguishes between 'culture as a process' and 'culture as fixed, race-like': he sees culture 'as a verb' rather than as a noun. I have found this distinction useful for analysing the literature on international students: to what extent do these writers see 'culture as a verb' rather than as a set of characteristics associated with the group of students from outside the UK? As Magyar (1996: 23) comments (in relation to a comparative study between UK and Soviet classrooms), 'culture is the unproblematic commonality shared between the writer and his British audience'. In my own research, both in Nepal and now in the UK with groups of students from different country contexts, I have been interested in how 'culture' (as a noun) is often set up as a barrier to prevent further critique or discussion. For example, in many research studies on girls' lack of access to schooling in remote areas of Nepal, the term 'cultural barriers' has been used to explain exclusion due to restricted mobility, parental opposition, early marriage and language difficulties, thus preventing a more complex and integrated analysis of these very different factors.

As Magyar (1996: 31) reflects, the methodological challenge facing comparative educational researchers lies in the question: 'how can comparison across cultures be used . . . in a way that enhances and enriches meaning rather than acting reductively, merely confirming cultural stereotyping, reiterating socio-historical differences?' In the context of our university research student seminars, I remember a PhD student from Malaysia who when presenting on his research into physical education in schools was interrogated by other students as to why the girls had to wear veils in a PE lesson. His initial reply was that this was a 'cultural difference'. As facilitator of the seminar, I felt uneasy about pursuing the implications of this 'cultural difference' further (particularly in my position as a Western female academic) – though eventually an interesting debate about our differing cultural perspectives emerged (see concluding section of Chapter 4).

How far we can generalize about the group known as 'international students' is a question raised by those keen to 'fix' cultural attributes. As Barker (1997: 112) notes, 'overseas students come from such a variety of backgrounds that they may not have much more in common than that they are students and come from overseas'. Nevertheless, there have been many attempts to categorize students into different cultural types, notably those with 'collectivist' cultures (as opposed to individualistic) and to generalize about prevalent learning styles. An example is Elsey's (1990: 54) observation that 'Arab students seemed uninterested in the discussion approach'. These cultural stereotypes are closely related to preconceptions about how students behave in the classroom, particularly the assumption that lack of response may be interpreted as 'passivity' on the part of South Asian students. As Elsey and Kinnell (1990: 2) suggest, these generalizations are then applied to all 'overseas' students, who are said not to 'respond easily to discussion methods when being taught. There was a reliance on rote learning, together with excessive deference to teachers'. It is noticeable that some of the students' own accounts start from these cultural stereotypes. An example is the reconstructed dialogue between a Thai student and a British Council officer where Nakornchai puts forward characterizations of the typical Thai student 'as patient and tolerant' in an education system where 'students tend to be spoon-fed, generally accepting a fairly passive role in the teaching/ learning process' (Hawkey and Nakornchai 1980: 73), then gives the reasons behind this appearance. In my own teaching, I have also found that students are often eager to generalize about 'their' culture, referring to 'we Saudi Arabians', rather than emphasising that even within our seminar group, individual Saudi students from differing backgrounds often hold contrasting beliefs. This may relate to the discussion of 'face' (see Todd 1997; Ryan 2000; Lie 2004) – that it is more important to avoid direct conflict between classmates and teacher, than to encourage criticism that might embarrass a colleague in public. I will return to this point in later chapters in the context of 'being critical'.

Moving away from cross-cultural as comparison

Though it is easy to dismiss cultural generalizations and stereotypes, I am aware that within my own field of international and comparative education, much research has been based on comparisons between the UK and 'other' educational cultures. Such accounts were often 'driven by empiricist notions of comparison' (Magyar 1996: 16). Comparative education has now begun to respond to the challenges of post-colonial writers who question 'the implicit values, analytic assumptions and over-generalisations that underpin such "dualistic" classifications in principle (Tikly 1999)' (Crossley and Watson 2003: 8). Some writers have also identified globalization as a 'threat' to the field of comparative education – in that the central assumption is that 'education systems are set up and run by individual nation states and that this is the basis of their difference' (Dale in Vulliamy 2004: 262).

Interestingly, Crossley and Watson (2003: 9) discuss the terms 'comparative' and 'international' education more in relation to 'two distinctive communities – those that have tended to specialise in detached, comparative study (often of Western industrial nations) and those whose primary interests lie in "international" educational policy and practice and active involvement in the direct experiences of developing countries'. The distinction made between practitioners and theorists, in relation to the ' "comparativists" who saw their work as less directly practical in nature than that of the "internationalists" '(ibid.) can perhaps contribute more to our understanding of culture with a small 'c' (than Culture with a capital 'C') within this book. The differing cultural practices and values of various academic communities could be analysed in a similar way to this distinction between the comparativist and internationalist research communities.

Post-colonial writers have increasingly drawn attention to the impossibility of comparing one culture with another: 'The very concepts of homogenous national cultures, the consensual or contiguous transmissions of historical traditions, or "organic" ethnic communities – *as the grounds of cultural comparativism* – are in a profound process of redefinition' (Bhabha 1994: 5). Bhabha goes on to discuss the 'way in which cultures recognise themselves through their projections of "otherness" ' (p. 12) and makes a key distinction between cultural difference and cultural diversity: 'Cultural diversity is an epistemological object – culture as an object of empirical knowledge – whereas cultural difference is the process of the *enunciation* of culture as *"knowledgeable"*, authoritative, adequate to the construction of systems of cultural identification' (p. 34). Within the discourse of globalization, the corresponding shift towards recognizing diversity has meant that minority rights groups, like the Maori groups in New Zealand, are concerned with defining their cultural difference. Western and Maori culture have thus tended to be polarized within writing by Maori researchers as two fixed entities in order to develop a strong political stance. This could be related to Street's (1999a) question (in the context of promoting nationalism), 'what does it mean to conceptualise culture as a process where it is being used in a reified sense for political purposes?' (p. 55).

Towards a wider definition of 'cross-cultural' in this book

When I began this piece of research, I started to explore the body of writing emerging on Maori approaches to academic discourse and research methodologies, which appeared similar to the 'cross-cultural' perspective on doctoral research that I intended to develop. Written from the perspective of a cultural group who have had their indigenous practices and knowledge colonized by the invaders, these communities were suspicious of any kind of research: 'the term research is inextricably linked to European imperialism and colonialism' (Tuhiwai Smith 1999: 1). The 'transition of the Maoris as researched to Maori as researcher' (Tuhiwai Smith 1999: 163) is traced not just in terms of challenging these hierarchical relationships (as in participatory research approaches). Tuhiwai Smith describes how this process is also about discovering and developing a 'Maori' indigenous research methodology: 'having been immersed in the Western academy which claims theory as thoroughly Western, which has constructed all the rules by which the indigenous world has been theorised, indigenous voices have been overwhelmingly silenced' (p. 29). This is not just a question of researchers becoming 'culturally sensitive' (such as learning the language) when working with Maori communities, but also about bringing Maori values into the research process.

In her chapter on 'Research through imperial eyes', Tuhiwai Smith (1999: 47) describes how 'Western ways of viewing, talking about and interacting the world at large are intricately embedded in racialised discourses', such as privileging the written text over oral and disregarding Maori ideas of time and space. She also discusses how knowledge is created through the Western frames of analysis. This is similar to Goody's (1977) discussion about how anthropologists have used classificatory tables to reach an understanding about how indigenous groups viewed the world: the anthropologists' conclusions may be 'a result of *our* tables rather than their thoughts' (p. 65). He suggests that tables 'may simplify reality for the observer but often at the expense of a real understanding of the actor's frame of reference' (p. 73). In other words, the visual frame determines what is analysed as 'knowledge' and which perceptions people put forward. More recently, similar dangers have been identified by development workers using a methodology known as PRA (Participatory Rural Appraisal), which is based on the creation of graphics such as matrices and maps. PRA practitioners have raised 'the question of how their [community's] knowledge is analysed and into whose categories (researchers tend to fit material into preconceived concepts)' (Chambers 1998: xvii).[5]

Relating these ideas to the PhD research context, the higher value put on written than oral accounts in higher education is often identified as 'Western influence' and has been challenged in particular by Maori communities of students on the grounds of cultural imperialism. Similarly, the idea of 'good' academic writing consisting of an argument backed up with references has been addressed by more collaborative writing practices. Teasdale and Teasdale (1999: 255) describe the dominance of Western 'systems of knowledge analysis' through an account of how a Maori student decided not to use the PhD framework but to 'approach her research question by walking round it'. Tuhiwai Smith's book is particularly useful in extending the more bounded discussion of 'academic literacies' to consider the wider social practices associated with academic research. For example, she analyses the assumptions in Western research about research ethics: giving consent is not an individual responsibility in the case of Maori communities but a collective responsibility. The ethical guidelines developed by Maori researchers also outline more explicitly the values that should inform a researcher's behaviour: 'Look, listen, speak, be cautious and don't flaunt your knowledge' (Tuhiwai Smith 1999: 119). I will discuss these ideas about indigenous ethical practices in more detail in Chapter 4.

Tuhiwai Smith's writing is based on a fixed distinction between ourselves and 'the other', which for her is around the differences between Maori and Western. It seems surprising to me that the term 'culture' is not problematized within her work. She writes only within a model of one Culture and leaves unexplored the implicit tensions between 'Westernized' and indigenous Maori, between male and female Maoris, elders and the young. Reading her book made me realize the importance of taking a wider concept of 'culture' within my own work, to bring in the complex relationships between UK and other academic cultures, and between different cultures within the student's own home context. While the critique of 'Western' paradigms is important in enabling us to focus on assumptions that may be taken for granted in research and also to begin to analyse how 'Western' academic practices might be viewed, I am aware that there are many stereotypes of 'Western' students, academics and institutions. Drawing again on Bhabha's work, I see the challenge facing me here as how to develop a more political and complex notion of the cross-cultural within research: 'Terms of cultural engagement, whether antagonistic or affiliative, are produced performatively . . . the representation of difference must not be hastily read as the reflection of *pre-given* ethnic or cultural traits set in the fixed tablet of tradition' (Bhabha 1994: 2). Rather than attempting to characterize 'Arabic' or 'English' students (and academics), I am interested in opening up that 'interrogatory, interstitial space' (p. 3) referred to by Bhabha: 'The interstitial passage between fixed identifications opens up the possibility of a cultural hybridity that entertains difference without an assumed or imposed hierarchy' (p. 4).

Locating this book – in theory and practice

I have looked above at the concept of 'cross-cultural' through an analysis of how the research literature has constructed 'the overseas student' and 'culture'. I have been keen to move away from cultural stereotypes to look at the processes involved in representing 'culture', especially from the perspective of the 'other' (whether that is 'the Maori' or 'the Academy'). Through introducing the more political notion of 'cultural difference' (as compared to 'diversity'), I have emphasized the need to analyse international students' experiences in relation to their positions as 'novice members' of the university (facing similar issues around academic research practices as other professionals entering the UK Academy), as well as in relation to their home 'cultural' identity. Although the title of this book includes the words 'educational research', it will have become clear through the above account, that I am situating my discussion of 'cross-cultural' perspectives in the more defined context of educational research conducted by PhD students. This decision is partly for reasons of economy (as my remit would otherwise include the vast debate on 'international educational research') but largely because of my belief as an ethnographer that we can learn much from a focused study of a small research community in a specific institution.

The issue that I have not addressed so far is my own position as author: the apparent contradictions of me as a white UK university lecturer speaking 'for' international students through the form of an academic book. Although this book contains writing by international students conducting educational research at the University of East Anglia, I would not suggest that this account fully represents their voices or perspectives, since they have agreed to my invitation to participate in this particular academic discourse on my terms. Seven students[6] responded by writing reflective pieces on their experiences, which we then circulated to each other and commented on as a small group of writers. I have positioned their accounts as interludes between my own chapters in an attempt to add a further dimension to the issues that I raise in each (for instance, Scholastica Mokake's discussion of complex ethical dilemmas encountered in her fieldwork in Tanzania follows Chapter 4 on 'Research ethics'). I was particularly excited to receive articles from two former students now back in their home countries (Karim Sadeghi in Iran and Howida Mostafa in Egypt), reflecting on the cultural adjustment they had to make on their return to their former professional contexts. In addition, Ayedh Al-Motairi and another student (who prefers to remain anonymous) offered to share their experiences in the form of an interview, rather than a written account. Their reflections – particularly on language and academic literacy issues – are included within my discussions in Chapters 5 and 6.

This book, however, is only one part of the 'cross-cultural' interactions that we have on a weekly basis through seminars and needs to be read as my individual perspective on that process. As part of my role as research supervisor, I convene weekly seminars for research students that are intended both as training sessions in research methodology, as well as forums for discussing our work-in-progress. I have learnt much about our differing cultural assumptions and practices through these seminars and this is reflected through the way that I have drawn on our seminar discussions throughout the book. I circulated the first draft of this book to the students who had been quoted from seminars – their responses to my text (and in some cases, their request to 'rewrite' some of their comments in seminars[7]) contributed greatly to this final version.

As I mentioned at the beginning of this chapter, there is a noticeable bias in the literature towards lecturers writing about their international students – rather than students analysing their own experiences in UK higher education. This is no doubt related partly to the more pressing imperatives of gaining a PhD before their funding runs out. My hope is that some of the international students included in this book (as case studies and contributors) will later feel inspired to write about their experiences in their own way.

The aims and structure of this book

Aims

In the previous decade, much of the literature on international students took a deficit approach: seeing the student as the problem, and stressing the need for better support, culturally appropriate teaching or language tuition. More recently, with the 'widening participation' agenda in UK higher education, attention has turned to the ways in which all students could be better supported in their roles as 'novice members' of the Academy. As Elsey (1990: 57) observes: 'it's worthwhile noting that perhaps overseas students are not that more difficult to teach than mature students returning to full-time study after several years working or conventional-age students with no real experience of life to call upon'. While I may be seen to contribute to this critical analysis of how universities could better respond to their increasingly diverse student population, this is not the main aim of this book. By taking a cross-cultural perspective on the PhD research process, I am not simply asking whether 'we' or 'they' should change viewpoints, through the kind of questions sometimes posed in the literature on international students: 'Do we attempt to bring their [overseas students'] view closer to ours or ignore the whole problem?' (Watt 1980: 40). My aim is to deepen understanding about educational research approaches and assumptions, through analysing and bringing together differing cultural practices around learning, teaching and research.

Sharing our perceptions on the PhD process is an integral part of the supervision and assessment system – and we need to acknowledge where the power dynamics of this relationship lie. In this respect, as I mentioned earlier, we already have a very formal dialogue about what is 'good' research or a good PhD thesis in the form of the 'viva' examination. What I am hoping to do through this book is to open up new opportunities for a more creative debate between international students and their supervisors about their assumptions and practices. In collaborative writing between international students and UK academics, this process has already started, giving a greater insight into how 'Western' research writing appears to Chinese students, for instance:

> In the science reports written by westerners, they normally give an introduction which reviews the research done by others, very wordy. When they discuss the new techniques or new methodology, they put in quite a lot of irrelevant quotations from others and their previous writing. In the end, they again give reviews and prospects and implications of this research.
>
> (Cortazzi and Jin 1997: 83)

As well as focusing on the written texts – the visible products of research – I am keen to expand this kind of analysis from a cross-cultural perspective to the other aspects of doing PhD research.

As Teasdale and Teasdale (1999: 255) point out in relation to Australian academics: 'Their own academic successes have been achieved by conforming to the Western way. Indeed, a doctoral thesis has prescribed parameters and deep-seated cultural expectations of its own'.[8] By looking at these 'deep-seated cultural expectations' through accounts of our seminar discussions, analysing PhD theses and other writing by students, I intend to explore our implicit assumptions about PhD research. Like the research into academic literacy practices that has already been carried out with undergraduate students, I see one outcome of this book might be for both university teachers and research students to be stimulated to carry out collaborative action research into their own practices in higher education (Chapter 7 focuses on this aspect). To some extent, these discussions may already take place through critical attention to the international student as an 'insider' carrying out field research in their own institution back home. However, the insider/outsider debate could also be usefully extended to the whole process of doing PhD research in a UK university. In the writing-up process as well as proposal design, students may find themselves constantly shifting between roles – as a government employee trying to ensure that they are following government policy objectives, while also trying to 'assimilate' to the new UK university context through reflecting critically on their previous workplace from a personal angle.

The project of 'multiculturalism' has taken on a more political edge than the relativist notions of recognizing 'cultural diversity' that were prevalent in the UK in the 1970s (see May 2001). In the context of higher education teaching, Trahar (2003: 2) refers to 'transculturalism' as a stage 'beyond interculturalism where a common and different culture emerges from the dialogue of the transcultural spaces between teachers and students'. Similar to Bhabha's concept of 'interrogatory, interstitial space', the 'transcultural spaces' can enable us to participate in transforming the underlying inequalities in current educational practices. The theme of Trahan's article and much recent writing on international students (see Ryan 2000) is that rather than being the domain of 'overseas' students, we can all gain through looking critically at the cultural bias within UK higher education. Implicit in this approach is the desire to build on and acknowledge students' prior experience, rather than dismissing it as irrelevant on 'cultural' or linguistic grounds. As I discuss in Chapter 6, even constructing an argument may be a quite different process in Chinese than in English: understanding these differences in logic may be the first step for both student and tutor to explore their own implicit assumptions about academic writing.

This book, then, has a strong pedagogical thrust, in that I write from the perspective of a university teacher and my writing is informed by inter-action with a group of research students. I hold the belief, like many of the writers promoting a more politicized multicultural approach to higher education teaching, that this is not just about improving education for a minority, but for all those engaged in education (including the educators). As Todd (1997: 174) comments: 'Improving postgraduate education for overseas students can help us to develop an appropriate culture to operate in the bipolar world of the 21st century'. The main purpose of my writing is to bring together the many fragmented reflections and arguments started but never finished within our seminar discussions on research methodologies. I hope to explore in this book how taking a cross-cultural perspective on the research process can enable us all to look more critically at how we carry out research, how we write it up and, above all, how we use the findings.

Structure

I began with the idea of structuring this book around different stages of the research process, based on the order of activities within a doctoral course of study (such as planning fieldwork, choosing a research approach, writing up). I was, however, concerned that such an account would fit closely with the 'how to do a PhD' genre of guides currently available. While my critical take on the process might gain meaning through being presented in a similar genre to those texts, I was concerned that the book might prove a disappointment to the student who bought it hoping for some tips for successful study! My unease about focusing on 'stages' of research was confirmed when I read Ivanic and Weldon's (1999) account of their collaborative research project: 'we call these "aspects" of the research rather than "stages" in order to emphasise the fact that they are not in any strict chronological order, but rather they are recursive pro-cesses' (p. 168). Their idea of 'aspects' of the research fits well with my intention to focus on discussion of key issues (such as 'being critical') that arise in doctoral research from a cross-cultural perspective. The 'aspects' of doing research that I have chosen to structure this book may not appear very different from 'stages' but by choosing to write a chapter on 'which language', for instance, I can look at wider issues around academic writing and conducting field research in multiple languages, rather than regarding in isolation the task of writing the thesis in English.

The 'aspects' of doctoral research that have shaped this book have emerged from analysis of seminar discussions with doctoral students in my department. As the majority of the students who attend these seminars come from outside the UK, an unanticipated outcome has been that much of the discussion has focused on their differing approaches and beliefs about research, as well as the challenge of understanding their supervisors' assumptions about the research process. To include part-time students and members of our group away on fieldwork, I started to write summaries of our discussions to circulate by e-mail. This material documented from seminar discussions has set the agenda for issues to be addressed in this book and is developed here by some of the students reflecting in more depth on their experiences as researchers. The first half of the book in particular draws directly on these discussions, case studies and extracts from students' writing in order to immerse the reader in the research community whose debates shaped the book as a whole.

An overview

To set this chapter in context, as well as to give an overview of the aspects of educational research addressed in subsequent chapters, I will end with a brief outline of the book as a whole. This chapter has focused on the concept of 'cross-cultural' in relation to theoretical debates about post-colonialism and academic literacy practices. Situating issues raised by international PhD students within this framework, I have looked, for instance, at the relevance of work with Maori communities to develop an alternative research methodology (to what they consider to be the 'colonizing' influence of Western methodologies; Tuhiwai Smith 1999). I have indicated the ways in which this book will look at educational research as a social and cultural practice, through analysing the perspectives of international students as they become part of a new 'community of practice' within the UK Academy. I have emphasized my aim of challenging the 'deficit' view of international students dominant in earlier research accounts and also of widening the more limited discussion of 'cross-cultural communication' within classroom situations, to consider differing values and viewpoints on the PhD process and educational research more generally. Building on academic literacies research, which analyses outsider/insider issues in the writing up stage of a thesis, I take a similar starting point to explore the other practices associated with PhD research (such as interviewing, analysing data and developing ethical codes of conduct). My intention in the book is not simply to critique the practices of UK universities from the standpoint of international students, but also to suggest how taking a cross-cultural perspective can enable us all to re-examine our assumptions about educational research. Rather than seeing 'Culture' as a barrier to effective communication and learning or as a way of polarizing two groups of people, we can begin to use 'culture' as a lens for developing a more reflexive approach within our research and teaching.

In Chapter 2, 'Defining the research question', I look at how power relationships, institutional priorities and cultural assumptions come together to influence a student's research agenda, drawing on the experiences of research students in my department, CARE. International students come from a range of countries and differ in how far they have a choice about the direction of their PhD research, partly due to sponsoring requirements. Chapter 2 compares the experiences of students who have a 'choice within limits' and those who have little or no external pressure on what they study – and analyses how they develop and negotiate change within their research question. Questions arise around values and priorities: How far can we challenge dominant values or policy priorities in their own institutions? If a student intends to do their PhD on information and communications technology (ICT) because it is currently a government policy area, should they or can they challenge this? Are there advantages in following government policy objectives if this means that research is more likely to have an impact? These issues relate to the PhD criteria requiring a student to make a contribution to 'knowledge'. For the international student, this may mean asking what and how do I intend to contribute to 'knowledge' through doing a PhD? Whose knowledge do I intend to engage with and build upon during the course of my study? How far is that knowledge valued/recognized by my supervisor or employer? How do I place myself within what is considered legitimate knowledge? Implicit in this discussion is the recognition that the researcher has to respond to specific audiences. For the PhD student, this may mean that if their reason for doing the research is primarily for promotion and to meet their employer's requirements, they also need to consider an audience beyond their home institution. If so, what complexities does this introduce to their research study?

The choice of a research approach is often assumed to be taken on methodological grounds, perhaps also indicative of a researcher's ideological stance towards their subject matter. However, as I discuss in Chapter 3, 'Choosing a research approach', a research student's decision to introduce a qualitative research methodology in their home institutional context may need to be considered in relation to political and cultural pressures. This chapter draws in particular on theses written by former CARE students describing how they dealt with the contradictory pressures from UK university staff and their national colleagues/ employers and how they tried to adapt case study and action research approaches within their home country context. Chapter 3 analyses what it means to conduct qualitative research in a 'quantitative environment' (in a research student's words), analysing the demands of donors or employers in relation to the expectations of host institutions. How have students made this transition? How did they 'sell' qualitative approaches to colleagues back home? Does quantitative research lend itself more readily to students with English as a second language, who find writing descriptive accounts difficult? This chapter also looks at action research and case study in an international context and how these approaches (closely identified with the research culture in CARE) have evolved in response to differing cultural practices. How do you go about doing action research within the constraints of a PhD and in circumstances where employers want questions to be defined in advance? Is case study inappropriate as an approach in some cultural contexts because of the emphasis on 'democratic values' (see CARE 1994)?

My starting point in Chapter 4, 'Research ethics', is the understanding that PhD research has often been influenced by the dominant development discourse (see Escobar 1995) where the ethical procedures and values of Western research institutions shape and provide the standards by which others are judged. I look at how research ethics procedures in the UK have been shaped by cultural factors (not least the growing culture of litigation), and relate this discussion to anthropological research that has analysed ethical concepts and practices in other cultures (such as the assumption of individual rather than community consent). This chapter extends such debates by looking specifically at educational research ethics in differing cultural contexts: What does it mean to conduct 'ethical' research in Kenya as compared to the UK? How can practices associated with ensuring ethical practices in the UK (such as signing consent forms) be adapted in other contexts? How does working within more bureaucratic structures (with greater mechanisms for accountability) affect research ethics? What ethical guidelines are offered by other research institutions/governments and how do they compare with UK guidelines? Do we have alternative moral codes/ethical practices to offer researchers in the UK? For many international students coming from countries with restrictions on open speech or writing, political and ethical concerns tend to converge: Why should I ask critical questions within my PhD research? What does this imply in a strongly hierarchical society? Can we introduce a critical edge to our research without being overtly critical? This chapter explores 'being critical' in relation to cultural context, looking at how students communicate with supervisors about cultural differences and less explicit ways of presenting criticism or giving an opinion.

Unlike most UK-focused PhD students, international students are often working with two or more languages in their fieldwork and writing up. Chapter 5, 'Which language?', looks at the implications for research rigour (how do you ensure that the way you write up in English accurately reflects what people actually said in another language?), ethical practices (research respondents often cannot read your final product in English) and practical constraints (the additional burden of translating transcripts). Questions raised by students and discussed in this chapter include: How do I handle several languages in my research – two different languages for interviewing, English for writing up? Should I translate as I transcribe? What are the implications of using one language for interviews and another for reporting? Should I analyse the findings in my own language or in English?

Chapter 6, 'Writing the thesis', builds on recent research discussed in this introductory chapter about how students are introduced to and learn 'academic literacies' (see Lea and Stierer 2000) in relation to other ways in which they have previously expressed themselves in writing. In the context of writing a thesis, this chapter looks at form and structure, in particular decisions about whether to produce a conventional or non-conventional thesis. How far can international students experiment with the form, while also taking into account factors around writing in a second language and their colleagues' expectations back home? Similarly, conventions around thesis style are rapidly changing, allowing students to bring in a personal perspective on their research and to include auto-biographical details. This may be the expectation in many UK educational institutions, but how would such a personalized text be read in the student's home culture? This chapter looks also at the practical dilemmas faced by international students: I would like to write in a more personalized style, but how do I do this in a second language – my English is too formal? Above all, the writer has to respond to the expectations of their audience(s) and, in the case of international students, this may imply trying to write two theses, not one. If an international student writes the thesis that the examiners in the UK appear to prefer, would they have to produce a different thesis to take back home? How far do they compromise to please the audience here or their employer there? While these may be the immediate concerns faced by an international student writing their thesis, the underlying tensions relate to our notions of what constitutes 'good' educational research in general: Is there a single 'true' knowledge that researchers can create or reflect? How is 'knowledge' shaped by the institutions within which it is produced?

All the themes addressed in the first six chapters have implications for the ways in which teaching staff organize research methods courses, relate to students in supervisions and provide ongoing assessment. There has been some previous research into the different 'learning styles' of international students (see McNamara and Harris 1997) but little attention as to how we interact about differences in beliefs and research practices (such as the need to be critical in the UK higher education context). Recognizing that our experiences and beliefs about teaching and learning shape our approach to educational research, Chapter 7, 'Reflections on the doctoral research process', looks at the pedagogical assumptions of both supervisors and students from a cross-cultural perspective. Analysing the case studies and reflections documented in previous chapters, this chapter asks: What can be learned from international students' perspectives on their experiences and dominant practices in UK higher educational institutions? How far can formal research methods courses build upon and support students' informal and peer group learning?

Though Chapter 7 may suggest otherwise, this book is not intended to be about or for international students exclusively. My own role as a PhD supervisor and research methods teacher has led me to consider the pedagogical implications of these differing cultural perspectives on research. To some extent, I see my major professional challenge as lying in how to better value and build on the prior experience of the international students I teach. However, this book is concerned with more than bridging the gap between students and their supervisors in terms of research methods or teaching approaches. By taking a wider view of 'culture' to embrace differences between policy and academic research contexts as well as between countries, I am developing ways of enhancing any research which aims to address multiple audiences with contrasting assumptions, practices and ideologies. My hope is that this cross-cultural exploration will enable educational researchers to begin to transform what are often hierarchical relationships between differing cultural groups (whether Malaysian students and UK lecturers or government policy makers and academic researchers). Recognizing that these axioms of difference are not just around culture but also around power is the first step towards creating a more equal interaction with other cultural groups about what constitutes 'good' research in our own educational context.

Impressions

By Manal Ibrahim Madini

When Anna suggested to me to write about my perspective on cross-cultural educational research, I did not hesitate for a moment, for I felt that this topic touches upon an important issue for me. I readily obtained pen and paper, sat alone contemplating and recalling my relevant experiences. The experience of moving from one country to another to study, which may take a few years, is both rich and diverse and during which researchers not only learn from the course they are allocated at the university they attend, but they learn from the new society as a whole. Here I will elaborate on some differences in the style of writing and research designs, in addition to some social differences inside the university.

It is worthy to note here that differences between cultures and societies I refer to above do not mean that some cultures are superior or inferior to others. I see that every society has its own specific culture and personality which differentiates it from others and which reflects a number of factors, such as the geographical location and religion. Adapting to the new environment is, in my view, one of the most important elements of success for the researcher and one which may be reflected in the researcher's performance positively or negatively. Some students have returned to their countries of origin because of their inability to adapt to their new surroundings.

I came from the city of Jeddah in the Kingdom of Saudi Arabia on which the sun shines almost all year round, and the times of sunrise and sunset do not change significantly during the various seasons of the year. On the other hand, the weather in Britain is cold almost all year round and the times of sunrise and sunset differ according to the seasons of the year. Many winter days can go past without the sun shining at all. These conditions require some kind of adaptation, since some students prefer studying during the daytime, while others prefer studying at night. This is particularly problematic during winter months, when, naturally, nights are much longer than days.

Teaching relationships

Inside the university campus, there are some interesting differences: for example, students at most Arab universities are used to addressing faculty members and lecturers by their titles and first names, whereas in Britain faculty members and lecturers are addressed by their first names directly, without their titles. At the beginning, it was very difficult for me to address the teaching staff by their first names directly, for whenever I did so, I felt I was not being polite, something that I certainly did not want to do. As for the teaching staff, some of them did not comment while others said that I could call them by their first names – just as they call me by my first name. As time went by, I discovered that the whole matter is relative and that certain behaviour or sayings may be accepted at a time and a place but might not be accepted elsewhere. Anyhow, not using titles may remove certain barriers and formalities when dealing with people. After all, the value of the individual lies in what she/he does, not in their title. What has always been important in my view has been to maintain respect between people, whether titles are observed or not.

Conducting educational fieldwork

It is important to adapt to the culture of the country in which fieldwork is being undertaken, and this can cause difficulties for the researcher as methods which are appropriate for one country might be inapplicable in another. For example, the Saudi Arabia education system strictly separates schooling for male and female students, and the school staff are from the same gender. There are some exceptions, such as kindergarten classes. On the other hand, in Britain, universities and schools have mixed gender classes. Accordingly, in Saudi Arabia, the researcher when collecting data for his/her research, must conduct it via non-direct methods (if he/she from the opposite sex), such as by questionnaires or by delegating the work and sending someone from the same gender on behalf of the researcher. Filming of teachers and students is totally prohibited for religious and social considerations.

Writing conventions

In addition, as is the case at King Abdul Aziz University (where I worked as lecturer), there is a particular order in organizing the chapters of the research, and this must be followed: that is, the first chapter must be the research introduction, the literature review, and so on, whereas this is not required at the University of East Anglia. Organizing the research in a certain manner may facilitate the extraction of information by the reader and there is a general form that most theses adhere to. However, not adhering to a certain organization for a thesis may in fact enable the researcher to work with a wider freedom and to choose the way in which she/he feels is the most suitable for the work at hand. This may assist the researcher to focus primarily on the research question, although they may need some time to break away from the forms to which they have become accustomed, in order to eventually benefit from other schools of thought.

This is in addition to the fact that in most Arab universities, studies must be written in the third person ('the researcher'), while at UEA they can be written in the first person. This may carry some interesting differences; the first person is not preferred in the Arabic writing style, as to use the word 'I' many times indicates selfishness. When I started my university studies, I remember asking one of my Saudi teachers at that time about the reason for using the third person. She answered that research is something for everyone and does not only belong solely to its writer, a fact which may reflect and enhance the objectivity of the research.

As a researcher studying and writing in English, I have found that expressing myself in a foreign language has been an enriching experience for me, though it has occasionally been fraught with difficulty. Language is a very important tool for any researcher to convey ideas and feelings in a precise manner. As for the style, I realized that some styles of Arabic writing tend to be redundant and general, particularly at the beginning of the article. On the other hand, where Arab writers enjoy the opportunity to be expansive, and to discuss an issue broadly and in general terms before attending to detail, in English the beginning of a piece of writing tends to be more specific and includes many details and examples. As for translation, there are some expressions in one language that can be translated into another, while other expressions may not mean anything when translated. For example, it is said in both languages (English and Arabic) that a 'bird in hand is worth ten on a tree', which conveys the same meaning in both languages. However, if we translate the English expression 'a piece of cake' into Arabic, it may not convey the intended meaning of 'easiness'. There are also some words in every society that are known to describe a particular thing, although it is more than the literal meaning of that word. Such literal translations may not work if used in these situations. For instance, private schools here in Britain are called 'public schools', while the word 'public' obviously means something general: not private!

Concluding reflections

Such differences can be beneficial to the researcher as they enrich and feed his/her experiences, and he/she may return to his/her country having gained many experiences which may aid his/her development. However he/she might equally find him/herself in an uncertain situation while attempting to bridge a gap between two extreme views. While some may think that such experiences are personal and only relevant to the researcher concerned, I believe that passing on such experiences to others is very beneficial in two ways. First, these experiences may benefit other researchers, for one may feel comfortable when sharing one's feelings and experiences with others. This is exactly what happens in my case, as I was given the opportunity to live in the university's residence where I lived amongst a multinational and multicultural group from Asia, Africa, America, Europe and so on. At times, we would gather in the residence's garden and exchange different experiences and feelings of nostalgia for our homeland. Secondly, such exchanges of experiences may benefit academics and administrators working at the universities alike, for they are supposed to be aware of such experiences and differences because they greatly assist in understanding others.

Manal I. Madini is a lecturer at the Department of Childhood Studies, King Abdul Aziz University in Saudi Arabia. She has taught and studied various subjects related to children's education. She was assigned a number of administrative roles during her work, which included the directorship at the faculty's cultural committee. She has contributed to a number of media-related activities, which were mostly aimed at raising awareness in society of the importance of the childhood stage of development. Recently, she has been completing a PhD at the University of East Anglia, where her research focuses on kindergarten teachers' stress in Saudi Arabia. E-mail address: m_madini@yahoo.com

Defining the research question

Introduction

> One long lasting defect in our system, in my view, is our belief in the
> superiority of anything that is Western. They theorise and we take for
> granted. They think and we think they think better. So they produce
> and we consume. I wonder: when is this going to end? I strongly
> believe that this perspective has to change.
>
> (Saad A.S. Al-Nasser 1999: 360)

These concluding remarks in a PhD thesis by Al-Nasser, a former student from Saudi Arabia in my department, caught my attention as conveying the paradox faced by many international students. In the context
of his thesis, Al-Nasser was arguing for both an alternative research
paradigm (from that dominant in Saudi Arabia) and a more participatory approach to curriculum development to 'plant the seeds in our
curricula for the coming generations to create in them the kind of spirit
of autonomy we need' (Al-Nasser 1999: 361). However, within his discussion on the methodological issues faced, Al-Nasser conveyed strongly
some of the tensions and contradictions encountered when trying to
carry out case study research in a culture where such approaches
were considered 'alien'. Seeing case study as a 'Western' approach, he
described the difficulties faced by 'non-European' students (in his UK
university) in understanding the methodology when they had no prior
experience to draw upon and yet not being able to 'give up' the PhD,
since they were government-sponsored. The paradox facing Al-Nasser,
therefore, seemed to lie in the realization that he had to adopt what he
saw as a Western paradigm of research to be able to put forward his
above critique of Western ideological domination. However, there is an
even deeper irony in that his comment is being given greater validity
through me as a Western researcher now quoting it in a higher status

published book, as compared to the unpublished thesis in the university library.

I have started with Al-Nasser's penetrating comment to give some idea of the layers of contradictions and meanings that need to be explored in relation to the question as to why someone chose to research a particular topic in a particular way. As I discussed in the opening chapter to this book, I feel uneasy about polarizing 'Western' and 'other' in the way that Al-Nasser does – not least because 'case study' may be equally unfamiliar to many people working in the UK (particularly in policy-making contexts). However, this chapter is concerned with people's feelings of being pulled in two contradictory directions. This dilemma tends to be more directly addressed in terms of methodological choices and paradigms (as I will discuss in Chapter 3). But here I want to start one step back by looking at the context in which international students make decisions about how to define their area of study and research questions. This relates to their personal and institutional objectives for doing a PhD, as well as to the whole political and cultural environment within which they operated before coming to the UK.

This chapter differs from many research methodology texts in that I consider the choice of a research topic and question as an ideological rather than technical task facing the researcher. Other texts often start from the assumption that the student has a free choice regarding their topic and it is simply a task of identifying a 'manageable' and 'answerable' research question within the scope of the PhD (Andrews 2003). In his book *Research Questions*, Andrews (2003: 79), for instance, advises: 'you should always find a topic in which you are interested, not one which has been suggested to you by someone else and in which you have only a passing interest'.

As will become apparent in this chapter, I learnt much about my own cultural assumptions about what it means to 'define a research problem' through participating in seminar discussions with PhD students from a range of backgrounds. For this reason, I draw directly on reports of our research seminars to illustrate some of the key issues.[1] For ethical reasons, I have chosen to use extracts from my seminar reports, rather than to quote directly from students' words in seminars – since these reports are already negotiated texts which are in the public domain (on our department website). After I circulated drafts of this book to the seminar participants included here, some of them also decided to add to and expand points in the extracts I have quoted.[2]

Although I am focusing on international students' perspectives on the PhD research focus, my discussion draws too on the interaction between UK and international students and between students with differing cultural beliefs or backgrounds. This relates to observations in the research methodology literature about the benefits of being an 'outsider' in fieldwork: being able to ask questions about the obvious or seeing things from a different angle (see Vulliamy *et al.* 1990; Crossley and Vulliamy 1997). For example, during a presentation by a UK part-time student on his research in East Anglia, it became apparent that even the idea of 'choosing' a research question lay outside the experience of some of our group:

> Sam encouraged us to look at the 'why' of our individual research projects – to answer not just 'what' we are researching, but 'why'. Also, to ask 'where do I get the right to do this?' Sam suggested that the purpose of much educational research, including his own, is to influence some body and that it is rarely just for ourselves. Several students commented that they had not had the opportunity to ask 'why' this research, since they were sponsored by their institutions/ government to carry out a certain kind of research.
>
> (Seminar report: 9/2/01)

This discussion about who felt they could or could not decide on the topic of their research made us realize how for some members of the group, putting forward the rationale for their research was less pressing than determining the parameters within which they could choose a research question. Within the group of international students, there was great diversity in terms of the political systems and educational institutions in which they worked. These factors influenced how far they could have a say in what issue or topic they focused on. Above all, their source of funding or sponsorship affected their autonomy as researchers. In the next section, I look at individual cases of international students to analyse how these factors came together in their search to prioritize a research question or problem within their PhD.

A choice within limits

Most international students in our group were sponsored by their government or employer (whether directly or indirectly via British Council scholarships). Their starting point for doing the PhD was invariably for career development reasons, in a country context where qualifications were greatly valued for their exchange value [see Dore's (1976) classic analysis of the 'diploma disease']. As Al-Yaseen (2000) explained in her thesis, the career motivation was also linked to a desire for self-development and the confidence that came from having studied abroad:

> In addition, I was shocked to know that obtaining an MA degree does not add much to my chances to hold leading posts such as the Dean of the School. So the key to any future posts is to get a PhD. Such a

feeling made me think to do my PhD as that will enable me to have a voice and to be taken seriously. Yet, my motivation was not only career driven. I hope that through this degree I help future teachers and prospective graduate students look at the academic life as a process to be creative and build creative thinking in our children.

(Al-Yaseen 2000: 93)

Given the desire to enhance their position in their home institution, it is therefore likely that students would choose to focus on a government or institutional priority for their research area. They might also be inclined to select an area where they already had expertise or knowledge to build upon. Though the initial boundaries were thus already set to some extent, there was still scope to decide which questions would be interesting to pursue within the defined area of government/institutional interest.

In a presentation on her research, Alina, a student from South East Asia, explained how she had begun to define her research investigation:

Alina explained that she will be looking at the use of ICT [Information and Communications Technology] in TESL [Teaching English as a Second Language] in the institute where she has been working as a teacher trainer. She has been involved in an intervention . . . which aims to give the staff the tools for changing from an institute to a university (a recent change in status). Alina explained that her starting point is to look at how technology can be used in education, rather than if it should be there or not. Within this focus, she intends to explore issues such as whether there is a need for special IT courses or whether IT should be integrated within all the courses.

(Seminar report: 7/10/02)

As a teacher trainer within an institute with a defined agenda to promote the use of ICT, Alina was concerned that her PhD should support the institute's policy priorities, rather than go in a completely different direction. During her presentation, she was tackled by fellow students who asked, 'Why focus on ICT? Is ICT being promoted at the expense of other kinds of education? Aren't there other kinds of priorities, such as teacher salaries, updating resources and "survival"?' She justified her stance, explaining that her research focus was related to her actual role within the teacher training college. The general government policy move towards ICT was to ensure that students were not left behind in the global market and were able to enter new areas of work. She also felt that ICT was the new 'trendy' area to be researching and working within, and that a lot of the studies on ICT in classrooms involved students in schools, rather than trainees in teacher training institutions (her focus).

Alina was keen to point out that she had defined her research questions within the context of her own role as teacher trainer and taking into account government educational priorities. This had influenced her decision to look at the use of ICT within education, rather than whether it should be there or not. However, another student expressed concern that 'we might be swallowing our government's policies', suggesting that we needed to question the parameters within which we made decisions about research questions. Significantly, Alina felt confident that she would be able to take a critical perspective on her research question and use the findings to improve teaching and learning in her institution.

Other students felt less secure about their potential position as 'critics' within their institution, particularly when they were more directly under government control. As a student explained to me, he had to ensure throughout his fieldwork and writing up that his work was not considered to be 'sensitive':

> I have to send my work to the [government sponsor] to make sure there is no political point . . . You have to be sure – give it [transcript] back to participants to get approval that nothing will harm them, if presented anonymously. I check again and again and delete any sensitive sentence. I make the equivalent for my thesis. The committee in the Ministry of Higher Education will read and check if anything is sensitive and ask me to delete. If there is a problem, they may ask me to change one sentence.
>
> (Interview notes: July 2004)

This student's concern was both at the individual level (protecting participants through not presenting any critical comments – a point which is explored further in relation to research ethics in Chapter 4), as well as worries about how he expressed his own opinions in the thesis. He also described the constraints he faced in obtaining information, having chosen to research an unusually sensitive area in this cultural context: 'Even to get statistical reports is difficult – drugs, divorce, social communication are very sensitive problems and it is difficult to get statistics. They try to give small numbers, not the real number for divorce, for example' (ibid.).

The choice as to which area to research could therefore involve a conversation in two directions – between the student and their academic supervisor as well as their former employer or sponsor. For instance, Azhar, a Ministry of Education officer, had to respond directly to advice from his employer when at the early stages of trying to define his area of research:

> Being within the Ministry, Azhar was keen to look at the new preschool curriculum in detail and had intended to do his research around the development and implementation of the curriculum. However, following a visit from two friends who are higher up in the Ministry, he decided to change his approach as they warned him that the documents he was intending to analyse were confidential and

could not be used in his research. He therefore decided to look at his topic in a different way, through focusing on parents' views of the pre-school curriculum.

(Seminar report: 17/12/02)

Explaining that his revised research question would now draw on his experience and interests as a parent, Azhar suggested that this would be a less politically sensitive area than his previous focus on the implementation of the curriculum (which required analysis of confidential documents). He had been concerned to find an area of research that could be more 'technical' (than political) and had decided to look at 'the decision maker in the family who chooses a pre-school, the criteria that they use and exploring what parents want their children to learn from a pre-school (the "why, when, where, what, who and how")' (Seminar report: 17/12/02). Although he had not yet started the investigation, Azhar was very aware of the gap between policy-makers' and parents' views of the new national curriculum. As a ministry official, he saw his role as a middle-man, 'raising awareness' among parents as to the underlying objectives of the new pre-school curriculum, while also 'helping the Ministry of Education to understand how various groups of parents make decisions about pre-school education'. Azhar acknowledged that in the context of top-down curriculum planning, it was unlikely that his findings from parents would be able to influence the content or aims of the curriculum, but he hoped that his research would enable the Ministry 'to identify a "target group" who might need to be "educated" further about the new pre-school curriculum' (Seminar report: 17/12/02).

As Azhar was working in a more politically sensitive context than Alina, he already had had to consider not just the parameters of his research question, but also how his findings might be analysed within the context of top-down planning procedures. Even before having carried out his fieldwork or beginning writing, he was trying to work out how to respond to the pressures of having two audiences: his ministry colleagues and the UK university. This was not just about choosing an area of research that would be seen as appropriate in career terms (like Alina's), but also about anticipating how his findings might be received. He presented his decision to focus on parents' views rather than the curriculum itself as partly pragmatic: '[this] does not require any government permission around research with parents . . . as compared to researching official documents' (Seminar report: 17/12/02). When questioned by others in our seminar group about what he would do if 'the parents' voices challenged government?', Azhar replied that at the moment he was not engaged by the government, so would focus on his academic audience.

In our discussion, it became clear that speaking to these two audiences meant that Azhar had to 'translate' some of the key concepts and assumptions behind his research question. He explained that his intention was to see how far parents understood that the new curriculum was based on the national philosophy of 'achieving firmer solidarity among its society, securing a democratic way of life and creating an unprejudiced society where the nation's prosperity can be enjoyed together, fairly and circumspectly' (Seminar report: 17/12/02). When a UK student pointed out that these seemed similar values to those being promoted in the UK educational system, students from other countries stressed that the 'Western' view of democracy was quite different from theirs, which was more around 'promoting moral values'. Azhar described how the aim of 'democratizing' education in his country meant that every parent, regardless of economic or ethnic background, should have the opportunity to send their child to a pre-school. This would not necessarily imply sharing power or control over the education system, as might be assumed in other cultural contexts. Discussions such as these led us to realize that as a group we gave different meanings to the same English terms. Sharing our implicit assumptions about these terms (particularly in relation to methodologies, as I will explore in the next chapter) was essential for understanding both the aim of a research study, as well as the factors that shaped that investigation.

Setting the boundaries: what makes a good research question?

Many international research students set out on a PhD course with an area of study that is closely defined (and monitored in some cases) by their sponsoring institution or employer. However, as they begin to explore their initial research question and the underlying assumptions, they may find themselves in the difficult situation of wanting to research different or wider issues. This relates to the whole question of what is a 'good' research question, and whether a good research question in a student's home political or institutional context always makes a good PhD question. In my role as PhD admissions officer, I am often aware that my criteria for assessing a 'good' research question guiding a student's proposal at application stage could conflict with a sponsoring government's objectives. For example, I would tend to dismiss a very narrowly focused research question (such as comparing two English language textbooks) as not providing enough scope for three years' study, whereas an employer may want to have an in-depth investigation into national textbook development from a technical point of view – rather than a more critical perspective on curriculum development that might take political factors into account (such as Azhar's first research topic). My own assumption that a narrow and tightly defined starting research question is limiting in a PhD thesis could be related to discussions in the literature (see Chapter 1) about the learning styles of international students, such as debates about how far learning is about opening out, rather than focusing in [see Cortazzi and Jin's (1997) analysis of the 'repetitive learning' associated with Confucian education]. Given also the tightly prescribed political parameters within which many educationalists have to work, there would be a danger of excluding many potential students from PhD courses, if we were to reject PhD applications of the type above. I am beginning to realize increasingly that many such students may develop a 'critical' take on their specific subject, which could be influential within their home institutions, whereas other more overtly 'political' research would be immediately disregarded.

Karim is an English language university teacher in Iran who focused his PhD research on the effectiveness of 'cloze procedure', a technique used in English language teaching for measuring the validity of communication between writer and reader. He described to our seminar group how he had come to develop this piece of research:

> [Karim] first began to question some of the assumptions behind this test when he did his MA and realized that reading comprehension of a complete text (a text with no blanks) was quite different from reading the same text in cloze format (where the student is having to construct the text by choosing the missing words). He then began to explore why this particular test is being used so widely for testing reading comprehension – one of the main reasons being 'economicality'. Compared to multiple choice tests for example, cloze tests are easier to construct and mark.
>
> (Seminar report: 15/11/01)

Compared with Alina and Azhar, Karim appeared to have less visible institutional pressure to define his research question according to certain policy objectives. Yet, he himself had set far more definite boundaries about what he was or was not interested in at the beginning of his PhD and about what he considered appropriate to research within these limits. It should be noted that Karim had been through a long pre-application process in Iran to get approval for applying for a PhD place in the UK.[3] His research seemed likely to strengthen his identity as a technical specialist and he was keen to stress the originality of his research within the Iranian context: 'All this I decided, provided sufficient grounds for a re-investigation of cloze in a context not previously investigated, namely, that of Iranian EFL [English as a Foreign Language] learners' (Sadeghi 2003: 3). Unlike Azhar, he did not consider the research aims of his academic UK audience and his home institution to be in conflict. When talking to Karim about his research question ('Given the widespread use of cloze as a measurement tool in Iranian secondary and higher education, is cloze procedure a valid measure of EFL reading comprehension?'), it was clear that as a practising ELT lecturer he was deeply concerned and committed to his topic and did not feel restricted by the parameters that he had set himself.

Even within the small sample of international students I have described above, we can see that there is a continuum from those with closely prescribed limits on what they can research, to those who have relative freedom within a more general area of research defined by institutional or political priorities. As I have suggested above, individual students might also see themselves positioned differently on this continuum, partly due to their personality. Karim could be seen as situated on the far extreme of having little flexibility in his research question (in that he defines it narrowly in terms of his 'technical' role), though he might consider himself as having great freedom to critique the technique of cloze procedure. By contrast, Azhar appeared to have a wider possible range of research questions but was more conscious of being constrained in trying to downplay the 'political' aspects of his research. Alina appears to have the most independence, having flexibility to research and report on her findings, so long as her general area of research enquiry was related to her institution's policy priorities.

Although many students start out with a clear idea of institutional or political priorities and the intention to frame their research within these, some find that the experience of doing PhD research brings into question these parameters. This also relates to the general experience of many PhD students, that only after carrying out your research do you find out what you really want to research! In our group, there were several students who recognized that their initial research question (and that approved by their sponsor) had imposed limits on what they could look at in their thesis. For example, Howida, a teacher trainer from the Middle East, had set out to compare the UK PGCE teacher training model with that in her own country. Although, like Alina, she had intended to limit herself to considering ways of improving educational practice in her home institution, she soon felt that she was focusing on too narrow an area in looking at one particular teacher training course. She found she was suggesting remedies for minor symptoms, and so ignoring the underlying causes of the problems she observed in her teacher education college:

> Many of the changes [Howida] would like to see could not be separated from the wider context of poor pay and status for teachers (and supervisors), few material resources in schools and colleges and hierarchical social structures where to initiate change is to take a considerable risk . . . She identified a gap between theory and practice, in that there was no link between what was taught in the college and the reality of rural schools.
>
> (Seminar report: 9/3/01)

In discussion, Howida also expanded on what she regarded as the 'cultural' changes that would need to take place for her to be able to take ideas from the UK teacher training course to her own institution. For instance, she felt that her institution regarded supervision of students more as 'inspection' than as supporting professional development and this meant that the meaning of criticism was more negative in her home context. Howida thus felt frustrated that she was limited to looking at how to improve practice within her own department, rather than having the opportunity to analyse what she saw as the wider constraints facing the education system as a whole. Howida was also concerned that any criticism expressed by her might be interpreted in a negative light and was aware of working in a very politically sensitive environment.

Tsegay, a student from a college in Ethiopia, faced a similar situation. Like Howida, he had set out to research a course on which he worked – an English language course for law students. He had intended his research to lead directly to changes in the teaching of English language for legal purposes for civil servants. The objective of his study was to 'determine the kind of problems adult students of law face in using English for academic purposes and assess their learning and target needs that would inform syllabus design for English for Academic Legal Purposes (EALP)' (Tsegay 2002). However, after discussions with colleagues in the Law Faculty, he realized that 'though students learn all the legal subjects in English, they work using Amharic or other regional languages because the Ethiopian Constitution dictates that and that almost all students work in courts using regional languages, so there is very limited use of English in the workplace' (Tsegay 2001). There was thus a contradiction in trying to develop an English language syllabus that could address their English language needs when they were working in Amharic and other regional languages. Like Howida, he acknowledged that because his research question was focused on his day-to-day teaching, he was unable to address the wider issues in any depth.

The above account reinforces the discussion in Chapter 1 about the diversity of the international student population. Even within apparently similar cultural or political contexts, people will respond in different ways to institutional pressures to research a certain question or issue. Students from the same country may identify different factors that influence the direction of their research enquiry – such as the recognition that a PhD can enhance their career development and contribute to their identity as a technical specialist. What all the students discussed above share is their starting point: that none of them had a free choice about what to research. In the following section, I will consider international students who were in the position of determining their own research question with few or no external constraints.

A choice without limits

Although a relatively small group, it is useful to compare students in the unusual situation of having the freedom to choose their own area of research. Inevitably such students are usually self-funded. However, within our seminar group, there were also a few individuals who had sponsorship without conditions attached and who felt that they were not accountable to produce a certain piece of work for their home institutions. This is not to say that they were uninterested in the career development aspects of doing a PhD. They saw it less in terms of strengthening their position within an institution, and more as a valuable personal development experience that might lead to other more tangible career outcomes, including a change in career.

Judith, a university lecturer from Mexico, explained to our seminar group how she had decided to embark on a PhD and why she had decided to focus on 'Gender, education and citizenship: a divided self':

> Working as a professional woman in a higher educational institution in Mexico, Judith had become increasingly aware that though a transition to more 'democratic ideals' was taking place, issues on gender had not been addressed . . . Having worked as a lecturer in a school of education, Judith found that she and many of her female colleagues felt 'isolated, lonely and ungratified'. She feels that most of the frustration that women in education experience is not due to their 'sexual identity' but to their 'segmented self or outlaw emotions when trying to live up to the contradictory prescriptions for being a caring woman and productive academic'. Judith intends to focus her research around two key questions:
> – Why do women in education consent to a system of class and gender oppression, which appears to offer few rewards and little benefit?
> – What are some of the signs of resistance or subversion that women in education respond to as a catalytic of oppression?
> (Seminar report: 3/4/03)

Judith went on to describe how having an open agenda presented different challenges to those who had objectives pre-determined by their sponsors. She was aware of opening up more and more questions through reading and discussion of new ideas in seminars, to the extent that it could become difficult to narrow them down to a manageable piece of research for her PhD. She also had no constraints on how she should carry out the research, so faced a dilemma about whether to do field research back in Mexico or to base the thesis on theoretical analysis instead.[4] Judith related her research closely to events in her personal and professional life:

About five years ago, she had started to write and edit a newspaper which was considered too 'critical and outspoken'. She then suffered from exclusion within her institution and felt she needed to take a break and move outside her country. The Mexican government has been creating funds for PhD study so it was relatively easy to come to study in the UK and she faces no constraints in terms of what she writes or studies here.

(Seminar report: 3/4/03)

The close connection between Judith's research questions and her own life events emphasized that she saw the PhD as a journey in every sense of the word. Like the students who had little choice in what they studied, she also saw the PhD as an important milestone in her career:

In terms of her own reasons for coming to UEA, Judith explained that she wants to find out how to negotiate with structures of violence and oppression and that she believed she needed to do a PhD to be an effective critic. Referring to the history of colonialism in Mexico, she explained that she needs to understand the West – 'it is my enemy, yet it is part of my identity'. She feels she is now able to negotiate from a new position.

(Seminar report: 3/4/03)

Rather than valuing the PhD only for its extrinsic value and status, Judith stressed the opportunity to extend her own learning and capacity for criticism. She pointed to the similar paradox that I opened this chapter with – the need to acquire familiarity with Western models and practices to be able to critique them, 'to negotiate from a new position'. Within our group, some students felt that Judith 'ran the risk of excluding the cultural background of her country' through drawing on such Western concepts of gender. Judith referred more explicitly to her changed identity and position, which she associates with doing PhD research – others suggested that she could choose to switch roles between the 'cool Western researcher' and the 'passionate South American'. This links to the observations by Howida and Tsegay in the earlier section about their changing perspectives on their initial research question. However, unlike Judith, they felt that they did not have the opportunity to redefine their area of research and pursue a different direction, due to institutional and political constraints.

Turning to another student with similar personal motivations to do a PhD, Scholastica, a counsellor from Tanzania, gave us an insight into how she had decided on a research direction:

She had become interested in this area of research through her own personal experiences of living with and looking after her brother when he was dying from AIDs in the early '80s . . . As his condition deteriorated, Scholastica found herself affected by the attitudes of other people in the community – her friends didn't want to study with her and their relations would not eat at their house. She and her former lecturer in the School of Social Work in Tanzania decided to set up an organization where they worked as volunteers to raise awareness amongst the community about HIV/Aids. They realized that even the orphans of AIDS patients had little idea about their own bodies or why their parents had died. This led Scholastica to begin to explore how children and parents could begin to communicate about sexuality and other issues related to HIV/AIDS.

(Seminar report: 17/6/02)

Scholastica's account of the origins of her research proposal (which she terms 'from not communicating with children to counselling') focused on the personal experiences which had shaped her gradual move towards doing PhD research. Like Judith, she was keen to make positive changes in her organization back home through the skills and knowledge gained doing a PhD. She had had to raise her own funds to do research, which she saw as feeding directly into her work as a counsellor with a non-governmental organization in Tanzania. In contrast to Judith, she was less interested in the PhD as a way of pursuing theoretical knowledge and was determined to make practical links with youth counselling services in the UK and to learn first-hand from the comparison with Tanzania. She emphasized that counselling could be seen as a Western import to Tanzania and that she wanted to look critically at how practices could be adapted to her differing cultural context. She described, for instance, how the role of a counsellor was sometimes seen as similar to that of a mother in Tanzania, shouting at the young girl for having done something wrong! Like Azhar, she recognized that even the use of certain terms like 'counselling' had to be 'translated' in her research question to get across the concept of counselling in a cultural context affected by different ideas of confidentiality and a greater respect for elders.

In the second half of this chapter, I will look more closely at assumptions implicit in many of the research questions I have described – often expressed by students in terms of the tension between the need to produce research valued both by their home institution and their UK university. As we have seen in the above account, some students commented on how they (or their peers) were being pulled in one direction or the other ('swallowing our governments' policies' as compared to 'running the risk of excluding the cultural background of your country'). The relationship between 'Western' and 'other' practices or theory was seen as essentially problematic and was a constant source of debate within our seminar group, especially in relation to defining a research question or problem to address – and, as I will discuss in the next chapter, when choosing a research approach.

Whose values? Whose knowledge?

A question commonly posed to a PhD candidate at the stage of their viva is to ask what they believe they have contributed to 'knowledge' through their research. This aim can influence someone's starting point too, as they strive to identify gaps in the existing literature or unanswered questions. For an international student, the first question may however be 'whose knowledge' to contribute to, as my opening quotation from Al-Nasser's thesis suggests: 'they theorize and we take for granted'. Concepts such as 'democracy' and 'counselling' were regarded by some students as Western in origin, and could be redefined within different cultural contexts. In some cases, this involved students taking a concept from the Western literature, such as 'teacher stress', and not only exploring another name or term (in this case, perhaps 'stress' was referred to as 'problems') but also whether the concept of 'stress' could be said to exist in other cultures.[5]

While some students welcomed the challenge to take Western concepts and adapt them, others were more ambivalent, feeling that this implied devaluing indigenous beliefs [similar to Tuhiwai Smith's (1999) stance discussed in Chapter 1]. In our seminars, these conflicting ideological perspectives often emerged during discussion. For example, Ted, a student from Taiwan, gave a presentation on his ideas of combining concepts from Western and Chinese philosophy to look at how 'personal salvation' (as compared to 'collective salvation') could be the first step for thinking about education and the curriculum. Ted contrasted the separation between one and the whole ('man and the world') within Western philosophy with the concept of Tai Chi, where the personal and collective can be integral in each other, not necessarily opposites. During our discussion, several students expressed unease with the idea of fusing Western and Chinese philosophy, as well as with Ted's research approach, which was not based on empirical data. In particular, they raised questions about his research objectives:

> What benefits can this kind of research offer? Some of the group felt it presented a threat to educational systems ('it would ruin our whole system in Malaysia') and to individuals, but others felt it offered a different approach for looking at the world and at education.
>
> (Seminar report: 18/3/02)

A student from Malaysia pointed out that their government had a national education philosophy around producing 'a balanced individual', suggesting that this differed from Ted's ideal: 'How can we expect governments to adopt the philosophy of "personal salvation" as compared to "individualism" when the objective of the education system usually lies in economic advancement?'

> (Seminar report: 18/3/02)

Though the objectives underlying the Malaysian education system ('the balanced individual') could be seen as more influenced by Western educational philosophies than indigenous concepts, the discussion implied that Ted was threatening indigenous objectives through his fusion of Western and Chinese philosophy. This discussion brings out the dangers of polarizing 'Western' and 'the other' (which I referred to in Chapter 1 in the context of post-colonial theory), as the colonial-influenced educational systems in countries like Malaysia may now be regarded as 'Eastern' by the younger generation population [see Lie (2004) for an account of the indigenization of colonial educational practices in Malaysia]. Research such as Ted's could then be challenged for bringing into question the 'new' indigenous values (even though these were 'Western' in origin).

Those students who had a 'choice within limits' did not usually set out with the intention of challenging indigenous assumptions or their government's values. However, during the course of their research, they sometimes found that their initial research question had led them in an unanticipated direction (as I suggested in the case of Tsegay, who by focusing on English language teaching had to give less attention to the pressing concerns he identified about the 'functionality' of language policy for law students). In several cases, students were left with a dilemma about whether to change direction if their initial findings suggested that their research question had been based on assumptions which they later questioned. For example, Halim had set out to research the implementation of a government programme to introduce ICT and more child-centred learning approaches into Malaysian schools. He presented his research through a table comparing the differences between the traditional and the new learning environment which the government hoped to create through this programme. During the seminar, Tsegay (from Ethiopia) questioned these underlying objectives: '[Tsegay] suggested that sometimes it might be more appropriate to promote "traditional" education, rather than new approaches . . . and that we need to ask "why" (this approach) as well as how to implement it effectively. Why should teachers and schools want to make this change?' (from Seminar report).

The challenge posed by Tsegay, as an outsider, was whether the Malaysian government should accept approaches that originated in the West: to question the underlying values rather than just evaluate their implementation. As an insider, Halim had intended to focus on the effectiveness of implementation of the programme, rather than analyse its rationale. During his pilot fieldwork, he discovered that there were problems in convincing teachers to adopt the new approaches: 'Only two out of the 24 teachers he sampled with a questionnaire were using IT and some of the teachers, when asked what IT integration meant to them, replied "nothing"!' (Seminar report: 17/6/03).

He was then uncertain about how to report his findings to the policy makers and how far to change his approach to look at the ideology behind the intervention, rather than focusing on the effectiveness of implementation:

> He had mentioned to a government official that so few teachers were using ICT and she suggested that the schools he had studied were not representative of [the programme], insisting that he should have sampled an area where the teachers were less laid back about ICT! In shaping his findings, Halim now faces a dilemma around how far to focus on the minority of classes sampled where IT was being used (i.e. the 26 classes (36%) out of 72 classes that used Smart School Management System, 10 schools (14%) out of 72 classes that used Overhead Projector (OHP), 42 classes (58%) out of 72 classes that used hands-on experiments in the teaching process).
>
> (Seminar report: 17/6/03)

It was interesting that the criticism by a government official had been made on methodological grounds (that Halim had not sampled a representative area) – suggesting a technical weakness in his research design, rather than his findings might be politically sensitive. During our discussion of this educational intervention, students from Malaysia differed in how far they felt 'the criticism might be around the method of implementation rather than the objectives of the programme'. However, there was agreement that the underlying assumptions about the cultural values informing the education system needed to be taken into account within Halim's research:

> The Smart School project implied a huge cultural change that was not going to happen overnight – the assumption [by the government] was that a collaborative culture could be developed, whereas an individualistic culture was still very strong within the schools. There were also assumptions about the links between IT and creating a more child-centred approach within the classroom or enhancing learning – in fact, Halim had observed teachers (who had been given free laptops) absorbed in their own computer and ignoring their students!
>
> (Seminar report: 17/6/03)

Although policy, planning and implementation are often regarded as separate stages that can be evaluated in isolation from each other, Halim's research illustrated how ineffective implementation may be related directly to assumptions behind policy objectives. However, having intended (and obtained official approval) to research the implementation stage of the programme, Halim faced a dilemma as to whether to take a more holistic view (including policy assumptions and objectives) or to focus narrowly on the mechanics of implementation.

In a situation where a student is sponsored or supported by their employer to research a certain problem or issue, asking 'whose values count?' can be seen as a challenge to their professional loyalty or even patriotism. In the cases I described above, this was not necessarily a matter of 'Western' values transplanting indigenous beliefs, but a concern about political priorities: that research into implementation of a programme might be more useful (to a national government) than questioning the original policy objectives in a wider context. As I discussed in the case of Malaysia, this might mean a student was criticized for attention to indigenous educational practices, as opposed to focusing on new 'Western' approaches.

Responding to the UK supervisor

Looking from the opposite perspective, I mentioned earlier the tension that many students experience between their 'home' values and knowledge and the Western university academic culture. Once in the UK, it may be more difficult to challenge (or even discover) the assumptions in the UK university than to cast a critical eye on your own culture – partly because of the relationship entered into by student and supervisor. Although rarely intended to be hierarchical, the supervisor/student relationship tends to reinforce the assumption (often held by students) that the supervisor's knowledge is somehow superior to that of the student. As I will discuss in the last chapter of this book, some international students may be familiar with and prefer traditional pedagogical practices – which makes it difficult for both parties to begin to transform the relationship into a more equal partnership. Though students may feel uncomfortable with the new knowledge and values they encounter through their supervisor, they might be understandably inhibited about challenging this with alternative frameworks of belief – not least because the supervisor's perspective on their research question is likely to give an insight into their future examiner's views on the research. During a seminar on 'writing a PhD thesis', students described the difficult balance they tried to ensure:

> Some students felt it was important to keep the supervisor on your side, that it might be difficult to ignore advice or appear to go a contradictory way. Others stressed the need to consider whose research it is and not be diverted if you feel the supervisor is encouraging a direction which does not fit with your own aims or context.
>
> (Seminar report: 17/5/02)

Elliott's e-mail conversation analyses the choice of research focus in terms of responding to the 'preferences of the supervisor' (Elliott *et al.* 2004: 7). John discusses with Hasani (his doctoral student from Malaysia) as to whether he saw himself as 'obeying his supervisor' in changing his research to focus on experiences of student disaffection. It can be difficult for students to challenge a supervisor's suggestions for their research – whether it is a question of introducing a theoretical concept that carries little meaning in their cultural context or a research methodology that they consider inappropriate. However, as I discussed in relation to Ted's study of Chinese and Western philosophy, the tension between differing cultural beliefs can also be regarded as a source of learning and personal development during the PhD. This is an aspect explored in Elliott's e-mail conversation with his doctoral students through the question 'who is the research educating?'

Notions of change

> How do we deal with change when we are doing the research itself? How does it affect us as researchers (particularly if we are 'insider' researchers)? What do we do if we find that our intended research has already been done by someone else? Tsegay raised these issues in relation to his research in Ethiopia, suggesting that many of us found that our situations were constantly changing. As Steve said, it would be nice 'if the world stood still' while we got on with our research.
>
> (Seminar report)

Implicit in the discussion so far in this chapter has been the idea that research questions develop in response to changes in the people and situations involved. This is a point supported by the discussion in Elliott *et al.* (2004): Grace reflects on how the data she collected 'changed my belief in the relationship between work and play' (p. 13) and John Lam describes how his 'focus was constantly changed by the findings generated and flowed out of my conversations with teachers' (p. 16). The idea of research design having to be flexible enough to respond to changing environments is much discussed in the literature on qualitative methodology (see, for instance, Mason 2002), drawing from Glaser and Strauss's (1967) influential work, *The Discovery of Grounded Theory*. There is also growing recognition of the need for reflexivity within PhD theses to explore how the researcher has affected the researched, the final text and research process – the kind of issues raised by students in the extract above. However, what is less commonly addressed is how we deal with change in ourselves as a result of doing PhD research[6] ('How does it affect us as researchers?') – and in the context of this chapter, how that change affects decisions about the direction of our research question or the data we collect. As Firth (1966: ix) discusses in relation to conducting studies of a community across time, 'He [the researcher] intends to record social change and he is supposed to be able to do this by comparing the main patterns he [*sic*] observes today with those he observed in the past. But he who applies the measuring rod has himself also changed'.

Looking at my earlier discussion about 'whose values', it appears that students were aware of shifting between differing identities during the course of a PhD, as an 'outsider' (in the UK higher educational context) and as an 'insider' within the Malaysian educational system, for example. Resistance to differing values or research priorities could be related to a student's desire to preserve their 'insider' cultural identity. In their final thesis, many students refer however to their research journey, identifying a gradual transition over the three years towards more of an 'insider' identity within the UK institution – as discussed in relation to 'communities of practice' (Wenger 1998) in Chapter 1. Although this changed identity seems to be welcomed by individual students in the end, I wonder how many students (or employers) regard this as an unintended side-effect of doing a PhD abroad.[7]

The experience of living and working in the UK can affect students' attitudes and values more deeply than their academic courses (as Manal Madini describes in 'Impressions': see Chapter 1). In our seminar discussions, several students commented on how their personal experiences of education in UK schools had made them reflect differently on the research they were intending to do in their home countries. For example, in a discussion about 'traditional' approaches to education, students drew on their own children's experience of going to school in the UK to think more critically about what education meant to them:

> What is it that people feel is worth holding on to from 'traditional' approaches to education? Sharah and Hisham described the experiences of their own children coming to UK schools from what could be termed a more 'traditional' form of education in their home countries (Saudi Arabia and Malaysia). They felt their children now regarded school as enjoyable and fun, and that the emphasis was on learning new skills, rather than memorizing, doing mountains of homework and cramming facts . . . in Saudi Arabia and Malaysia, children were being well-trained in how to work hard for long periods of time, which might be key to later economic success.
>
> (Seminar report: 22/11/01)

This extract suggests that these two students were not only learning about different educational approaches, but also valued the 'new skills' that their children were being introduced to. In this respect, they were aware of constantly comparing and evaluating differing practices and educational philosophies. Another Saudi Arabian student compared himself as a child to his young daughter who now attended a UK primary school:

Think about children. There are better teaching methods here, insisting on self-actualization for children, to express themselves, not just memorizing or receiving information. My daughter can speak with anyone, but I couldn't at that age. We found it the right way, but we should start from an early age. We can't change our society as we grew up with this method.

(Interview notes: July 2004)

The researcher as an agent of change

The differences between the two educational systems (of home country and UK) could be related to the notion of change and to reproduction theories of education (whether schools are intended to reproduce or challenge existing class or gender relations: Bowles 1977; Kuhn and Wolpe 1978). Transposing these opposing views of educational change to the research context, students could also distinguish between research approaches that set out to change (society, systems, people, educational practice), like action research, and those which fitted more easily with the desire for stability and predictability. A student from Saudi Arabia commented on her worry about writing a research proposal for her PhD, relating this to our discussions about the need to be flexible within qualitative research: 'In my country you have to stick to the proposal once you have written one. In case you change, you have to explain their queries. Once you commit yourself on paper about a research proposal, you have to do it' (Seminar report: 5/2/03).

Caught between the expectations of the UK department that she should be flexible and respond to changing circumstances, and her home institution's insistence that she should keep faithful to her original research question, this student could find herself in an impossible situation. Other students, however, met less resistance if they wanted to make changes, the proposal being regarded by their employer less in terms of a blueprint. Half-way through his PhD, Hisham (from Malaysia) reflected on his research in relation to his initial proposal:

Hisham began by giving us the context in which he wrote this proposal – it was during his first eight months and he had to produce a more detailed proposal, partly for his sponsoring institution to know exactly what he was doing in his research. He had submitted a proposal before arrival at UEA, which had a greater emphasis on discovery learning but changed after he started the PhD to focus mainly on distance learning. The change came about because he realized that there were so many aspects to take into account once he started to read more about distance learning (i.e. not just discovery learning). Hisham pointed out that he had not looked at his proposal since writing it and it was quite a shock to see the terminology he had used then – for example, he wondered why he had used the word 'voyage' so much.

(Seminar report: 28/2/03)

This account gives an insight into how the research proposal could be used as a measure of change: Hisham reflected on how his research question evolved in relation to the literature he read and also on how he now read his own text (the proposal) differently. He described how part of the challenge of doing a PhD was also 'how to leave behind what you think you already know, when working in a familiar environment'. Although sponsored by his university in Malaysia, Hisham did not face the same constraints as some of his fellow students, and was in the position of having a choice of research topic within relatively wide limits: 'Hisham explained that the ownership of the research is his and that his sponsoring university is more concerned that he gets the degree – they don't mind a slight change but not a whole change of focus' (Seminar report: 28/2/03).

Change within limits

The whole issue of change within limits can be related to my opening section on choice within limits: individuals, even from the same cultural context, may position themselves in differing ways through their research question and the methodology they adopt. As I discussed earlier, by choosing a tightly defined technical question within ELT, Karim prescribed his own boundaries and did not set out to explore the potential social and cultural dimensions of his research area. His desire for change was therefore focused clearly on the linguistic testing tool he investigated, rather than encompassing any structural or political changes to the educational system. Other students were cautious about how far they could directly hope to initiate change, more for pragmatic reasons. Tekleab, a student from Eritrea, explained that though he would like to make changes in the system, it could not, he believed, be done with a single dissertation and that he did not have the scope to work at macro level. A student from Malaysia explained that as he was an inspector back home, his status sometimes worked against his capacity to initiate change through his research in his immediate context. He was concerned about when change might take place – like several other colleagues, he was aiming to implement changes after his PhD rather than alongside it.

These questions about how, whether, when and what kind of change is intended to be initiated through research were not always anticipated when students began their PhD. However, influences from the theoretical literature, their new cultural environment and interaction with their new colleagues sometimes caused them to re-examine the assumptions embedded in their original research question. The students' own perspective on education, and how far this was changing due to their (and their children's) experiences in a differing culture, influenced whether they regarded changing or expanding their research question as a problematic step. Whether they took educational change for granted or preferred to minimize the possibilities for change within their research design was reflected in their choice of research question and methodology. As I will discuss in the next chapter, confidence in how far students could make changes in their own thinking and personality greatly affected their choice of research approach and how to adapt research methods to their own country context: 'how would I be able to convince the participant to accept taking part in a research that is of a tradition I myself have not yet got the grip of?' (Al-Nasser 1999: 83). It is not just a question of whether the sponsor or employer recognizes and supports a desire for change, but how far individual researchers want to challenge their own established educational and research practices.

Finding a 'good' research question: the double audience

> What is doing a PhD about? While some people felt it was about self-discovery, so the personalized approach was essential, others felt they had been requested by their employers to research and present recommendations on a specific subject.
>
> (Seminar report: 17/5/02)

Any group of students will hold diverse aims for doing a PhD. As the above comment suggests, their objective for doing a PhD not only influences the question or issue they decide to research, but the style and form of the thesis (see Chapter 6). Though the 'personalized approach' was not considered appropriate for research supported by an employer, students sometimes felt that they were expected by their UK teachers to bring in an element of personal reflection. As I mentioned earlier, there was a sense in which they were being pulled in contradictory directions through studying for a PhD in the UK, and this related to the issue of quality. It was not just a question of responding to the demands of two different systems of education (home country and UK) or institutions (employer versus UK university). Students were aware of differing criteria as to what constitutes 'good' research and that they had to make strategic decisions about how to succeed on both terms. Once in the UK context, they had learnt what the criteria for 'good' research consisted of: being reflexive (the 'personal' element) and being critical were two key differences that many students identified in comparison with their home academic culture. They then had to work out how to carry this off successfully in their thesis. As

Scholastica commented in relation to her research in Tanzania, this implied a major change in the way you related to people and looked at the world:[8]

> How do you become critical after a lifetime (and an educational system) which has discouraged criticism? This question from Scholastica was not just around the dangers of being critical in certain political contexts, but the difficulties she had felt in adopting this approach, coming from a culture 'that does not allow us to be critical: how do you go about this in a society that doesn't ask those kinds of questions?'
>
> (Seminar report: 9/7/02)

I will look in later chapters in more detail at what it means 'to be critical' in differing cultural contexts, but here Scholastica's comment that her 'society doesn't ask those kinds of questions' related to students' concerns that a 'good' research question by their employer's or colleagues' standards might not be considered 'critical' or penetrating enough to guide a PhD study, by their UK supervisor's criteria. Since I am looking at educational research in this book, rather than research in general, I am constantly aware of the link between the students' educational experiences in the UK university and their practice as educational researchers within their home schools or universities. In other words, their experience as students in a differing cultural and institutional context enabled them to learn first-hand about contrasting educational practices and concepts (which they may also have been reading about) – a point which is developed further in Chapter 7. In this instance, learning new academic practices as research students in a UK university involved evaluating what was considered 'good' in their old and new academic context – which might prompt them to look more critically at their research question.

Comparing notions of quality

Within our seminars, we often focus on differing views of quality in relation to the educational practices being described and researched by students from very contrasting backgrounds. The following question arose when teachers from Ethiopia commented that a Saudi Arabian teacher's description of crowded classrooms and poor facilities looked idyllic from their perspective of 120 children in a class with no equipment at all. They then went on to compare how teaching approaches were influenced by physical conditions, as well as notions about 'quality' and learning objectives:

> Whose criteria do you use to judge a 'quality' teacher? It was pointed out that often Western criteria around 'quality' are imported into

non-Western contexts, where people may have different criteria. What is considered 'good' language teaching by Saudi teachers may not be considered good in other contexts (and vice versa). How do these issues feed into Ayedh's research around how the context affects quality of EFL teaching? Are there different teaching styles?

(Seminar report: 2/7/03)

Here a distinction had been made between Western and non-Western criteria of 'quality', though as my earlier discussion has implied, there were differences between values held even within one culture (for example, the teachers who preferred 'traditional' education to the 'new' approaches in Malaysia). In another seminar that focused on the idea of 'different mirrors on quality' (Seminar report: 18/5/01), we looked more closely at how to problematize quality in relation to teacher education and came up with these questions:

– Who defines 'quality'?
– What is the purpose of evaluating 'quality' and how far does this influence the relationship between researcher and researched? Whose purposes will the data serve?
– What is it most useful to evaluate in relation to 'quality'?
– How can we move away from the idea that assessing quality is simply a technical act?
– How do we avoid the imposition of one educational philosophy when discussing or judging quality?

(Seminar report: 18/5/01)

If we transpose these questions, which arose in relation to assessing quality of teaching, into the context of educational research, we can begin to illuminate the tensions faced by an international student. We can see a parallel with the student who has a double audience for their PhD – employer and UK examiner – and the possibility of imposing one set of criteria for evaluating success or failure ('one educational philosophy') above another. The danger of ignoring these ideological differences and considering 'assessing quality' to be a 'technical act' links to the earlier comment by Halim's colleague who said that his sample had been wrongly constructed because he came up with negative findings. As this section has emphasized, for many international students it is not just an issue of deciding which research topic or question you prefer, but identifying an area that will be judged 'good' by institutions and individuals with differing agendas and value systems.

Conclusion

Choosing and redefining a research question could be assumed to be a personal and individual activity. As I have tried to convey in this chapter, for many PhD students, simply focusing down on one topic, issue or direction within their subject area can however mean responding to the priorities of different parties: both within the UK institution and their home political and educational context. An employer's or government's decision to support an individual to enrol for a PhD in the UK may have been made on the basis of institutional rather than personal goals. How a student decides to position him or herself in relation to these often competing pressures will be influenced by their personal objectives for pursuing a PhD abroad, as well as their anticipated future role in their home institution.

As this chapter has shown, the very process of undertaking a PhD, living in another culture and participating in educational practices with differing values and norms can mean that an individual begins to change their perspective on their initial research question. The choice of a research question is therefore not a one-off decision but for many students involves a constant re-assessment of their starting aims and the theoretical assumptions behind their research. The relatively autonomous UK student may regard this process as the fulfilling aspect of pursuing a PhD. However, for the student who had a limited choice regarding their research topic, the gradual pressure to move in another direction may present ethical dilemmas, raising questions such as: How far can I challenge dominant values or policy objectives? The decision as to whether to address two audiences arises at an early stage for such a student. When developing their research proposal and exploring ideas from differing ideological perspectives, they may need to ask: Whose knowledge do I intend to engage with and build upon during the course of my study? How far is that knowledge valued or recognized by my supervisor, by my employer? Faced with a two-way challenge, from both the UK university and home institution, the student may try to reconcile differing criteria of quality or conflicting values – or decide to go one way or the other.

Learning to be a student in a new academic and institutional culture is a major challenge in itself, as I will discuss later in this book in relation to learning academic literacy practices. Conducting empirical PhD research often involves moving between the two cultures for fieldwork too and the added responsibility of having to justify any changes in your educational approach, research practices and even in your perceived identity to colleagues and family back home during your course of study. Though some students need to receive official approval for their research question, a greater hurdle may be to convince colleagues that an unfamiliar research approach can lead to valid findings. Many international students feel that they have to take on the role as advocate for a particular research approach in their home institution. Rather than a bureaucratic procedure similar to getting a research proposal approved, they saw this as an educational process where they had to raise awareness informally about the benefits of their research approach. Since decisions about research methodologies were often regarded by their colleagues as 'technical' in nature rather than ideological, this meant that they otherwise risked being dismissed as 'bad' researchers (as opposed to 'different'). The issue of whose criteria is used to judge the quality of research came to the fore when they realized that 'good' PhD research (by UK university standards) could be considered as worthless personal anecdotes by their colleagues back home.

This is, of course, a concern shared by many qualitative researchers working in UK policy environments where the quantitative paradigm is dominant, pointing to the importance of recognizing the influence of institutional cultures on research practice (see my distinction between 'Culture' and 'culture' in Chapter 1). The tensions identified throughout this chapter, between the need to closely define a research question and to open up possibilities, between 'Western' ideologies and indigenous beliefs, were often related to what students saw as the polarization between quantitative and qualitative research paradigms. This tendency (to polarize quantitative and qualitative) could be seen as common to most PhD students. However, the cross-cultural perspective adds complexity to the debate, since many international students identified the differing cultural values and practices in the UK with the 'new' research approaches they now encountered. In the next chapter, I will look in detail at how such students learned to conduct research within what they first considered an 'alien' paradigm and how they developed and 'sold' qualitative approaches once back home.

Challenges facing a PhD graduate from the UK: an Iranian context

By Karim Sadeghi

Every year, a number of Iranian candidates are sponsored by different governmental organizations, including the Ministry of Research, Science and Technology (MSRT), to pursue their studies at PhD level in first-class universities in other countries, including the UK, Australia and Canada. Most of the graduates to whom I have spoken find themselves at a loss when they return to Iran and start their career here. Recounting my own story will clarify the issue properly, I hope.

I begin with the process before a PhD candidate starts his/her PhD. A candidate in Iran has to pass several barriers before he/she is allowed to apply for admission for a PhD programme abroad. The first step, of course, is for candidates with an MA or an MSc to pass a competitive nationwide PhD written exam in their relevant fields held by the Organization for the Measurement of Education (OME). Although this part of the PhD candidature selection procedure is mainly objective, the rest of the process is very much subjective. Namely, after passing this test, a candidate is sent to at most three universities (those in which the candidate has shown an interest to be employed by after finishing his/her PhD) for oral interview. If a candidate is successful at this stage too, then he/she should pass another selection bridge which has nothing to do with the speciality or knowledge area of the candidate and is a form of 'security check'. All these processes successfully accomplished, the final list of the eligible candidates is issued, and these candidates are introduced to the Scholarship Office of the MSRT, where they have to go through still some other processes in order to be issued with a scholarship or a confirmation letter that will authorize them to study abroad. Only after their names are issued by the OME can the candidates contact universities abroad to apply for admission. The whole process, from enrolling in the PhD exam in Iran to leaving the country, may take an average of two and a half years and sometimes less or more. In my case, this period took 45 months (nearly four years). Of course, the process and the length may differ for candidates sponsored by other organizations or for university instructors who are allowed to apply for PhD admission abroad, and sponsored if successful, without taking part in the PhD exam mentioned above.

The issue is if the selection procedure takes such a long time, the outcome should be highly important for the scholarship bodies, and they should, therefore, take all necessary measures to make the right decision as to which areas they would like their prospective employees to be trained in. There is, however, much mismatch between the needs of such organizations and the skills that the candidates gain during their PhD. In other words, while most of the PhD candidates, especially in the UK, are trained in carrying out research in a very narrow area of their field, this is not what they are expected to be able to put into practice when they return home, and even if they would like to pursue the research themselves, there are no academic facilities on the one hand, and no financial, organizational or social support on the other.

In my case, for example, having done my PhD research project on the validity of cloze procedure as a measure of EFL reading comprehension, I find little connection between my theoretical findings (that cloze tests should only sparingly be used to test the comprehension of a passage) and their application in the university where I am a lecturer. Namely, although I myself try to apply my findings in the tests that I construct (i.e. use cloze tests as the last resort for testing reading comprehension), there is virtually no other teacher or lecturer who would like to refer to my research and use the findings in their teaching and testing. It seems as if I have done a 'private' research study only to inform myself and the results of which have nothing to do with the rest of my co-professionals. Other professionals would neither care nor show an interest in finding out what I have done research on or whether there is something useful for them in it. The striking issue is that rarely ever would any lecturer bother himself to refer to the latest research findings and try to apply them in their own class.

Simply put, research or research-based practice has no meaning here for the majority of the teachers in the English Language Department where I teach, and the priorities are different things for a variety of reasons. There is no research culture here mainly because of economic problems: most of the teachers spend a lot more time on teaching (with an average of 30–40 hours a week), some having to teach in other higher education centres or language institutes even on Thursdays and Fridays (which are 'off' days in our university). A lecturer like me earns a little more than £250 a month and he/she has no other option than working overtime, teaching either university English courses or English conversation classes in private institutes. Mainly because of economic hurdles, a university lecturer is obliged to move away from research which not only does not offer him/her short-term financial benefit, but also may require him/her to suffer some financial loss in order to disseminate it, for example, by presenting the findings at international conferences.

As a PhD graduate from a Western country, one would be expected by both the students and the administrative staff of the university to have returned as a better teacher and not as a better researcher – while as a PhD candidate one never receives training on teaching. The reality is that a lecturer engaged in teaching a course after getting his/her PhD may actually under-perform compared to the time he/she taught the same course before doing a PhD because, in the meantime, he/she has lost some teaching experience by taking distance from teaching for a couple of years and by focusing on a very narrow issue in his/her subject area. Such expectations on the part of the university community and the inability of the newly graduated lecturer clearly show the wide gap between the research training gained by the candidate and the practice he/she needs to put his/her knowledge, experience, skills and expertise into. Has the time not become ripe to rethink the role of research-based PhD candidature in fulfilling the educational needs of the Iranian university sector? Or is it not the time to revise Iran's present university education system and make it more research-based? Although choosing one over the other may not be so easy for some social, economic and political reasons, as an academic who has experienced alternative routes to better university education, I would recommend the Iranian educational authorities to invest more on the latter.

Karim Sadeghi has a PhD in TEFL/TESOL (Language Testing) from the University of East Anglia in Norwich, UK. Since his return to Iran in September 2003, he has been lecturing and researching in Urmia University, Iran. His main research interests include: process of second language learning, language testing, alternative assessment tools, reading comprehension and error analysis. He can be contacted at: Department of English Language and Literature, School of Literature and Humanities, Urmia University, Urmia, Iran or k.sadeghi@urmia.ac.ir

3

Choosing a research approach

Qualitative research in a quantitative environment

Dear Researcher
Do you call this research? What are you researching? What is it
you are measuring? I suggest you first learn how to construct a
questionnaire, construct one, and then start your project.
Good luck.

Signed

Dr . . . . . .

(Al-Nasser 1999: 85)

The choice of an appropriate research approach is often assumed to be
taken on methodological grounds, perhaps also indicative of a researcher's
ideological stance towards their subject matter. A research question can
imply a certain research methodology, as Lewin (1990a: 213) points
out: 'There are good reasons for favouring different styles of research.
But these, as has been argued, are likely to have their roots in the
research questions. Some types of question do not benefit from qualitative
approaches, others do'. However, as the above letter from a parent to a
PhD student carrying out research in Saudi schools illustrates, by choosing
a methodology unfamiliar to participants or sponsors, a student could be
jeopardizing their status in their local community. Al-Nasser (1999)
reports how the problem he faced was 'not the sarcastic tone of the letter',
but the fact that 'his letter was read by the headmaster and his deputy;
and probably every teacher in the school heard' (p. 86). The researcher
goes on to describe how he had to 'retaliate' by composing a letter back to
the parent, justifying his approach and pointing out that there was not
just one right way of doing research. As the letter indicates, Al-Nasser

faced practical difficulties as well, in persuading people to participate in his study because his research tools were unfamiliar. When he tried to convince another father to participate in a semi-structured interview, he was advised again, 'Construct a questionnaire. What you want to do is not research' (p. 87).

This chapter explores how students like Al-Nasser came to choose an unfamiliar research approach and the implications of adopting case study methodology or action research in differing cultural contexts. Many international students accept that the decision about how to conceptualize and conduct their research needs to take account of certain political and cultural factors. This is not just so that they retain their status as researchers and can persuade people to take part in interviews, but also to ensure that their PhD will be used and acted upon when they return home. As I discussed in Chapter 2, students are often conducting policy-orientated research to meet institutional goals and the choice of a research approach is similarly regarded as partly strategic. For this reason, even someone who is convinced that quantitative data would be limited or not provide the kind of answers they are looking for, may decide to conduct a small-scale survey alongside a case study, to ensure that their research as a whole is taken seriously.

An introduction to the CARE research tradition

As in the previous chapter, I will base much of my analysis on discussions and presentations with research students in seminars, as well as PhD theses written by past students in my department. At this point, I need to emphasize that the unusually strong tradition of qualitative applied research within the Centre for Applied Research in Education (CARE) shaped the international students' view of what 'UK' educational research consisted of. This account of CARE by Rob Walker, the current director, gives an insight into the influences shaping that tradition:

> CARE was established at UEA in 1970 as a research and development centre to continue the secondary school curriculum work begun in the Humanities Curriculum Project, a project which challenged convention by engaging young school leavers in the discussion of contentious social issues. During the 1970s, CARE became internationally well known for its development of new methodologies for studying educational change, we established an influential MA programme based on this work and began supervising doctoral students. This distinctive methodological focus, on action research, case study methods and democratic evaluation remains a CARE hallmark.
>
> (Walker 2003: 1)

Lawrence Stenhouse, the founder of CARE, saw the role of the teacher as 'researcher' as central to this work:

> Only in curricular form can ideas be tested by teachers. Curricula are hypothetical procedures testable only in classrooms. All educational ideas must find expression in curricula before we can tell whether they are daydreams or contributions to practice.
>
> (Stenhouse in Elliott 1983: 108)

In the UK as well as overseas, CARE was thus presenting a challenge to established approaches to educational research through emphasizing more involvement of participants in determining the research agenda and outcomes. As Rob Walker goes on to explain, this implies being explicit about the values and objectives underlying the research process:

> For CARE, 'applied research' does not just mean providing an information gathering service commissioned by clients, but building the capacity for informed judgement into the practice of a range of organisations, networks, institutions and those whom they serve. In the way that we realise it, 'applied research', is independent, critical and challenging. We claim that when we complete a project we leave behind, not just findings, but a process.
>
> (Walker 2003: 1)

Placed in the context of the previous chapter, the values highlighted by Walker – 'independent, critical and challenging' – could be considered as directly contradictory to the kind of research anticipated by some sponsors and employers of international students. I have provided this brief background on CARE's philosophy to suggest that, as in the international students' own departments 'back home', there was a similarly strong view of how research should be conducted within the UK department where the students would be based. The fact that the new research approaches were labelled 'qualitative' and were underpinned by values that appeared to be on the opposite end of a continuum encouraged students to polarize the two methodological approaches. 'Quantitative' became a composite term to describe not just quantitative tools, such as questionnaires or surveys, but to suggest the opposing values (to those democratic ideals of CARE) – such as lack of researcher autonomy or even political oppression.[1] As I will discuss in the next section, certain research approaches were associated with negative attitudes and values – which implied that the researcher had to take a moral stance (ironically) similar to that identified by Al-Nasser above, that all quantitative research was necessarily 'bad' and misleading because of 'statistical manipulation imposed by researchers' (Al-Nasser 1999: 77).

Learning about qualitative research: the hidden curriculum?

I have added this account because as a newcomer to CARE four years ago, I was struck by the contrast with the department where I had studied for my PhD – notably, the encouragement by CARE faculty to adopt a specific research approach or ideological stance. I am aware that – particularly in relation to this chapter on choosing a research approach – the specific context of CARE presented dilemmas and challenges for international students in a more intensified way than in other UK educational departments. By comparison with other institutions, in the past CARE has been more determined to articulate their underlying values to students as part of their immersion into qualitative research methodologies. Within the CARE PhD theses I have read, this sometimes comes across through images likening the transition the student made from 'quantitative' to 'qualitative' researcher to a religious conversion. Al-Nasser describes his attempts to understand what 'case study' is like chasing a mirage: 'But is case study a method? Questions such as these need to be raised, and answers to them need to be sought before any endeavours are made to go after what might seem at first, a mirage . . . I read and read . . . Weeks and months went by, but mirage was all there was' (Al-Nasser 1999: 68).

Another student writes about 'wandering around the corridors of CARE searching for the Holy Grail' (Pillay 1995: 274). By contrast, in the department where I studied for a PhD, students tended to regard the transition into the department in pragmatic terms as a question of obtaining sufficient technical support for their research (such as finding someone with quantitative expertise to supervise their project). I did not have the sense of being inducted into a department philosophy or the need to adapt to a new 'community of practice'. The international student arriving in CARE was, however, compelled to take notice of the new research practices – and as Pillay comments, there was so much at stake for individuals, they usually struggled to understand and adopt these approaches in their own research: 'At this point, the research student in CARE has certain options. One can give up (unlikely if you are a government sponsored student like me) . . . but perhaps if I go out and do some fieldwork, I might "see the answer"' (Pillay 1995: 274).

Given the specific cultural context of CARE that I have described above, the focus of this chapter is less about *why* students made a decision to adopt a qualitative research approach, and more about *how* they did this, particularly the ways in which they adjusted methods to their home context and countered resistance from colleagues and donors. I have suggested above that because research approaches are often seen as linked to department ideologies and established practices, the question of 'why' to choose a certain methodology may be seen only in terms of adapting to a new academic department (or continuing to respond to the expectations of former colleagues). However, to balance this account (which might imply that students were brainwashed into a certain way of doing research within CARE!), I will end this section with some reflections about how individuals feel that they have benefited through their experience of and learning about qualitative educational research.

Al-Nasser's discussion in his thesis of his research journey reveals both the struggles and commitment involved ('I held on mainly because I was attracted to the term "qualitative" mainly for being "discovery based"'; Al-Nasser 1999: 77). Significantly, he ends his thesis with a statement about the need to challenge the dominance of quantitative research approaches in Saudi Arabia, as well as his recommendations about English language teaching. He had begun from a position of dissatisfaction with these research approaches, particularly the 'statistical manipulation imposed by researchers and based on hypotheses derived from theories coming from research conducted in second language contexts or in contexts completely irrelevant' (ibid.). He gradually realized the value of case study research as a way of generating theory at the local level and giving voice and role to 'the silenced' (p. 81), and he later valued the experience of doing the PhD for the opportunity to learn about another research approach whose values he supported:

> Perhaps the most exciting and most beneficial experience this study has given me is the coming to terms with a research tradition which is pluralistic, holistic, flexible and most important gives partnership to the 'other'. Although I cannot claim to have learnt enough skills to be a good qualitative researcher, nor have I learnt enough about the nature of the diverse qualitative approaches, I have already fallen in love with this tradition and this love increases as my understanding of it and how and why people do it broadens.
>
> (Al-Nasser 1999: 80)

Given my discussion above of the dominant CARE research discourse, it is possible that Al-Nasser was consciously drawing on this discourse to ensure his thesis was positively received by his UK examiners. However, the fact that several ex-PhD students have gone on to establish qualitative research networks once back in their home environment suggests that this was more than a temporary 'conversion'. What is interesting is how they succeeded in bridging or narrowing the gap to this extent – both through convincing colleagues of the value of qualitative approaches and questioning deeply embedded assumptions among quantitative researchers. Looking at how CARE has evolved as a research centre – and particularly at changes in research culture – I am aware that the interaction is no longer the one-way learning process that Al-Nasser and others implied ('the meaning of case study which one is convinced must be in the head of some member of faculty or tucked away in the archives of CARE'; Pillay 1995). Just as it is now more difficult to generalize about the research culture in Malaysia,[2] the idea that CARE has an unchanging research tradition has also been challenged by new influences internationally and locally.

Selling qualitative approaches

Many international students are in the unenviable position of constantly shifting between two or more cultures and having to convince their colleagues at both ends that they have adopted the right course. As I discussed above, adopting a qualitative approach could not be seen in isolation as an academic decision as to which kind of data or analysis might be appropriate to one's research question, but a decision fraught with political implications. Many of our seminar discussions and presentations by students focused on the difficulties of how to convince colleagues back home to participate and support the PhD fieldwork, or as several students described the process, how to 'sell' qualitative research.

Why resistance?

Understanding more deeply why there was opposition to qualitative research approaches was partly a matter of self-exploration as 'insiders' of that institution and culture – since students had often shared the same perspective and initial resistance to qualitative research. However, as Al-Nasser's comments above suggest (and I discussed in Chapter 1), in many ways people coming to study in the UK could also be considered atypical of their colleagues (see James 1980). They may, like Al-Nasser, have already mistrusted quantitative approaches or begun to question established research traditions back home, and this was part of their motivation for doing a PhD.

The distinction between research methodologies and methods (or tools) is perhaps key to understanding the different kinds of resistance to qualitative research and also, with regard to case study, could be the 'holy grail' that Pillay sought. As I will discuss later, 'case study' may be considered as a research tool, rather than a methodology, particularly within a context where quantitative approaches are more familiar. In this chapter, I have tended to conflate the terms 'methodologies' and 'methods' by referring to 'research approaches' in order to reflect the ambiguity that I detected in discussions of resistance to 'qualitative research'. In many contexts, the resistance from colleagues seemed to be at the level of tools, which were unfamiliar:

> While doing my fieldwork, I was frequently asked the following question which is 'What are your research tools in collecting your data?' I replied that 'I am doing a case study and I am depending on different methods in so doing such as classroom observations, interviews and document collection'. I always get the reply that this is not enough and that I need to have something more concrete to base my analysis and findings on. 'The magic tool is a questionnaire'. I got this suggestion from the language inspectors and from the PhD holder who is involved in ELT in government schools as well.
>
> (Al-Yaseen 2000: 77)

Al-Yaseen described how she had to convince colleagues and research participants that her research methods would provide equally 'concrete' evidence to the information collected through a questionnaire, with which they were more familiar. Significantly, both she and Al-Nasser describe the main opposition as coming from PhD holders, whose criticism could threaten others' participation in the study through undermining the students' credibility as researchers. The resistance from other Saudi researchers in this case could be seen to be linked to a desire to preserve their own status as 'experts' in the face of unfamiliar new methods. As Al-Nasser notes in relation to his own experience, this was also to do with not knowing the language and terminology of such approaches: 'When I first came to CARE I had not the slightest idea what terms such as qualitative, naturalistic, case study and action research meant' (Al-Nasser 1999: 77). In Ethiopia, Tsegay found that it was more a fear of the unknown (rather than a threat to academic status or norms) that made people suspicious of qualitative research tools:

> He found from the fieldwork in his pilot stage that many people reacted negatively to the idea of qualitative research, as they were more familiar with quantitative approaches. This influenced his ideas for the main fieldwork and he decided to use a mixture of both quantitative and qualitative approaches.
>
> (from Seminar report)

Tsegay therefore recognized the need to engage colleagues in the research through using tools familiar to them (such as questionnaires), though he later reflected that it was difficult to predict people's likely reactions to any research method.

Though criticism of research tools such as unstructured interviews tended to be a reaction to the unfamiliar – 'do you call this research?' – people also gave objections on pragmatic grounds. A Malaysian government official suggested that opposition to qualitative research in the Ministry of Education was 'mainly practical: quantitative research gives clear results in a short period of time and they do not have time to read a lot, so they want a quick summary' (Seminar report: 16/12/03). It is worth noting that this is an objection raised by many policy makers in the UK, and not specific to overseas governments, as Lewin (1990a: 213) comments: 'Bureaucratic organisations – and much research in developing countries takes place within bureaucratic frameworks – treat such approaches [case study and ethnography] with suspicion since they appear to be subjective and too close to "story telling"'. Research participants were also sometimes reluctant to devote the time required to have informal discussions or interviews, as noted by Tsegay, and by Al-Nasser who commented that parents were not willing to spend more than 15 minutes talking to him.

Related to these practical constraints was the concern expressed by some PhD students that people were not accustomed to participating in less formal interactions with researchers: 'People are not used to this kind of research, with someone enticing them to talk while his tape recorder is on' (Al-Nasser 1999: 83). Al-Nasser was particularly concerned about how the quality of data might be affected by his participants' lack of confidence, as he recognized that the research interactions were shaped partly by informants' previous educational experiences. After he encountered difficulties persuading pupils to talk in a group, he concluded that: 'the probability was that the boys were not used to being informants; to being asked what they liked and what they did not like . . . Our pupils have always been made to believe they are recipients and nothing else' (p. 89). Placing the research participants' responses in the context of the behaviouristic learning theories prevalent in Saudi schools, Al-Nasser concluded that pupils were used to being treated as 'passive respondents rather than active participants' (ibid.).

These observations suggest that resistance to new research tools might be due also to lack of confidence (on the part of respondents as well as the researcher, to some extent) about how to participate in new and unfamiliar social practices. As Pillay pointed out, this could also mean that participants became less guarded in their responses than they would be when responding on questionnaires. Teachers participating in her study told her, '"teachers know how to answer questionnaires", meaning they knew the kind of answers bureaucrats wanted and responded accordingly' (Pillay 1995: 290). In this kind of situation, the PhD research student had to take on a new role as educator – not just raising awareness about the value of different research tools but also giving ideas about how to participate. Al-Nasser saw this learning process (on the part of informants) as being dependent on personal qualities that were not normally expected from research participants in his home context: 'Would the people I like to include as informants in my study have the kind of endurance, co-operation and understanding expected from informants in qualitative research?' (Al-Nasser 1999: 82).

Resistance to the methods or methodology?

There was thus a resistance identified at the level of research methods – both practical and ideological. People might be reluctant to participate in unfamiliar research activities that appear more time-consuming than filling in forms. There were also concerns about the ways in which these new research practices transformed hierarchical relationships (between teacher and student, researcher and researched) through their informal nature. Qualitative research tools presented a potential threat to the established status of traditional educational researchers who did not understand the terminology, or the purpose behind activities such as a focus group discussion. Open dissatisfaction was thus expressed by colleagues and informants about the unfamiliar research tools. Their criticism of the research methodology came across less directly, yet lies behind many of their comments about the research tools (for example, the insistence about one correct way of doing research through questionnaires).

As many students have found, the difficulties of conducting qualitative research in their home countries lie in the more explicit ideological stance that they are encouraged to adopt on their research question – in their words, the need 'to be critical'. During field research, a student may decide to downplay the implications of adopting a certain research methodology for this reason. They may choose to justify the different research tools they are using on the grounds of technical effectiveness, rather than attempting to explain a differing philosophical stance. In our seminars, however, several students commented on the perceived dangers of carrying out and participating in qualitative research: that 'being critical' is not only a differing skill from that promoted in many educational systems, but can pose a political risk to both researcher and participants (an issue discussed further in relation to research ethics in Chapter 4). Amir illustrated this in his account of his respondents' reluctance to use a tape recorder: 'Only two participants agreed to use the tape recorder. They were hesitant because of cultural reasons. They don't like to talk and use a tape recorder . . . These two said if you want me to talk about something sensitive, then turn off the tape. But they let me use my notes' (Interview: 30/7/04).

Returning to Al-Nasser, the resistance that he faced was not just to the ways in which he asked questions but to the kind of questions he was asking. He suggested that informants' reluctance to participate in his research activities was due to 'the fear of getting in trouble with politics' and that 'hierarchy appears to be another obstacle, i.e. only some people have the right to ask questions' (Al-Nasser 1999: 90).[3] The association of the right to be critical with status within the established hierarchy is key to understanding why someone might be reluctant to promote qualitative methodology, but happy to 'sell' the methods. Presenting oneself as a technical statistician is far less of a risk (politically and personally) than a researcher deliberately setting out to initiate change and reflection, as in action research. In many academic institutions too, the right to express criticism is associated with status, as explained by a student in a seminar: 'in her own country, she had been advised by her supervisor not to present critical views of her own because she was only a masters student – expressing criticism was something that came with the status of being a professor' (Seminar report: 17/5/02).

Being judged by the methodological principles of the quantitative paradigm was one of the hardest challenges faced by students who tried to convince colleagues of the value of qualitative methodology. While some students would argue that they were trying to find different answers to different questions (and so draw strength from the perceived gap between qualitative and quantitative research), others made a point of 'defending' their stance through stressing their similar goals or criteria. Hisham, a PhD student researching distance education in Malaysia, reflected on how the issue of generalization was a major concern for 'students like himself coming from Malaysia where the quantitative paradigm is dominant. In Malaysia the starting assumption that research findings should be replicable in other situations has meant that many people are not open to qualitative research' (Seminar report: 16/12/03). Hisham went on to say how he had found the concept of 'relatedability' in the research literature helped him to explain how the case study can 'extend the power to generalize' to readers.

The policy–research interface or cross-cultural?

This discussion about how to justify qualitative research approaches in an institution dominated by a quantitative paradigm is not specific to a cross-cultural context, or a problem faced only by international students. However, many students coming from countries where a quantitative approach is dominant have seen their role as 'advocate' for an alternative research paradigm as arising directly from their experiences in the UK education system. They believe that if they do not succeed in convincing others (both in the UK and at home) of the value of their research, their reputation could be at stake – as Hassan (Assistant Director in the curriculum department of the Teacher Education Division in Malaysia) commented in his PhD thesis, 'it was therefore a considerable personal risk and professional challenge in committing myself to a qualitative research methodology' (Hassan 2003: 378). As we saw in Chapter 2, adopting a critical stance, in terms of the question addressed and research approach chosen, could threaten sponsorship too: 'Tsegay contrasted his situation in Ethiopia where certain contextual circumstances would not allow him to be as critical as he would like, and significantly, no one would sponsor intellectuals to do this sort of research so it would be more on a personal basis' (Seminar report).

Comparing my own experiences as an ethnographic researcher in Nepal conducting evaluations for local projects, I was less conscious of the threat to my own position (possibly because I had more initial confidence in using qualitative approaches). I was, however, more concerned about whether the resistance from people in authority would mean my research was not used or useful in the end. Like the students I have quoted above, I became increasingly aware of the need to educate people about ethnographic approaches so that my reports were not dismissed as 'anecdotal'. I came to realize that recognizing whether this resistance was at a methodological or methods level was essential before working out a strategy for awareness-raising among colleagues or sponsors.

A case study from Nepal

To look more closely at the implications for 'selling' qualitative methodology within a policy context, I will draw on a specific study with which I was involved while based as a researcher in Nepal. I had been commissioned to carry out an analysis of the linkages between health outcomes (especially family planning uptake) and literacy in a women's education programme running in several districts of the country. The study had been designed by the sponsoring aid agency in Washington, though I was invited to make any (minor) changes that I felt necessary. The study was termed 'qualitative' because the tools included life-history interviews and focus group discussions, but the way in which the research question and the design had been constructed suggested that the project belonged more within a quantitative paradigm. For example, there was to be a control group of 'literate' women to compare with the 'illiterate' women and their knowledge was to be tested through a questionnaire to produce scores in literacy and health knowledge which could be statistically correlated. I felt uneasy with many of these elements – particularly the assumed divide between literate and illiterate, which implied that the sponsoring agency was working within a different ideological framework from myself. My own belief was that there was a continuum rather than a divide between literacy and illiteracy, and that we all learn different literacies at different times in our lives. Similarly, the idea of non-contextualized health 'knowledge' that could be quantified through a test ran counter to my understanding of how people negotiated their own and 'outside' health knowledge within these communities. However, rather than discussing our differing theoretical perspectives on literacy, I decided to adapt the design through changing the control group to 'non-class participants' to compare with the 'course participants' (rather than illiterate/literate) and adding unstructured observation of adult literacy classrooms and community interactions (for example, in health centres) to the research activities.

As I was not tampering with the overall design of the study, the sponsoring agency was happy with the changes I had made to the methods and all went according to plan. It was only when we began to discuss the findings of the project that I realized the implications of not having discussed our differing theoretical perspectives at the outset. As the observation in classrooms revealed more and more 'difficulties' in implementing the family planning programme which we were evaluating, the sponsoring agency became increasingly insistent that we should find statistical linkages between literacy and health outcomes, not more complexities. The detailed accounts of classroom interaction revealed that the course book was attempting to give women messages about the benefits of family planning ('Small family, happy family' slogans), rather than actual information about family planning facilities (which is what rural women wanted). Our research outside the classroom showed that women (both participants and non-participants) had much knowledge about family planning but faced great pressure from in-laws when they tried to adopt new practices (not least because their mothers-in-law wanted them to produce more sons) or that they did not have access to family planning facilities.

During the research process, we were visited several times by the director from Washington and each time she would ask whether we had 'found the links' between literacy and health. As findings emerged that could usefully shape the programme in a different direction, she would become more insistent with the young research assistants that they were to search hard to find some changes in the group of class participants (as compared to non-participants)! I became increasingly aware that we were offering the sponsoring agency something different from what they had expected and that I had introduced an unwelcome complexity through persuading them initially to adopt qualitative methods. Eventually, they accepted that perhaps the links were less direct than anticipated – being around the confidence that women gained in literacy classes to speak out in their own families about family planning decisions.

The outcome of all this was that the Washington office immediately cut funding to the programme on reading our report, but they managed to use the test score results to produce graphs showing that participants had more health knowledge than non-participants. Though I pointed out that these graphs were often based on samples of only a few women and were statistically meaningless, they found these findings to be more useful than the pages of penetrating but lengthy analysis of qualitative data. By the end of this research project, I had realized that my attempts to 'sneak' qualitative methods into the study were misguided. The sponsoring agency were not going to act on the findings of our research because their overall aim was still to use the quantitative data. I had also not 'educated' them as to the value of the qualitative findings – in fact, they considered these data to be less accessible than graphs or tables, and as complicating the situation, by 'raising new questions'. By limiting our discussions on our research approach to the level of methods rather than methodology, I realized that we had closed off opportunities for sharing ideas about what a more critical perspective on the project might entail.[4]

I have focused on this case study of a research project in Nepal to illuminate the difficulties of carrying out qualitative research for an agency whose research assumptions are informed by a quantitative paradigm. My difficulties could be seen as similar to the PhD student who tries to convince an employer of the value of a qualitative study and the account gives an insight into the convenient way in which both parties may choose to conflate methods and methodology. However, I do not identify the key issue in this instance as being 'cross-cultural', except in the broadest sense of the tension between research and policy contexts. The opposition to a qualitative research methodology was from the American funding agency, not from the Nepali communities where we carried out the research.

Looking back at my earlier examples of students' accounts of the resistance they have encountered in introducing qualitative research approaches, many of the problems they describe (such as the time-consuming nature of qualitative methods) could be associated with any policy-focused context in the UK too. However, they do face an additional hurdle in that both they and their colleagues identify these research methods and theoretical assumptions as a 'foreign' import, since the researcher has returned from study abroad. Compared with my own experience, students have to defend their research methods and methodology on the ground against accusations that they have adopted a 'Western' (read 'critical') approach. In some cases (as we saw in Chapter 2), approaches (to education or research) which are now considered 'indigenous' may actually be 'Western' in origin because of their colonial inheritance. As Pillay, a Malaysian PhD student, commented: 'I realized in the course of my research how much a product of the British colonial education system I was' (Pillay 1995: 3000). This whole debate about how far a research methodology can be considered 'Western' relates to the issues raised by Tuhiwai Smith about the need to develop indigenous research methodologies (to meet Maori needs).[5]

The international student as advocate

Deciding to carry out qualitative research in the face of perceived opposition from employers and/or research participants often means that a student has to take on the additional role as advocate for a certain research methodology and methods. This need to raise awareness and gain support is particularly important at the beginning of the fieldwork process. As Tsegay explained to our seminar group after returning from his pilot study in Ethiopia, his colleagues had been reluctant to participate in the study because of the qualitative approach:

> [Tsegay] felt that this was largely due to lack of awareness (95% of studies in educational research here, he found used a quantitative approach) and he has now decided to give orientation sessions to staff and students when he returns for the main fieldwork. We discussed the need for a common research language – how referring to 'interviews' and 'questionnaires' is more acceptable to colleagues than talk about 'ethnography' or 'case studies'.
>
> (Seminar report)

As Tsegay suggested here, he had to become an 'educator' within his old institution – teaching about the value of qualitative research and explaining the unfamiliar terminology. As I mentioned earlier, he felt the need to compromise by including quantitative tools that were more familiar to his colleagues. He also did not attempt to initiate change alongside his research but afterwards: 'He wondered whether this piece of work could be considered "action research" as he will be actually implementing and evaluating the proposed "action" only after he finishes his PhD' (Seminar report). Tsegay had seen the purpose of his pilot study partly in terms of trying out and evaluating research tools that were new in that institutional context:

Objectives:

1. To test the efficiency and efficacy of the questionnaire and focus group discussions as instruments for a case study meant to identify the English language needs of law students. In other words, to see how a qualitative approach could work in a mainly quantitative tradition in educational research.

(Tsegay 2001)

As a result of the feedback to his pilot study methods Tsegay altered some of his tools, but during his main fieldwork period he found people had changed their minds again. This suggested that their responses to the research tools had been on a more pragmatic level (i.e. not enough time) rather than the ideological opposition prevailing: 'For example, whereas in the pilot phase his former colleagues preferred informal discussion to structured interviews or written questionnaires, when he came back for a second visit, they said they had no time to discuss issues and would prefer to give written information' (Seminar report).

It was not only in the fieldwork phase that students had to raise aware-ness about qualitative research, but in particular when they wrote up their thesis. During a presentation by a member of staff on how PhDs are assessed, this idea of having to argue the case for a particular research methodology came out clearly:

> [He] went on to describe his dislikes [as a PhD examiner assessing a thesis], suggesting that it is not always necessary to discuss the advan-tages of qualitative research over quantitative (though some students pointed out that in certain cultural contexts, this is necessary to con-vince sponsors or their home institution of the value of qualitative approaches).
>
> (Seminar report: 13/12/01)

The students' comment about the purpose of listing the advantages of qualitative research made us (UK researchers) aware that they saw their thesis not just in terms of analysing and reporting findings, but also as a way of defending their new research approach. This written justification for their research approach was essential in their eyes, for ensuring that their thesis and findings were taken seriously on their return to their institution. Some students also decided to continue the 'awareness-raising' process once they were back home. When asked how his col-leagues had regarded his PhD research when he returned with his thesis, Othman Lebar, a former research student from CARE, explained: 'that he had conducted seminars and workshops on qualitative research to raise awareness but that it took time to convince them of the value, particularly as quantitative research is "very fast" but it takes time to collect qualitative data' (Seminar report: 28/10/03).

The above account gives insight into how students set about 'selling' their approach to their former colleagues and employer. The research process involved not just carrying out research interviews, but also raising awareness through workshops or informal discussion about qualitative research and presenting a written justification in the thesis or research proposal. In this respect, the international student was consciously aware of adopting a new identity as a qualitative researcher, which could be criticized as inappropriate to the institution or cultural context. As a novice qualitative researcher, the student might also lack confidence in his or her own ability and skills to follow through a new approach. The next section will look in more detail at the constraints students faced in implementing unfamiliar research approaches and how they went about adapting these approaches to their specific institutional and cultural context.

An evolving research approach

In CARE international students' accounts in their theses of how they decided upon and designed a research strategy, there is a common concern to work out what would be feasible or realistic to attempt in response to their particular circumstances. As well as taking account of the anticipated resistance from colleagues, students often suggested that they themselves were not fully convinced that an approach such as case study would work as well in their country as in the UK. Their worry was not just about whether or not people would participate in the research, but also about whether, for instance, 'case study had values and approaches that differed from the values of Malaysia' (Lebar 1995: 372). They were also conscious that as 'outsiders' to what they perceived as a Western research approach, they were at a disadvantage and needed to understand more about the practices and ideological assumptions behind the approach.

One step behind?

In their PhD theses, several international students from CARE commented on the frustrations of learning about qualitative approaches, indicating that they had a different starting point from other students:

> The participants in the course were mostly Europeans who, one way or another, had prior knowledge about what case study is. So the concentration of the course was on treating problems arising in the field. I think that more attention should have been given to the fact that there were students who knew nothing about case studies.
>
> (Al-Nasser 1999: 68)

I discuss ideas about how university research methods courses could build more explicitly on students' prior experience and knowledge in Chapter 7, in response to comments such as these, which imply that the international student's perspective was not fully recognized. Although Al-Nasser suggests that the European students automatically had 'prior knowledge' about qualitative research approaches, it is also likely that CARE attracted students with a particular interest in these approaches. Just as the CARE 'international' student may not be typical of his or her institution or country, we need to be careful about generalizing about the 'European' student with regard to research approaches. In her thesis, Al-Yaseen also recognized the differing ideological positions that students came from and how this affected their willingness to learn about qualitative research. As a novice to any kind of research, she felt at a particular disadvantage during the introductory research methods course compared with other students. Al-Yaseen vividly conveyed the effort she had to put in to learning the new approach, a point echoed by Al-Nasser, who stressed the personal investment in learning and conducting qualitative research: 'There were moments when I stopped and asked myself: Why do I have to do this? How long can I go on doing it? Why am I not doing what many researchers do, follow a formula?' (Al-Nasser 1999: 99).

The difficulties of teaching about qualitative approaches such as ethnography (as opposed to 'doing' them) have been well documented in the anthropology literature (see, for example, Ellen 1984). The frustration expressed by international students (Al-Yaseen's 'confusion') was that they were being asked to do something – but they did not yet understand what it was. The intangibility of qualitative approaches, versus quantitative methodologies with which they were familiar, comes across in students' accounts of their research journey: 'the meaning of case study which one is convinced must be in the head of some member of faculty or tucked away in the archives of CARE. The uncertainty can sometimes be intolerable' (Pillay 1995: 274).

Besides the difficulty of learning what case study or other qualitative approaches consisted of, international students also felt at a disadvantage compared with native English speakers in producing narrative accounts or thick ethnographic description instead of tables of figures. As Lebar explained in his thesis, this was related to gaining confidence in a more informal style of writing English: 'Portrayal is a significant piece of the whole case study. Being new to this kind of reporting, at the beginning I was having great difficulty in how to get started' (Lebar 1995: 59).

As Chang and Swales (1999) note, writing in a personalized and informal style can present a greater challenge to international students than producing a concise formal account in the third person. As I discuss further in Chapter 6, some students found the English language and writing style requirements a barrier to reporting and carrying out qualitative research. Dilemmas such as these – based partly around the students' recognition that they were at a disadvantage compared with UK students, whose mother tongue was English and who had some embedded knowledge of qualitative approaches – influenced how they decided to go about using qualitative methodologies in their home context. It was not just a matter of gaining confidence in written English or learning new skills, but also working out how a research approach might need to be modified in a different cultural context. In the next section, I look at how individual students decided to adapt case study and action research approaches to be more acceptable within their culture and also to address the constraints identified above. In this respect, compared with 'outsiders' coming to do case study research within their country, they were perhaps a step ahead – as insiders, they could anticipate the possible problems they would face.

Case study

> Am I any nearer to answering the question 'What is this a case of?' It is a question I have to answer with a 'Yes' and a 'No'. Yes, because in some ways I have been able to make some sense of the data and write the case, and No, because I am quite sure there are some layers of the case to unravel. What I can say is that I am comfortable in a sense with 'not knowing' because I realise one can never really know all of what can be known of a case.
>
> (Pillay 1995: 298)

These reflections by Hannah Pillay at the end of her thesis and of her three years in the UK provide an insight into the uncertainty that she and many of her colleagues found difficult to accept initially. They had arrived in CARE expecting to find out what the term 'case study' meant and how to do it, yet as Pillay points out, they often left with a greater sense of what they did not know about their case. She describes her gradual transition to being 'comfortable with the idea of not knowing precisely what it is I am looking for or what I will find. Allowing the field data to speak to myself as it were' (Pillay 1995: 297) and sees her 'tolerance for uncertainty' as one of the greatest benefits of her UK educational experience.

This tension between wanting to present recommendations or definite conclusions and the recognition that case study necessarily involves presenting complexity and uncertainty comes across in other theses too. The student is faced with a choice as to whether to attempt to present the case study in a form that might be better understood within their home country. This relates partly to the intended purpose of their research – how far their research problem had been decided by the employer or sponsor. If they were asked to go out and find the answer to a specific question, it would be much harder to come back armed with a case study that led to more questions or uncertainty. Zuber, a student evaluating PE (physical education) teacher education in Malaysia, struggled as to whether presenting recommendations at the end of his thesis (for the benefit of policy makers) would undermine his intention that the case study should 'speak for itself'. Students like Zuber arrive at CARE with a research proposal, often to be told by their supervisor that it is 'a good starting point' but 'too straightforward' (Hassan 2003: 13). Having broadened the research through conducting a case study, they then find they need to narrow it down again to fit with employers' expectations. Related to this concern, was the issue mentioned earlier about whether to attempt a personalized narrative style.

Responding to cultural expectations

In the range of theses presented for examination within CARE, it is clear that students responded in different ways to the expectations of their employers or colleagues as to what a case study should consist of. Pillay was perhaps unusual in describing how she had 'cased' her study. Other students felt that they had to indicate more definite boundaries and completeness in terms of findings. Again, this could be an experience common to UK researchers too, when presenting their case study to a funding agency or policy-oriented institution. However, in the CARE context, international students related the need to compromise on form or style of the case study in response to 'cultural' expectations. As Lebar discussed in his thesis, there was a shared feeling that, as they were pioneers of the case study approach in their countries, they should adjust the form and methods so that they fitted easier with the dominant quantitative approach: 'I decided that case study cannot be introduced in a drastic manner if it hoped to take root [in Malaysia]. It needed to be introduced by showing its complementary and reinforcing relationship with the survey method to obtain more valid and authentic data' (Lebar 1995: 372). This might mean including statistical data within the case study or writing up in a less personalized style than was the expected practice in CARE.

Being critical: asking questions

Once in the field, the researcher was often faced with a dilemma about how far he or she could challenge traditional practices and norms. For example, Marzita Puteh describes the difficulties of asking direct or implicitly critical questions in Malaysia:

> In the Malaysian culture, feelings are not easily articulated by many people, especially students. It is culturally more polite to keep one's feeling to oneself. In fact, the whole idea is not to hurt anybody's feelings by being outspoken and articulate. These two words, outspoken and articulate do not seem to have a dividing line in the Malaysian culture.
>
> (Puteh 1998: 85)

This worry about asking direct questions was not just related to 'the fear of getting in trouble with politics' (Al-Nasser 1999: 90), but also of offending cultural sensitivities and, in the end, getting things changed. During a period I spent working within government ministries in Nepal, I heard frequent complaints from Nepali officials about foreign consultants who 'appeared angry' because they asked loud, direct (and often critical) questions. Their recommendations were rarely acted upon, though officials agreed politely with them in public. As I began to recognize the more subtle ways in which people put forward criticism, I realized increasingly that their indirect suggestions were often more likely to be implemented.

In the context of carrying out case study research, students had to make a decision whether to appear 'Western' through asking direct questions in a culture where this was not common, and then whether to present the case critically within the thesis. Lebar (1995) suggests that case study goes against 'Malaysian values' in that the aim is to generate information from the bottom-up. He quotes previous Malaysian students who feel that 'a case study approach in the democratic mode would not be practical in the Malaysian situation because of the different values, culture, professional background of those concerned' (Zin in Lebar 1995: 35). Given this belief, a student might decide to 'play down' the critical perspective on their case study, and would be reluctant to negotiate accounts with participants: 'doing it would appear to be outside their social and professional experience' (Lebar 1995: 35). Students were also aware of the implications of being an 'insider' carrying out case study research, particularly in a culture where social and political connections carried greater weight. Al-Nasser reflected on his intended case study research in Saudi Arabia: 'Would I be, politically, able to work my way through? In other words, would it be possible to drive the research process without any contacts with politics?' (Al-Nasser 1999: 83).

Case study at a distance

The greatest challenge facing the international student in the UK was that of time constraints and logistics: how to conduct case study research at a distance. Although CARE had developed a methodology of 'condensed fieldwork' (Walker 1980) involving short periods of intensive fieldwork, restrictions laid down by sponsors or employers often determined when and for how long students could return back home, rather than students being able to work out their own research strategy. Attempts to structure field research in a way that would produce a good case study fitted uneasily with the requirements of employers – which were usually based on a fieldwork pattern associated with quantitative research, notably a short period of time in the field to collect data that that would be analysed back in the UK. Pillay reflected in her thesis on the 'difficulty of doing "long distance" fieldwork in short bursts, over a period of time, where things do change. It represented further problems of tracking down participants in order to negotiate accounts of the case' (Pillay 1995: 286). The time constraints and difficulties of communicating with participants at a distance meant that students were sometimes frustrated that they were unable to present a holistic account of the case (particularly over an extended period of time) and that they were unable to follow their intended ethical procedures. These factors also greatly affected whether and how students were able to initiate an action research study.

Reading students' accounts of their methodology (in completed theses) and how they adapted the case study approach to fit their cultural context, it seemed to me that they often felt in the position of having to justify not doing case study 'right' to the examiner or supervisor. They assumed that the adjustments they had made both to fieldwork practice and the form of the thesis in order to fit in with specific cultural and institutional practices would be seen as undermining the intended purpose of doing case study. It was as if they anticipated questions from the UK audience, such as how could a case study raise critical issues if the researcher was unable to ask direct questions? Or, as a participant in our seminar commented, the implicit assumption that: 'Strong questions make strong answers' (Seminar report, June 2003). As a UK researcher who has conducted most of my research in Nepal, I also recognize these constraints. But, perhaps because I came from a differing culture, these often uncongenial conditions also presented me with exciting opportunities to critique my own research practices and underlying assumptions. What also comes across in the students' reflections is that they were aware of building on previous students' experiences of case study research in their own country and that they were creating a new research tradition: that 'Malaysian' case study could evolve in quite a different way from the approaches they had learnt about in the UK. With this came the excitement of being a pioneer. As Al-Nasser remarks excitedly: 'I might take the risk of claiming that this study might very well be the first case study in education ever to be conducted in Saudi Arabia' (Al-Nasser 1999: 82).

Action research

The department where I am based has a strong reputation and a particular tradition of 'action research' that influences how students and faculty view research in general. Within CARE, the research student cannot ignore these influences – even if only to acknowledge that they have decided not to adopt this approach. Coming from a differing background of 'action research' in the development context (influenced particularly by PRA and PAR[6]), I have found it useful to analyse how the UK approaches differ or are similar. For this reason, I will begin with a brief account of my own learning within CARE. The founder of this centre, Lawrence Stenhouse, promoted the idea that not only should educational research aim simply to 'not harm' individual participants, but should also try to give all stakeholders an equal voice in determining the agenda and the content of evaluation. Similarly, in the area of curriculum development, teachers were to be enabled to have more voice in how subjects were developed and there would be a move away from centralized curricula. Within this context, an approach to action research evolved which still influences the practice of educational research in UK schools today: 'action research is concerned with the everyday practical problems experienced by teachers, rather than the theoretical problems defined by pure researchers within a discipline of knowledge' (Elliott 1978: 355).

Referred to by one critic as 'educational midwifery' (Kemmis 1981: 2), action research in the UK has been seen as a way of encouraging teachers to look critically at their own teaching practices and as an effective form of professional development. The UK government now offers small grants (Best Practice Research Scholarships) to teachers to carry out research in their schools, in recognition that this will help them to improve their performance as teachers. Though a few action researchers have chosen to extend the boundaries of the groups whom they consider as the 'subjects' rather than 'objects' of the research [e.g. Kirby (2001), who worked with children as researchers], most have not sought to challenge the authority of the teacher as owner and controller of the research agenda. While there may be more democratic sharing and generating of knowledge between teachers and university educators through action research, this has not often spread within and beyond the school to encourage, for example, children and their parents to participate as researchers too. This would seem to be a major difference as compared to PRA, which is focused on community action: that the 'action' within educational action research in the UK has more often been conceived in terms of the teacher's professional development and initiating a more equal relationship between university researchers and teachers.

The unpredictability of action research

International students arriving at CARE were thus introduced to an action research approach that emphasized professional development – the implication being that as teachers, government officials or health professionals, the PhD could enable them to reflect on their own practice and that of their institution with the idea of making positive changes. Given the conditions of sponsorship described in Chapter 2 (where many students had defined parameters about what they could choose to research), adopting an action research approach could present particular problems. If the intention was to go in with an open agenda and allow the research question and direction to develop through the action, this did not fit easily with employers' expectations that the research question and methods should be defined in advance. Similarly, the purpose of initiating change was more explicit within action research and was a difficult starting point within an educational and political system where people were expected to be passive recipients. Aiming to make changes from the outset implied that the researcher was critical of what went before and, as an 'insider', they would be taking a great risk in even asking the questions to prompt people's reflections. Judith, a student from Mexico,[7] queried:

> How far is it possible to conduct action research in other countries, where speaking your mind is not so acceptable? [Judith] questioned whether she would be able to use such an approach in her institution in Mexico . . . in other countries [from the UK] you cannot be so sure about trusting colleagues in case you lose your job.
>
> (Seminar report: 28/5/03)

In a sense, conducting action research meant addressing more directly and openly the embedded issues raised in this chapter: how to be critical or how to take a holistic view of a narrowly defined issue. Although qualitative or quantitative methods could be used within an action research approach so there was not likely to be the opposition from participants described earlier, the student would have to be more explicit about their differing ideological stance: as an agent of change.

In our workshops on action research, we discussed how action research approaches could be adapted within cultures where asking questions was not usual or institutions where researchers were expected to have a more defined agenda. Questions raised by students included:

– How far is research the 'product' (report, thesis, etc.)?
– How far is the decision to do action research made before starting fieldwork? Do the researcher and/or research participants have to have the intention to change something or tackle a certain problem, or can action research also be a more open-ended exploration, about discovering an agenda?
– Do we all set out with an agenda and is it just that in action research that the dilemmas about whether you impose your own agenda are more explicit?
– Is action research necessarily less rigorous than other approaches to research? Does action research imply the use of certain methods?

(Seminar report: 10/5/01)

The dilemmas about 'opening up' an agenda related not just to concerns about sponsors or employers, but also to the constraint of having to produce a PhD out of the research.[8] Students faced pressures from both their own institutions and the UK university to focus on the 'product' rather than the process of research, which appeared to be valued more within action research. The worry about whether action research was a 'less rigorous' approach was around the recognition that 'amateur' researchers, such as teachers or even children, might be carrying out the research activities and analysis. This is similar to the assumptions about quantitative research being higher status and being seen as more 'professional' in some country contexts.

A necessary compromise

For some students, the unpredictability associated with action research meant that they would not be able to negotiate the research direction sufficiently clearly to employers and they decided to do the action after the PhD. A practical constraint was also the time involved in such negotiation, both with employers and participants, if the researcher was going to initiate and research action alongside their PhD. Several students saw their position as a compromise, in that they were able to adopt some elements of an action research approach. As Tsegay explained:

> Although it goes only half way to becoming an action research, it seems reasonable to say that this research shares some elements of action research. The first two are also the main areas of focus for my research because it seeks to clarify the practical problems of teaching/ learning English in the college I work in and provides action-strategies by creating a syllabus to improve the situation. But it falls short of implementing the syllabus and evaluating its outcomes.
>
> (Tsegay 2002: 11)

Seeing the key element of action research as reflecting on current practice then initiating change, Tsegay suggests that he is only able to do the first stage of his overall project during the PhD. Other students shared his perspective on this, saying that they would do the action afterwards – partly because they could then adopt a more invisible role as insider and make changes subtly within systems where it could be risky to come along with a defined agenda. The role of action researcher for some students (especially if this was stated in their research proposal and thesis) implied taking a direct stance as critic, which could be counter-productive (as I described in relation to my own experiences in the Nepali Ministry of Education) in some contexts.

Conducting 'long-distance' action research – like case study – was a challenge faced by those who decided they did want to adopt this approach. Hasani, a student from Malaysia looking at pupil disaffection, told us how he was attempting to get round the distance and time constraints:

> A major constraint facing [Hasani] is how to initiate and follow up with this kind of collaborative research project, when he is only able to go for three months field visit (due to Malaysian government regulations). He has therefore established a relationship with a 'critical

friend' (or 'middleman' as Hasani suggests) from amongst the school staff, who will be able to continue some of the research process with those at the school (particularly on-going discussion of findings) once Hasani is back in the UK.

(Seminar report: 25/5/01)

Hasani's decision to appoint a 'middleman' enabled him to continue to monitor and contribute to the 'action' during his PhD. However, such an option would not be open to students who lacked supportive colleagues back home willing to take on this extra task. This may again be a situation where the student has to raise awareness as to the professional benefits for a colleague of becoming so integrally involved in action research. Even if a colleague was able to take over this role, Hasani was handing over control of the research enquiry to a greater extent than was usual in a PhD, as some of our group commented in response to his presentation:

> With this kind of collaborative research, where students and teachers are determining the lines of enquiry, might the PhD research lose its focus or be too wide to handle? Is there a fundamental contradiction between the tendency for academic research to move towards 'closure' and the collaborative process that Hasani intends, which is to open up more and more avenues of enquiry, stimulating further action and investigation?

(Seminar report: 25/5/01)

Moving nearer to the model of action research developed in CARE, through having a middleman, could therefore leave the student with the feeling that they were being pulled in two directions, by the research participants and by the PhD requirements. For this reason, perhaps, more international students opted for Tsegay's compromise – to envisage action as following research (as in many conventional research paradigms).

Conclusion

The aim of this chapter has been to analyse the influences on students' choice and development of a research methodology (and research methods). The choice of research approach, like that of a research question, was often viewed by international students as indicative of a certain ideological position. They regarded decisions about methodology as linked to their willingness to take an explicit political stance in their institutions back home and whether they envisaged their role as a change agent. Being situated in a department with a strong qualitative research tradition meant that students felt that they were being challenged to adopt a 'new' research approach or to integrate elements of an approach, such as action research, into their research design. They were aware that the decision to work within a qualitative paradigm meant that they would need to learn new skills and practices, some of which they saw as inappropriate to their culture (such as asking critical questions). Students learnt about qualitative research through their immersion in a different research culture, as well as through their reading of the research literature.

The process of engaging with the new oral and literacy-based research practices learnt in CARE was more often discussed by students in terms of their own changing educational beliefs[9] than in relation to their research approach. Although 'qualitative research' came to be viewed by some only as the 'product' (case study) – just as 'quantitative' was associated with questionnaires or surveys – others recognized that their learning through the 'invisible curriculum'[10] of CARE enabled them to begin to articulate and critique the implicit assumptions and values of differing research approaches. However, the greatest challenge for most students was how to convince their employers, sponsors and research participants that they were conducting 'real' research. While recognizing a need for awareness-raising in their home institution in order to be able to conduct effective research, they faced a dilemma about how to articulate their own learning about the importance of the research process to colleagues who did not see the value of looking beyond the research report to find out how it was produced. In one sense, this is a similar problem to that they faced on arrival in the UK – how to make sense of the 'product' (such as case study) without having familiarity with the cultural practices that shaped this research approach.

As we have seen in this chapter, methodologies such as action research and case study were sometimes adapted to fit the constraints within which students were working in their home context. This included the practical problems associated with studying for a PhD in the UK, where sponsors' requirements often did not allow for them to return to their home country for extended fieldwork. Aside from this, these cross-cultural perspectives on qualitative research reveal the ways in which international students felt they had to adjust their behaviour as researchers to respond to cultural and institutional expectations back home. For example, they needed to problematize research practices that were taken for granted in the UK – particularly 'being critical' and what taking a critical perspective in a country like Malaysia might imply.

Looking at fieldwork practice through a cross-cultural lens can help us to analyse assumptions underlying certain practices, such as asking participants to read and comment on transcripts – which may be a difficult task in an educational system where individuals are never asked to provide feedback. In a wider context, these differences and assumptions about pedagogical relationships have implications for the ways in which we expect international students to participate in UK university classrooms too. The comments from CARE students about the difficulties of learning case study methodology point to their isolation and feeling that they were 'different' from the European students because of their prior lack of experience in such approaches. As I will explore in Chapter 7, this may also be related to the unfamiliar pedagogical approaches they were encountering, as their supervisors insisted that they would find out what case study was by doing it (rather than by hearing a lecture).

In their attempts to create a 'Malaysian' case study tradition, CARE students were thus beginning to challenge research practices that were appropriate in the UK environment but which might present a 'risk' to the researcher and research participants in Malaysia. In the next two chapters, I want to move on from the idea that 'they' are commenting on 'our' research approaches – a tendency in many of the PhD theses I have quoted from here – to look at areas in which this kind of cross-cultural critique could contribute to better practice within the UK context too. Research ethics and language issues are two areas of particular concern to international students, and their differing starting point can help UK researchers to reflect more critically on their own communicative practices within research contexts.

Behind the scene: the 'culture' of interviewing in Malaysia

By Asmahan Abd. Razak

Introduction

As a researcher who works in one's own familiar scenario and setting, I had the pleasure of *seeing* the interview approach and research differently during my fieldwork in Malaysia. As I embarked on my research, my focus was on the strengths and weaknesses of the various research approaches which encompassed the principles and techniques of interviews – because of having gone through a series of research methods seminars. I was more concerned with the professional and academic aspects of conducting my fieldwork, neglecting the personal and cultural aspects. I took for granted the cultural aspects of my own society for it is 'at the back of my hand' and hence dismissed it on the grounds of being insignificant as I would be in a familiar setting – that is, 'I know my culture'. The common understanding of culture is the notion of shared beliefs, values, customs and meanings that distinguish one group of people from another and gives one identity. Having 'shared' the values, beliefs, customs, etc. sometimes does not give anyone exclusive rights to claim to 'know it all'. I, for one, was awakened by what I discovered of my own culture and customs. It was an 'awakening' for me to have such an invaluable experience, an experience which is distinctively 'Malaysian'.

The most striking characteristic of Malaysia is its cultural diversity: Malaysia comprises three major ethnic groups, namely Malays, Chinese and Indians. Although each ethnic group retains its identity, some values are common to all ethnic groups. There are a set of values and behaviour patterns that are ingrained in all of us and that we act them out unconsciously and involuntarily. I realized how value-laden it is when conducting my interviews – to see how Malaysians envisaged respecting those with power. The process of a research study in my case defines my understanding of interviewer–interviewee power relations in lieu of *respect*, which is multi-form. To understand power relations (P-p)[11], it is pertinent to understand Malaysian social values.

Interview culture

Malaysia is a hierarchical society, for having power is an exclusive right: thus one has to respect those who possess power. The person with power is seen as a significant and important person, since it is important to present what and who you are in the eyes of others, for it is important to be 'what others see and think of them'. The notion of 'looking up to' was taken literally. I was oblivious of a power struggle then, when I was conducting my interview. However, upon reflecting on it, I realized the struggle between the interviewer and interviewee in establishing a relationship. Thus, being an interviewer and an outsider of a new territory, I have to 'respect' those with power (P) in that territory. This entails the 'Kow-tow'[12] culture, which was a dominant feature during my interview. It simply means that, I, the interviewer, have to respect my interviewees by 'bowing' to them for having 'P'. They are the 'authority or boss' in their department: though it is my research, I have no power (p) over my research. I was practically at their mercy, unless I am 'somebody', that is, having as much power if not more. My interviewees are 'powerful' (P) in most matters, they dictated when and how my interview should be and/or if it should be conducted at all. Since I was in their territory, I had no choice but to bow, respect and abide by their rules. I had no rights or power to demand their time and effort in meeting me, for this entailed disrespect for them.

The power is being shared with and extended to personnel in the department as well for being in the 'right place'. This reflects their important and significant existence in the department. Just when I thought I knew what was going on, I realized that I didn't and I learnt new things about my own culture. Much to my chagrin, respect had to be extended not only to my interviewees but also to the gatekeepers, namely, the secretary, personal assistants or any personnel of the new territory. Interrogations after interrogations are expected most of the time before you are allowed to pass the 'gate'. The higher the position of your interviewee, the more you will be interrogated and the longer you will have to wait. Not willing to disclose or wait simply shows you are disrespectful. To be patient is a virtue in conducting the interview. The common 'call me back' and the convenient 'forget' would have to be entertained, even for turning up late or not at all for the interview session. My interview was not in their best interest and thus they felt less or not guilty at all for not having one. The public still has the notion that researchers are time-wasters and there's nothing to say for they are all 'confidential'. Confidential is the key word to subtly end an interview or avoid one. Therefore, an interview can be time-consuming most of the time, not to mention emotionally and physically challenging.

A sign of respect is reflected in the way you present yourself, such as dress, mannerism and addressing titles. The emphasis on presentation is Malaysians' core nature for they pay special attention to the way you dress, your fashion statement. Smart, formal dressing and appropriate attire in meeting with anyone at any level and for any reason reflects the degree of respect you have for them. The respect showed guarantees you with the key to most doors in setting appointments and eventually conducting the interview. Your dressing is the door to you and your work. To don a 'Power suit' to reflect who you claim you are is therefore an integral part in guaranteeing you a face-to-face meeting in most cases.

Respect in the Malaysian context is the notion of saving 'face'[13] of oneself or anyone to maintain social harmony in a multiracial nation. Respect for others is an important aspect in socializing that needs to be observed and is highly demanded by the society since Malaysians are relationship-oriented. This includes respect for those senior in age, as well as in social positions. Malaysians are very particular about titles or status too. Titles need to be addressed properly to show respect to the respective person. Thus, respecting my interviewees was upheld at all costs and times during my interview. I was not spared from the customary and obligatory smallness: an interviewer has to be 'small' during the interview because the 'smaller' you are, the 'better' the response or cooperation you might get in most instances. To show signs of superiority would and could be detrimental. This could mean that the interview could be cancelled or postponed indefinitely.

Conclusion

The crux of the matter is that the product of an interview is not as meaningful and significant as the instances of the process, which were not addressed in any research books. I realized that the success of any interview did not rely on the types of question and/or the quantity of information or data collected, but rather the depth of my understanding of the cultural context and the locality I was in. I appreciate investigating social relationships, social phenomena and the workings of my own culture, for I find it to be a creative, value-full, contested and dynamic activity. I have to work on various issues such as public perceptions, views as well as reactions on interview as a research approach. The process of conducting an interview has always been considered as a mundane routine; of having to go through red tape or the bureaucracy and the politics of interviewing in both government and non-governmental organizations, which is quite common I would think anywhere. However, there are certain issues or aspects that I discovered were predominantly and exclusively Malaysian. The experience, simply put, has unravelled the true characteristics of my culture that is highly 'political' even when conducting a research study.

Asmahan Abd Razak *is a lecturer at Universiti Teknologi MARA (UiTM), Malaysia. She used to teach proficiency English courses in the pre-TESL programme and general methods courses in the B.Ed (TESL) for the undergraduate secondary education programme, which includes education psychology, foundations of education as well as education and society. She is currently pursuing her doctoral degree at the University of East Anglia, UK. Her areas of research include instructional technology and innovative practices in teacher education, psychology of learning, and language learning and practices.*

The insider/outsider dilemmas in educational research – a Mexican experience

By Judith Castaneda-Mayo

Little qualitative research related to academic women and their identity has been undertaken in Mexico; therefore, wrong assumptions and perceptions about them in general persist. Academics are perceived as 'sacred cows' or the 'gurus' (Altbach 2003; Gil-Anton 2003: 43), so the whole idea of attempting to make them my collaborators for the educational research I am actually doing at UEA-CARE to get the PhD degree in philosophy of education almost paralysed me. My methodology focuses on the analysis of narratives from text about the life history of at least fifteen Mexican academic women. So I needed to interview respondents who had completed a PhD in any discipline and who were willing to share the story of their professional development.

Mexican academics are not strange to me, since I am also an 'academic' or 'professor' as they are called in the US. But the perception of who is who in academia in Mexico differs from that prevailing in the North or Western institutions. There, Gil-Anton (2003) argues, 'they have full-time professors with doctoral degrees'. I have been a lecturer for almost fifteen years in the University of Tabasco, Mexico and some of my colleagues are PhDs and many have studied abroad. They are professors and the perception most people have is that they are an elite who exclude others from their circle.

In fact, I have never been a member of their club, 'guru or sacred cow', although some are close friends. This was paradoxical or perhaps it was just my perception, but they look down on those who are not equal in terms of academic achievement. This of course is very subtle but there is a red code, which they enforce to exclude others and that adds to the tension prevailing in different academic circles. The intellectual profile for a professor or lecturer in higher education in the North has traditionally been of a PhD graduate, regardless of gender, and in fact all these academics have followed that model, including myself. This perception was shaped by my experience in the past when I did my first degree in the US and all my professors were PhDs. They were very open and kind with pupils and I remembered that the first advice they used to give us was that they appreciated if we would address them by using their first name or nicknames, rather than 'Doctor X' or 'Professor Y'.

They were friendly and open – whereas in Mexico, PhD academics are evasive and sensitive to critique, thus I was very judgemental and I still cannot look up to them. I found them very contradictory and shallow. Then I read about the psychological profile we Mexicans have in O. Paz's (1961) *The Labyrinth of Solitude* and it became clear that academics were just 'Impassionate hearts, disguising their sorrow . . . [Popular song]' (p. 29) and presumably they are not any different from any other human being 'who shuts himself/herself away to protect himself/herself: his/her face is a mask and so is his/her smile' (ibid.). So that aura is just another mask, another thread that makes up the fabric of their academic identity, thin as smoke.

I had to admit that there were some strong fears provoking my paralysis but it was evident that at the core I had a very low sense of confidence. But wait a minute, how can I say that – if in the past, my critical stance has taken me to scenarios where I have openly confronted and contested my rector and the dean of my school in Tabasco, Mexico and I have been successful, very assertive and with a strong determination? That did not make sense at all. The difference with these academic women stemmed from the fact that for them I had become an outsider: they were the 'Other' (PhDs, gurus, sacred cows) whereas myself, I was just a postgraduate student.

For the purpose of my research, I now needed to relate to these 'gurus' by asking for their collaboration in sharing the story of their life and being open about the personal, and perhaps the private, to a stranger, an outsider. *Pecata minuta*, a minor effort with three of them that I considered personal friends but the requirement was to interview fifteen at least. So even when I knew there were others in the university, for me they were the Other and the 'sacred cows' – hence the untouchable.

What a mess, I felt trapped and everywhere I turned in the literature, they just kept pounding on the same point that it was just a relatively easy task and my success was guaranteed if I followed the instructions: step one – prepare a questionnaire; step two – build up confidence with your respondents, create rapport; step three have a pilot trial; step four – always carry a spare tape recorder and please do yourself a favour, turn it on. If that was the case, why then all this uneasiness and anxiety? I guessed it was because this was the moment of truth and I was confronted with myself and my limitations. I was biting the dust, nowhere to turn but to face and deal with this ordeal. What was the worst that could happen, I thought: that they rejected me and I returned empty-handed or that perhaps they made too many queries about the purpose of my research and I had to confess that I was still in the process of constructing a focus?

The pilot process was relatively easy and that boosted my confidence. Another instance was when I contacted some of the prospect respondents by Internet and by telephone and they agreed to give me an interview. I was just delighted and in disbelief because they even suggested other names that I should include in my list whom they were sure would love to contribute to my research and share their story. Somehow what I had heard from Ivor Goodson and Les Tickle (who are professors at UEA) that summer in 2003, during the UEA summer school, also fell into place.

I remembered that Les Tickle made his 'Two Miles to Town' workshop seminar very practical and that the documentary materials that he presented showed me *vis-à-vis* the potentials of using life history as a research methodology. That collection of material was laid out then as his road map – with the 'longer mileage' he has walked to become the Professor, the academic and the 'guru' he is today: 'You reminded me of the 140 thousand miles my car has on the milometer, and I think it is ready for the scrapyard'. The group prepared questions where we drew on different themes and issues related to the personal and the academic. This exercise was another lift that built on my trust that a new sense of confidence invaded me. Now what Goodson and Tickle claimed about respondents in their theory – that 'they love to go on and on once you start them into talking about their life that you have to keep an eye on time or else they'll never stop' – became a reality. Ivor Goodson shared a capsule of the history of his life where he rekindled the voice that invited him to walk out of that potato chip factory and return to school so that he could pack his mind with greater thoughts instead – hence becoming the great researcher and professor today. Somehow at CARE, I felt close to family, an insider perhaps?

And then the moment of truth came and, to my astonishment, my expectations went beyond the boundaries. I have succeeded in my task. My respondents were more than willing to participate: their accounts were complete 'victory narratives' though. I guess I was not prepared for that and I had to make a second journey to get the 'real' side of their life filling in those big gaps. I found that their narratives fell into the category of what MacLure (1993: 320) suggests: 'People use (biographical accounts) to make sense of the present; to work out where they "stand" in relation to others; to defend their attitudes and conduct'. In other words, they were just 'victory narratives' as Lather (1994) observes, rather than 'ruins'.

It transpired that at the core, I still wanted to treat their stories as sacred text rather than as 'mundane autobiography' (MacLure 1993: 373). New fears and negative thoughts invaded me when I saw the risk of being judgemental and breaching the ethics. Again I fell into the outsider/insider dilemma on how to distance myself from the text and the subject and render a critique of their subjectivity just from the narratives through deconstruction. I still have no 'real' answers to solve these ambiguities and dilemmas, yet only a thought of consolation that I came across in the literature that educational research is just 'writing fiction under oath' (Bridges 2003: 171) – or is it not?

Judith Castaneda-Mayo is a full-time lecturer at the University of Tabasco in Mexico, where she has been teaching subjects related to communication, education and ESL for almost fifteen years. She is a graduate from the University of New Mexico in the USA, with a BA in Communication and English Literature (1989) and an MA in Education from the University of Nuevo Leon in Mexico (2000). Today she is a full-time student at CARE (University of East Anglia) pursuing her PhD in the philosophy of education. Her research interests concentrate mainly on issues related to gender and education, specifically those that explore subjectivity and the development of identity of Mexican academic women, from a poststructuralist feminist perspective.

Research ethics

Introduction

Concerns about how the 'outsider' researcher should behave and relate to
people in a different culture have been much explored in anthropology, a
discipline described as 'cross cultural inquiry at an interface of ethical
systems' (Appell in Akeroyd 1984: 154). In development studies texts too,
there has been recognition that development workers may face dilemmas
about how far to impose or even just articulate their differing moral
values. More recently, this discussion has been extended by writers like
Escobar (1995), who offer a macro perspective on individual development
actors through the theoretical framework of 'development discourses'.
Within this framework, research practices (including ethics procedures)
can be analysed in relation to how 'development' as a discourse positions
and influences interaction between the 'developer' and 'developed',
researcher and researched (Robinson-Pant 2001a). In this chapter, I
recognize the wider ethical dimensions involved in the theoretical debates
about whose knowledge and 'whose reality counts' (Chambers 1997).
As Lewin (1990a: 212) points out, there are issues around the products of
research as well as the generation of data or theory: 'What defences
are there to the charge that much research in developing countries on
education is another kind of cultural imperialism where the spoils are the
capture of data and enhancement of status of the researcher in the world
of international publication?' Though I have found the theoretical
framework of development discourses valuable, particularly as a way into
analysing the frequent mismatch between development policy and practice, I am aware of the potential criticism from practitioners on the ground
that deconstructing discourses can lead nowhere (in practical terms). For
this reason, I will focus in this chapter on the micro level of individual
researchers and research institutions. This could be criticized as a return to

earlier anthropological writing about how the individual researcher responds to and reconciles differing ethical practices and standards.

In relation to people carrying out research in developing countries, Warwick (1983: 315) notes that: 'The special circumstances of cross-cultural research, whether across or within countries, raise ethical questions that are different in degree and sometimes, in kind, from those seen in unicultural projects'. He was particularly concerned with the 'cross-cultural' aspect of fieldwork in a development context – Western researchers conducting field research or evaluating development interventions in countries where they might not be familiar with local practices and beliefs. As a former development researcher, I can remember the difficulties of carrying out interviews or observation in situations where I was still trying to piece together what an event or practice meant in 'their' terms, rather than my own. Comparing my perspective to that of international students, they may be carrying out field research in a familiar environment (though as Warwick points out, there are 'cross-cultural' situations within any one country too) but often have to respond to or anticipate ethical concerns posed by their UK university colleagues. In this respect, they are in a similar position to anthropologists such as myself – needing to become more aware of 'an interface of ethical systems' and making decisions about which value system to emphasize when writing up, analysing findings and conducting interviews. During the course of their PhD, they may have to address questions such as: What does it meant to conduct 'ethical' research in Kenya as compared to the UK? How can ethical practices common in the UK – such as signing consent forms – be adapted in other contexts, particularly where people have less everyday contact with written documents?[1]

The aim of this chapter is to explore such questions in relation to PhD research, in the hope of opening up a space where both UK and international researchers can begin to question their research practices on ethical grounds. My starting point is the understanding that PhD research has often been influenced by the dominant development discourse where the ethical procedures and values of Western research institutions shape and provide the standards by which others are judged. In this chapter, however, I am interested in looking not just at the implications for international students, but also how far can researchers in the North[2] draw on alternative moral codes and ethical research practices from the South? This has particular relevance for educational researchers such as myself working in countries with contrasting belief systems where questions about the 'outsider' researcher and their research agenda frequently arise. As Warwick (1983: 324) and Lewin (1990a: 212)[3] suggest, these questions are often around issues of bias, identity and purpose:

- What business is it of the researcher to be there? Curiosity? Self-development? Academic qualification? Assistance with a problem? Invitation to contribute to a policy debate?
- Whose side is the researcher on – who has the researcher's sympathy? How far is the position taken really value free or value loaded? Which/whose values count?

For 'insider' researchers, such as PhD students going back to conduct interviews with their own colleagues or community, these questions may be raised more directly by research participants or sponsors and are linked to my earlier discussions about the research question and approach adopted. Anticipating the potential ethical dilemmas that an 'outsider' researcher might not be aware of, the international student may also be asking:

- How far should I avoid some topics if they are controversial in my country?
- Should I allow my sponsor/employer to influence my research design and interpretation?

As the above questions imply, ethical concerns are integrally related to the quality of research and are reflected in the research design, objectives and methods. In this respect, this chapter examines critically many of the dilemmas embedded in the earlier and later sections of this book – on choosing a methodology and writing for audiences in the UK and 'back home'.

Research ethics in differing cultural contexts

Before turning to consider the ethical implications of working cross-culturally, it is useful to analyse what has caused people to reflect on the ethical dimensions of their research. In the UK, the growing culture of litigation has had an impact on how people view researchers and research. Alongside a concern to protect research informants from the negative 'side-effects' of research, there has been recognition of the need to provide researchers with safeguards too. From informal relationships between researchers and research subjects based on trust, there has therefore been a move towards developing contracts and written explanations as evidence that both parties entered consciously into an agreement. The emphasis has been on 'informed consent' and finding ways of guaranteeing confidentiality to the research informants. Such research practices need to be seen in the wider context of legal developments like the Data Protection Act. Seen in this light, the ethical dimension of research activities can become reduced to obtaining clearance for access to participants and release of findings. This concern with the mechanics of research ethics procedures (through committees with set criteria or principles) can lead to a 'bolt-on' view of research ethics, rather than the 'intrinsic' view that I outlined in the introduction to this chapter.

As research associations and institutions have developed more explicit ethical principles and procedures to ensure that these principles are adhered to, there has also been recognition that ironically these mechanisms could cause the researcher to look less critically at their research, in the belief that the ethical dimensions were already taken care of. As Vulliamy (1990: 112) warns, research ethics have a moral as well as legal dimension: 'I believe that the kinds of ethical problems discussed here [in his book] cannot be resolved by recourse to general statements of ethical principles or professional codes of conduct, although the latter may provide the useful role of alerting all researchers to such problems. Rather, they are matters for individual conscience'. Alongside this emphasis on researcher 'conscience' is the insistence that research rigour is also at risk if research is not ethically conducted. Wilson (1992) notes that this is not about the researcher taking a moral stance but about ensuring, for example, that remarks from informants are not presented as 'typical' when, perhaps only one person made such a point: 'the more "ethical" researcher is not necessarily the most vocal and eloquent advocate for a particular cause . . . but rather is the one who makes the most rigorous application of methods enabling objective understanding' (p. 182). The implications of this stance are that the researcher's attention is drawn to 'the ethics of validity' as compared to the 'ethics of release' (CARE 1994: 135). When researchers are working within a research paradigm that is unfamiliar to research sponsors or ethics committees, this can sometimes mean that qualitative approaches are dismissed as 'unethical' because of suspicion about the validity of so-called 'anecdotal' evidence.

Personal responsibility: the influence of participatory development approaches

In the UK (and many other countries in the North), there has been a visible transition in recent years from informal codes of practice (such as referring to research participants by pseudonyms) to more formalized procedures designed to protect both researcher and researched from unforeseen consequences. Within many countries of the South, there has also been a movement towards stating more explicit ethical principles, which make a useful comparison with UK research ethics. This movement has been influenced by participatory development paradigms (Korten 1980) and recognition of indigenous peoples' rights. The extractive nature of much research conducted by development agencies has been analysed in terms of the hierarchical relationship between donors and recipient countries, development workers and local communities. Participatory development research approaches, such as PRA and PLA,[4] aim to challenge these relationships through articulating the values that should inform research and development practice. The 'three pillars' of PRA – which could be seen as the underlying ethical principles of the approach – are defined as:

- the behaviour and attitudes of outsiders, who facilitate, not dominate
- the methods, which shift the normal balance from closed to open, from individual to group, from verbal to visual and from measuring to comparing, and
- partnership and sharing of information and experience between insiders and outsiders and between organisations.

(Chambers 1997: 105–106)

PRA training input on 'behaviour and attitudes' encourages development workers to reflect not just on why they are carrying out research, but to examine their own beliefs critically with the aim of making changes in their personal attitudes and behaviour. PRA practitioners emphasize the more holistic approach they have adopted towards research where ethical consideration has to be given to the whole research situation, rather than just focused on the methods or access to participants. A PRA workshop report from India (Kumar 1996: 25) documents the learning experiences contributing to changes in practitioners' behaviour and attitudes, including:

- realising that much development is imposed on people
- understanding the need for space to allow others to reflect and improve/change their attitude and behaviour
- learning to regard one's work in participatory learning and action as a way of life, not a livelihood.

The same report advises on 'how to offset biases' through 'being nice' (p. 57), suggesting that facilitators should 'be sensitive', 'show positive attitude to help others', 'respect people, their culture and social traits'.

Viewed from the perspective of research ethics, these could be seen as similar to the 'principles of procedure' in UK educational institutions. Emphasizing common 'human' values, the PRA statements imply, however, that a researcher is personally (rather than institutionally) accountable to research participants – stressing that this is an individual responsibility. By developing in personal terms (seeing research as 'a way of life, not a livelihood'), the researcher can learn to take on this ethical role. Unlike the UK context, the emphasis here is on looking critically at communicative practices between researcher and researched: using oral (rather than written) explanations of research objectives and developing visual and oral ways of collecting data so that it can be shared more easily with the communities being researched. The push for greater reflexivity and accountability on the part of the researcher can also be seen to parallel the ways in which anthropology has developed over the past decades (see Ellen 1984). However, whereas anthropology emphasizes these in terms of methodological rigour (the idea of the researcher's representation telling more about the researcher than the researched), PRA highlights the ethical dimension (of developers exploiting the researched through imposing their own agenda, if not held to account and encouraged to reflect on their actions).

Deconstructing 'Western' codes of practice

Indigenous groups who have previously been the subjects of anthropologists' research studies have now begun to challenge dominant research practices more directly, seeing their past oppression as linked to attempts to 'colonize' their knowledge as well as their resources. As I mentioned in Chapter 1, Maori groups have been particularly active in developing an alternative research methodology and articulating the embedded assumptions in Western research practice. With regard to ethics, they link the 'Western sense of the individual and individualised property' (Tuhiwai Smith 1999: 118), which lies behind concepts such as 'informed consent' and 'confidentiality', to the same principles that informed the laws introduced by colonial powers to govern, for example, land use and reform. Tuhiwai Smith explains that 'the social good against which ethical standards are determined is based on the same beliefs about the individual and individualised property. Community and indigenous rights or views in this area are generally not recognised and not respected' (ibid.). She discusses Kaupapa Maori practices, which 'are not prescribed in codes of conduct for researchers, but tend to be prescribed for Maori researchers in cultural terms' (p. 120). Explaining that Maori sayings (such as 'look, listen . . . speak', 'do not trample over the mana of people' and 'a respect for people') 'reflect just some of the values that are placed on the way we behave' (ibid.), she suggests that these values should govern a Maori researcher's behaviour. These proverbs bear a remarkable similarity to the PRA advice on behaviour and attitudes – again suggesting an alternative to legal definitions of ethics, based on a belief in common human values shared by researcher and researched: 'the term "respect" is consistently used by indigenous peoples to underscore the significance of our relationships and humanity' (ibid.).

Top-down versus bottom-up approaches to research ethics

Comparing the differing country contexts that I have described above, there appear to be two distinct approaches, with contrasting assumptions about research ethics and relationships. The development of written ethical codes of conduct (as in the UK context) seems to be based on an assumption that researchers are liable to exploit research subjects and is bound up with notions of control and legal accountability. In other countries too, guidelines for researchers' conduct are concerned less with identifying issues of ethical concern, and more with setting out visible parameters of responsibility. For example, the Malaysian government guidelines for researchers outline the need for research to 'be of benefit to the nation' and state that 'the researcher is barred from raising or touching upon controversial issues in their findings/reports' (Malaysian Government 1999: 4). Underlying both the UK and Malaysian approach[5] to research ethics is a mistrust of researchers and the intention to circumscribe the limits of their activity through guidelines or codes of conduct. By contrast, the PRA and Maori guidelines focus solely on the relationship between researcher and researched, in the assumption that if the researcher's behaviour and attitudes are changed for the better, ethical concerns will automatically be taken care of.

Taking a cross-cultural perspective on research ethics is thus not just about comparing one value system with another, but as much about understanding the cultural context in which ethical codes have been developed. The Maoris' alternative research methodology – and their emphasis of community accountability above individual responsibility in ethical guidelines – has to be seen in relation to their struggle against intellectual domination by Western researchers. Looking at the various situations I have described, the question arises as to how far ideas about ethics are ethnocentric. Are there universal values that researchers should hold (as PRA suggests – 'be humble', 'be sensitive'; Kumar 1996) and just different ways of going about ensuring that these values inform research (such as written contracts in place of oral interaction)? How far are the key concepts underpinning ethical codes of conduct – such as 'secrecy' or even 'democracy' – culturally embedded? For example, Warwick (1983: 327) identifies 'the wide cross cultural differences in the value and meaning of privacy'. If privacy is not a strongly held value in a certain cultural context, should protection of data and individual identity be a key issue to address with regard to research ethics? As many researchers have discovered to their cost, the meaning of 'sensitive information' also varies greatly between countries. Devereux and Hoddinott (1992a: 33) describe how 'individuals and cultures do not share the same sensitivities': they cite as an example Westerners' unusual (as compared with other cultures) reluctance to discuss their personal income with researchers.

The implications of all this are that two major ethical dilemmas face the 'cross-cultural' researcher. The first is the most evident and straightforward dilemma: whether and how to adapt to cultural differences in behaviour. This might include 'being critical' in less direct ways or even how to give gifts/payment within a culture where gift exchange is related to status and prestige rather than generosity (see Wilson 1992: 193). The second ethical dilemma is perhaps more difficult for the 'insider' researcher: how far to question or adopt new or contrasting ethical values within the research study in response to working within an institution with a differing code of practice. As I will explore in the next section looking specifically at international students working within two institutional frameworks (their home employer and the UK university), this is not a once and for all decision about following one set of guidelines or another but a dynamic process of self-reflection and adjusting behaviour to differing contexts: 'Doing ethical fieldwork is not about following prescribed formulae but precisely about thinking over the processes and situations that you are involved in' (Wilson 1992: 198).

Implications for the PhD student working in two cultures

As a UK teacher trainer going to work in Nepal, I was briefed on how to adapt my behaviour to another culture and not to judge people's behaviour on my own (culturally embedded) terms. As Wilson (1992) describes in relation to his fieldwork in Zimbabwe, there are many situations in which one would feel uneasy taking this neutral role, such as witnessing a child being beaten. He advises that 'being a member of another society, albeit temporarily, does not mean the suspension of a personal moral code' (p. 189) and that a researcher (even as an 'outsider') would be advised to intervene. Relating my situation as an ex-pat researcher, to that of an international student returning to conduct research in their own country, I am aware that the advice would not be so clear-cut. Although an international student would be familiar with the cultural norms of their country and be inclined to adapt to fit in, they could not afford to ignore the possibly contradictory ethical concerns of the UK educational institution. After all, their performance as researcher is being judged by that institution's values and procedures. Similarly, once back writing up in the UK university, they might be better advised to 'suspend' their moral code and beliefs (or, at least, appear to) if those came into conflict with the UK codes of practice.

This is a situation that I have frequently come across in development, particularly in relation to 'gender training' initiatives in Nepal. Such courses were intended to transform development workers' behaviour in the home as well as workplace setting to promote gender equity. However, in practice many colleagues learnt to speak convincingly about more equal gender roles and relations, yet continued to behave in the same way. The same gap between rhetoric and practice could be seen in health education programmes and in teacher training courses where new participatory methods were being introduced. Although this could be dismissed simply as hypocrisy, I would relate this inability to challenge different values and assumptions to the hierarchical relationships associated with development institutions of North and South, as well as to contrasting notions about change (as discussed in Chapter 1). Taking this perspective on the international student who is expected to follow different ethical practices in their own culture as part of the PhD field research, I would anticipate that he or she might have similar responses to the development workers I described above. As I discuss in Chapter 7, UK educators face a major challenge in creating a non-threatening classroom/ supervision environment where students are encouraged to discuss these differing ethical assumptions.

Meeting UK standards[6]

I am reluctant to generalize about ethical procedures and even about values promoted within UK education departments, though I have heard people talk about 'UK' ethical standards. However, I will outline my own department's stance on research ethics to illustrate how such guidelines have evolved and to provide the context within which the international students I describe later were studying.

A history and overview of research ethics in CARE

In contrast to the indirect ways in which they had to find out what 'case study' might mean (Pillay's search for 'the holy grail'), students entering CARE are given a research ethics briefing pack which describes clearly the department's expectations and procedures as regards research ethics. They are therefore made aware from the outset of having to meet or conform to the UK university standards in this respect.

Like many Schools of Education, we have established a research ethics committee whose responsibility is to advise on the ethical dimensions of research proposals and see that certain procedures are followed. Historically, researchers who were conducting studies around the 'caring professions' (such as nursing) were already obliged to submit their proposals to the local research ethics committee. As these committees within the health services were more used to examining proposals for new drugs trials, the kinds of questions raised tended to be around the 'side-effects' of the research. This question took on a new meaning in the context of social science research, though there was increasing recognition that a range of people involved in research – people working with children, teachers in school, social workers – all needed to consider the ethical side of their research and what the unintended 'side-effects' might be. The

School of Education Research Ethics Committee was therefore set up partly to help researchers to get through the local research ethics committees by ensuring that they took those regulations into account. But it was also intended that the Committee would help initiate a dialogue with researchers about the ethical dimensions of their proposals and in particular to minimize the risk to vulnerable participants in their research.

A research ethics briefing pack was developed as a resource for students and supervisors to draw on when discussing the ethical implications of their research. The pack specifies when a proposal should be submitted to the Research Ethics Committee: when the research involves vulnerable people (very young children), any aspect of health care or intimate personal information. There are also guidelines about how to address ethical issues within such proposals: 'the proposal should state whether and how confidentiality of information will be guaranteed to participants and the limits of that confidentiality' (UEA 2003: 7). The pack also advises that 'the research should guarantee anonymity to participants, unless they are to be asked explicitly to waive this right' (ibid.). There are examples of participant consent forms and information sheets within the pack. Students are advised that wherever possible 'participants should be offered an information sheet telling them about the research ... in simple, non-technical terms' (p. 9) and that: 'Ethical research depends upon participants freely giving their consent to being involved. Although verbal consent is sometimes acceptable, especially if this is tape-recorded, it is normal for written consent to be given' (p. 12). The pack also includes articles on background issues, such as the legal aspects of giving consent. There is acknowledgement that it may be necessary to obtain 'assent' rather than 'consent' when 'researching with people with limited capacity to understand and people who belong to groups whose cultural concept of consent is different from the researchers (e.g. asylum seekers, travellers, members of other cultures)' (p. 11). This is however seen as a compromise: 'This is a weaker form of consent, but better than nothing' (ibid.).

The Research Ethics Committee emphasizes that it does not intend to have a 'policing' role within the School of Education – in contrast to the research ethics committees in some health institutions. The Committee Chair in his briefing to new students introduced the idea of 'situated ethics' as an ethical code that varied according to context: 'you cannot make decisions that are final, but may have to keep reviewing ethical decisions that you have made' (Terry Phillips, quoted in Seminar report, 10/2/03). As the emphasis is less on giving rigid guidelines, than on encouraging critical reflection on the research in its cultural and social context, the approach and materials developed by the Research Ethics Committee are constantly evolving. Through discussion with international research students conducting fieldwork in their home countries, there has been increasing awareness that our ideas on ethics are ethnocentric and the committee began to reflect on its own procedures and practices in this light. International students and researchers working in contrasting cultural contexts have been encouraged to identify and reflect on some of the key issues, such as how concepts of 'vulnerability' differ from one country to another, or the implications of asking for written consent in a community where most people are non-literate. Students have also (just as Tuhiwai Smith noted in relation to Maori research ethics) questioned the assumption that individual as opposed to community consent is required, for example, when seeking permission to take a photograph.

The requirement for students to submit proposals to the Research Ethics Committee if dealing with vulnerable groups or sensitive issues has, however, meant that approval has to be obtained before fieldwork can go ahead. A formal letter is issued by the Committee stating whether or not approval has been granted and listing the reasons or requirements if it has not. This process implies that certain criteria have to be met – and international students can sometimes feel that they are being assessed by the ethical standards of a UK institution, when the field research is going to be carried out in another country with differing cultural norms and values. As Scholastica, a Tanzanian student, commented after her proposal was criticized by the Research Ethics Committee, 'we don't ask those kinds of questions in my country' (Seminar report). In other cases (as I will discuss in the next section), students felt that they could follow the procedures outlined by the briefing pack, but that it would negatively affect their relationships with research subjects. The international students therefore faced a dilemma similar to that outlined earlier – whether to propose certain procedures on paper but adapt their behaviour to the more usual research practices (often top-down) when back in their home country. However, as I have discovered from reading former CARE students' theses, many did address these ethical concerns in their research and wrote explicitly about the ways in which they adapted UK ethical practices to their own context. Unlike many UK researchers, their writing reveals that they were aware of being in the position of having to 'defend' or 'explain' their differing approach to research ethics to an audience who might not share their ideological perspective.

Following CARE research ethics procedures: exploring the constraints

Tsegay described how when he tried to discuss the ethical dimensions with colleagues whom he was interviewing (in Ethiopia), they laughed at the idea of written agreements, saying he could do what he wanted and if anything was very sensitive, simply 'don't mention our names'. In Tanzania too, Scholastica felt she 'could do anything' and that agreements were an informal matter of trust.

(Seminar report: 2/12/02)

The reactions described by these two students researching in African countries were typical of many contexts outside the UK – where attempts to negotiate ethical codes of practice are met either with non-comprehension or dismissed as a joke. In this section, I look more closely at the reasons why both PhD students and their colleagues expressed initial resistance to introducing practices such as signing consent forms in their home context.

The danger of formalizing relationships

In the Malaysian context, the procedures were viewed as legalistic and aroused suspicions when the researcher tried to get the participants to understand the principle at issue. This highlights a problem with the use of the concept of 'informed consent' . . . and the notion of democratic principles that case study tries to promote.

(Pillay 1995: 294)

Adopting the research approaches developed by CARE – like case study – implied becoming familiar with the ethical values, such as 'democratic principles', which lay behind them. In the 1990s, international students like Pillay were introduced to the 'principles of procedure' developed by CARE for establishing relationships of trust between researchers and research participants, particularly in the context of evaluation and case study. As Pillay describes, such principles could be viewed as 'legalistic' and set up barriers in cultures where relationships were negotiated less formally. Like other international students, she was concerned that by following the UK guidelines for ethical practice, she might make inter-action with her research participants more difficult. She did however feel uneasy that her easier access in the Malaysian context was probably because of her higher status as a researcher and what she terms 'naievety' about research on the part of participants: 'It also represented a certain naivety, a trust in the researcher which could and perhaps may have been abused' (Pillay 1995: 287).

Ching-Tien Tsai, a student conducting a comparative research study on curriculum change in Taiwan and the UK, described a similar reaction when he tried to introduce ethical procedures such as clearing transcripts with Taiwanese interviewees:

There were interesting cultural differences between interviewees . . . in Taiwan and England. While in England I needed to negotiate the clearance of transcripts, in Taiwan, the interviewees all agreed to allow me to use the data collected in any way I wanted and though I offered a copy of the interview report, they did not feel the necessity for this and did not bother to comment on it. This signified trust in the researcher.

(Tsai 1996: 26)

Like Pillay, Tsai explained the differing response of research participants in his home culture as due to 'trust' and recognized that this put a greater responsibility onto him as researcher not to exploit the relationship:

In Taiwan as in Malaysia, the researcher carries a different status from that which researchers carry in the UK, where there is a need for the interviewee to have a copy of the transcript and to have the right to edit it as they like and where there is an element of distrust of the researcher. This is quite a cultural difference from the response in Taiwan. However, this also places a particular ethical responsibility on me as researcher.

(Tsai 1996: 26)

Although the more trusting relationships put additional demands on the researcher in some respects, Pillay also recognized that the 'culture of hospitality', rather than negotiation of written procedures, enabled her to conduct her field research successfully: 'I would say it was the willingness and desire on the part of the teachers to help a researcher that made the research feasible. It is also part of a culture of hospitality where the visitor is warmly received and people try to be as helpful as possible' (Pillay 1995: 290).

Both of these students highlighted the different ways in which a researcher was received in their home country where interaction was more informal. They were understandably reluctant to adopt what might be seen as 'Western' behaviour by introducing written explanations of research and contracts explaining the ethical procedures. Their concern was both at the level of undermining social relationships and worry that the research findings could be negatively affected. This is similar to the concern expressed by many students about 'being critical' and asking critical questions in a culture where this was not usual.

Ethical procedures based on 'Western' values are not effective

Apart from formalizing relationships, students were sometimes reluctant to adopt CARE's ethical procedures because they believed such practices would not be effective in ensuring that the research was ethically conducted in the differing cultural context. Relating this partly to the hierarchical structures within which they were working, students emphasized that informants would be unlikely to contradict or criticize the researcher since he or she had gained access through their superiors. Lebar, a student from Malaysia, described how the dominant 'traditional' values which emphasize stability and consensus above conflict influenced the way people interacted with researchers:

> I think what makes the difference is the basic values of the people. Traditional values are still very much alive in Malaysian pluralistic society. Respect for others and follow orders are highly regarded values which govern most of the activities in everyday life of the people. A less direct mode in giving criticism is still favoured even in the official routines . . . All ethnic groups are fully aware of what should be disclosed and what not. Also the bureaucracy, in most of its functions operates in a secretive manner for the sake of maintaining political and racial stability.
>
> (Lebar 1995: 37)

In his thesis, Lebar implied that he was reluctant to put informants in the position where they would be more critical, since he understood the importance of following 'traditional values' of 'respect for others and follow orders'. While he recognized that the underlying assumption of the case study approach was to promote democratic values, he was equally aware of the unspoken values in the context where he was conducting research. For this reason, perhaps, he had doubts about the CARE procedures for negotiating accounts with participants and had to compromise by doing this only with gatekeepers, such as the college principal:

> I was unable to do this negotiation with every participant because some of them have been transferred and also the constraints of time did not allow me to do it. Therefore the negotiation of accounts was done with the Principal of the college and some lecturers. The negotiation was aimed at not only validating the account but also to ascertain the extent to which this procedure can be carried out in the Malaysian context.
>
> (Lebar 1995: 56)

Lebar suggests here that he was testing the relevance and practicality of the CARE ethical procedures in the Malaysian context. Pillay, also from Malaysia, described similar problems with negotiating transcripts and explaining principles of procedure:

> Although I had guidelines for the conduct of the research, with regard to the use of data, transcripts, negotiation of data etc, most people did not bother to read the document or to scrutinise it carefully or hold me to the conditions set out in the document. The interviewees usually did not want a transcript and looked taken aback when I talked about sending back the written case for them to

comment on. In a sense, I felt they had been used to research being done on them or to them, and therefore had never felt the need to have rights of control over how the information was used.

(Pillay 1995: 287)

Like Lebar, Pillay suggested that such procedures did not work effectively in the Malaysian context since participants were not used to being critical and were not familiar with the concept of democracy:

But in a country with a fledgling democracy where there is still experimentation regarding issues of open debate and the rights of individual citizens, participants would have little practice with these concepts and little training in how to exercise them. The reality may be that they do not know how to exercise their rights or feel they have the right to do so.

(Pillay 1995: 294)

By relating this to participants' lack of understanding of their rights, she suggested that the researcher could be left with the responsibility of determining what would be harmful to participants:

It left me with a dilemma. If the people I interviewed were ignorant of their rights, then what was my role with regard to the protection of their rights? Did I then have to make decisions on the selective use of data, taking into consideration whether the publication of some information would have consequences to their careers?

(Pillay 1995: 288)

Though Pillay encountered these constraints, she did persevere with trying to involve informants in validating their accounts and explained her educational role in raising awareness, for example, about transcripts (and the differences between written and reported oral speech). She also noted the implications of respondents not being familiar with qualitative research methods, suggesting that this put them at a disadvantage, since they were less conscious of what they were revealing through oral interviews as compared to questionnaires:

Interviewing represented not only cross cultural problems but also problems of ethics . . . the novelty of case study meant that the researched were used to answering questionnaires, which have an air of distance about them . . . The interviewees tended to become more unguarded about what they said as the interview progressed . . . partly due to the fact that for the first time, many of the participants felt that someone was actually interested in listening to their views . . . It may be because information in its oral form, cannot be 'seen'.

(Pillay 1995: 290)

Though face-to-face interviews appeared to be a positive experience for respondents ('someone was actually interested in listening to their views'), Pillay suggested that there were additional ethical implications for a researcher using 'new' methods in a context where people were more used to giving written responses, which are fixed and more visible on a form. She recognized that this put an additional burden of responsibility on the researcher (as compared to the UK PhD student), since she might have unwittingly 'tricked' respondents into saying more than they intended. This made it even more important, in her eyes, that they should validate and give permission for the release of these data.

A common constraint, however (shared by UK researchers too), is that informants were too busy or uninterested in reading through transcripts afterwards. Tsegay, a student researching in Ethiopia, found that informants were not interested in taking copies of the code of conduct ('when I suggested about everyone's right to have a copy, no one seemed to bother') and responded that he could 'transcribe and use the information in any way I liked' (Seminar report). The participants' apparent disinterest in the ethical codes of conduct which students tried to introduce indicated not only a lack of familiarity with their rights, but also that they placed their trust in the researcher's integrity.

I should mention here that some PhD students felt the ethical procedures served no purpose in a differing cultural context, as Syed Zin, another Malaysian student, explained in relation to his case study research (quoted in Lebar 1995: 35): 'The negotiation of accounts with the interviewees was not undertaken because it has never been the practice to negotiate accounts with the participants. Doing it would appear to be outside their social and professional experience'.

A comment by another PhD student, however, suggested that the cultural (as I discussed in Chapter 1) can sometimes be used as an excuse for not implementing ethical procedures that will make the research process more complex and cumbersome. Tan (1989) hinted at a problem not specific to Malaysia, but common to any researcher negotiating data with respondents – the possibility that they would not be able to use valuable data:

> In making decision about negotiation, I had to bear in mind the following:
>
> i. The cultural and political differences between my informants in Norwich and in Malaysia
> ii. The risk of an unproductive fieldwork in Malaysia if negotiation causes information and data to be withheld
>
> (Tan quoted in Lebar 1995: 36)

With the increasing influence of 'Western' values through globalization, it is likely that international students today face less resistance in introducing these ethical procedures than Zin and Lebar did in the 1990s. However, these reflections still have a relevance in that students may feel that meeting ethical concerns within their PhD research is about applying practices and values not held by participants in their own cultural context. It is worth noting that innovative development projects have often been met with similar responses to those noted above in relation to research approaches – that such interventions promote unfamiliar and alien practices (for instance, child-centred individualized teaching approaches). As 'new' cultural values and practices have become assimilated and disseminated, it has become increasingly difficult to adopt models of analysis based on this static concept of 'tradition' or 'indigenous'.

Bureaucratic procedures and confidentiality

Bureaucratic procedures for obtaining access to institutions being researched are not unique to international contexts.[7] However, as Lewin (1990a: 213) points out, 'much research in developing countries takes place within bureaucratic frameworks' and students sponsored by governments are under particular pressure to conform to bureaucratic requirements, including monitoring their movements and research activities. As Pillay described in her thesis, this meant difficulties in disguising the identity of informants and ensuring confidentiality was often impossible. Reflecting on the amount of paperwork she had to submit to gain access to research informants, she reflected: 'What this leads to is a trail of official paper following the case study researcher in Malaysia. Anyone who wanted to could more or less trace where I have been and whom I have talked to' (Pillay 1995: 288).

She emphasized that the systems of monitoring and regulating researcher activity in Malaysia placed extra pressures on the PhD student if they were going to respond to the UK expectation that they would protect informants' identities:

> No matter what strategies of anonymisation I have used, there is a possibility that my sources of information could be identified. So wherein lies the researcher's assurances of confidentiality . . . Case study researchers doing research and operating in different systems of government need to be sensitised to this difficulty and the ethical dilemmas involved.
>
> (Pillay 1995: 288)

Pillay's concerns suggest that even if informants were persuaded to sign written agreements regarding confidentiality, the researcher would face major practical problems in trying to keep to their side of the agreement.

As I discuss in the next section, this implies that international students may face ethical dilemmas of a different kind from the UK student that are not necessarily addressed in the UK codes of practice. Pillay, like other Malaysian students, was aware of having to meet two sets of contrasting institutional expectations. From the Malaysian government side, she was supposed to be transparent about whom she had met and interviewed and be willing to report findings openly; whereas the UK institution began from the starting point that data could be harmful to individuals and individual institutions if identities were not concealed.

Differing ethical concerns

I have discussed how international students adapted the ethical guidelines provided by the UK university to their own cultural context. This involved looking more critically at research practices that are taken for granted in the UK, such as signing consent forms or giving information through an interview rather than a questionnaire. In outlining the constraints faced by international students in implementing ethical procedures developed in the UK, I have suggested that the question of 'what could do harm' to respondents may be answered in different ways in another cultural context. In addition, conducting research in a different culture for a UK-assessed PhD may raise new ethical concerns not dealt with in the guidelines provided by the UK institution. In this section, I explore the question of ethics from the perspective of international students' own priorities: issues arising from the experience of writing in a language different from that of respondents, balancing differing institutional and political expectations, and experimenting with form.

Language and ethics

Writing the thesis in English and conducting interviews or observation in another (or possibly two or more other) language(s) can present ethical issues that are rarely encountered by UK-focused PhD students. The ethical dimension is related not only to the validity of the data, but also to the practical impossibility of informants being able to collaborate on the final text in English. Tsai described how this put an additional responsibility onto him as 'interpreter' – in the literal sense – of his interviewee's words: 'I have to check the transcripts again and again to find the exact expression for the Chinese language in English, so that I can represent the views of my interviewee fairly' (Tsai 1996: 26).

Given the time-consuming nature of transcribing a tape in the language used in the interview, then translating the whole transcription into English, a student may decide to translate directly from the taped oral version into English. From an ethical perspective, this could be seen as undermining the respondent's right to read and collaborate on the original transcript. Decisions about which language to use in interviews could also be related to Pillay's concern about informal interviews putting respondents in a disadvantageous position where they reveal more than they intended because the situation is unfamiliar. For instance, if research interviews are normally conducted in English with higher-level officials, they may become less guarded if the interviewer switches into their mother tongue. Linguistic strategies, such as code-switching, can be used by 'native' researchers to draw on their 'insider' identity and often provide more revealing insights than would be presented in English to an outsider. The international student may need to consider in advance of interviews and focus group discussions whether to make a choice about language medium with respondents in advance and whether to let respondents take the lead in these decisions. Conducting fieldwork in Nepal, I have sometimes faced this dilemma – when government officials wanted to have formal interviews in English rather than share informal conversations with me in Nepali – and this limited our interaction. As a researcher, I had to decide how far to push my own views on language choice (which, of course, was complicated by the fact that I was a foreigner speaking in a second language).

Balancing differing priorities: politics versus ethics

A basic premise in this chapter is that the politics and ethics of cross-national and cross-cultural field research are analytically distinguishable, but closely connected in practice . . . Politics refers to interactions revolving around power, influence and authority . . . Ethics deals with questions of moral goodness or evil and the proper standards for human action.

(Warwick 1983: 316)

The convergence of political and ethical concerns in the cross-cultural context within which all international students operate is perhaps the hardest issue to address. As Warwick suggests, in many countries it is impossible to discuss ethics without considering politics – particularly where the state is involved in determining 'questions of moral goodness or evil' (ibid.). Looking back at the CARE ethics pack, political considerations would need to come into play when defining what are 'sensitive information or issues' and which groups are 'vulnerable'. As well as putting a different slant on such guidelines, the political context within which many students work back home means that they have to consider different forms of 'protection' than could be offered by UK principles of procedure. In a seminar on research ethics, several international students raised questions about how to conduct research that could be considered critical in a sensitive political environment. A student from South America asked: 'What about ethics in certain political contexts? How can you protect yourself as a researcher in a country where people may not be free to express their opinions?'

In discussion, students suggested that it was a common personal dilemma they faced, partly because of their supervisor's insistence that they should be 'more critical' in their research. Being critical carried different implications for the researcher in a strongly hierarchical society, especially as an 'insider' who would return to work in the same country context after the PhD course. The UK ethical guidelines were developed to offer protection to the researcher in relation to possible disagreements with respondents about the data, but did not offer much protection for the researcher whose whole project came under attack from national government or sponsors. Though students were continuously aware of having to balance their academic and political loyalties, they were concerned that UK supervisors did not fully understand the dangers associated with being critical in their home context:

> Students in the group felt that supervisors needed to acknowledge more the tensions of coming from another culture and political context and that in many countries, to be critical at all is 'very risky' . . . Several people felt that the opportunity to study in the UK meant more flexibility, the change to challenge practices of a lifetime, but others felt that they would not be easily able to write up research in a way that satisfied both their supervisor here and their colleagues or government back home.
>
> (Seminar report: 17/5/02)

This political dimension affected not only how they carried out research activities, but also the kind of information that respondents were willing to give or sanction. A student said that his colleagues back home told him they were happy for him to quote their words if the point was 'academic' but not 'political'. Seen in this context, ethical dilemmas were closely related to anticipating political harm – in the choice of topic or approach as well as the conduct of the researcher. As Warwick (1983: 325) points out, this implies addressing the larger questions, such as 'Should some research topics be avoided, particularly when they are likely to touch off domestic or international controversy?' For many international students, the desire to introduce a critical edge to their research without becoming overtly critical was a response to the conflicting expectations and demands of their sponsor and the UK university. As I discussed in relation to the Malaysian government guidelines for researchers, some students were also aware of having to balance these differing priorities through responding to two sets of criteria for what constituted 'quality' research.

Whereas the Malaysian guidelines were shaped by political considerations about promoting the nation's interest through research that was not 'sensitive' or 'controversial', the CARE ethics pack was premised on the idea that research findings could be sensitive and potentially harm individuals. Referring to the dominant 'discourse of nation building' in Malaysia, Lie (2004: 74) points out that: 'Adopting a publicly critical voice is a major challenge for most Malaysians, especially when they are dismissed for risking social harmony and goodwill'.

Representation of findings

Today's PhD theses take a greater variety of forms than ever before – fictionalized dialogues or dramas, narrated life stories – but choices about writing styles or forms tend rarely to be considered in relation to research ethics. In research seminars, I have sometimes been made aware that resistance to adopting a less conventional form of thesis is not always about cultural appropriateness but can sometimes be made on moral grounds. An instance occurred when a UK student presented a fictionalized conversation constructed from real interview responses from his various respondents. Although they had not met in person but been interviewed on a one-to-one basis, the conversation implied that they had been in the room together. A student from the Middle East objected strongly to this text on the grounds that it was 'lying': 'He felt this way of presenting interview text "distorted the reality" as there was no indication of what had been invented or changed' (Seminar report: 11/11/02).

This made me reflect on other situations where students had objected to non-conventional presentations of data. Going back to epistemological debates about the nature of 'reality', experimentations with form can be regarded as an expression influenced by an ideological rejection of one absolute truth or reality. Yet, if someone strongly believes in one 'truth' (which is often associated with a certain research approach and written genre), does fictionalizing data present an ethical dilemma (both for the reader and writer) rather than only a methodological choice? Scholastica, from Tanzania, pointed out that 'the way people narrate their stories in different cultures is quite different' (Seminar report: 2/12/02). Although she was referring to oral narration, she was concerned about how to represent a different form of narration in her thesis. On another occasion, she explained how the form of a case study could be misunderstood in a culture where stories are used mainly for didactic purposes (to teach a moral). She suggested that a case study about boys who steal cars to buy drugs might be interpreted in her culture as promoting such (im)moral values. As I will discuss further in Chapter 6, the choice of narrative style and form in a thesis may be regarded in terms of an ethical stance, rather than a personal choice as to which representation best conveys the research findings.

Implications for developing ethical research practices in the UK

I will end this chapter with some reflections on how a cross-cultural perspective on research ethics could help improve current educational research practice in the UK. I am aware that many of the comments made by international students in the context of their home country (Scholastica: 'it would be a lot easier in Tanzania to simply go out and talk to people'; Seminar report 9/7/02) were equally applicable in the UK just a decade ago. Recently, I attended a seminar where a researcher working in Suffolk described how she could wander into a school in the 1990s and ask the head's permission to interview young children, without any query as to how the information would be used. This researcher was shocked in retrospect at the lack of control and accountability mechanisms, and reflected – like many international students quoted here – on the consequent ethical responsibility she carried. The field of educational research (encompassing health care too) is subject perhaps to more tightly prescribed ethical guidelines than other areas of research because of dealing with children, a vulnerable group, who are already subject to power hierarchies within schools, families and communities. The role of the researcher fits easily into these hierarchies, increasing the possibility for respondents to be exploited unless the researcher's power is regulated.

Having conducted research in both the UK and Nepal, I have had the experience of adopting ethical procedures, such as seeking consent to release information, as well as the situation where I alone had to monitor the ethical implications of my research. In the UK context – perhaps because I have previously worked in a country where there were no ethical guidelines or expectations of accountability – I have been aware of the danger of failing to reflect continuously on the ethical dimensions of my research. The fact that clearance has been granted in more formal ways (through respondents signing forms) can lead to the assumption that the research ethics are taken care of. The increasing tendency to associate research ethics with formal, often mechanistic, procedures – such as passing a proposal through a committee for approval – has had some unfortunate consequences, not least a 'bolt-on' approach to ethics. By contrast, a student trying to implement such procedures in a differing cultural context is made aware of the implicit assumptions about what constitutes ethical practice and to question concepts such as 'informed consent' in every situation. In my previous research in Nepal, I was aware of having to develop my own guidelines and draw on collaborative research approaches (such as PRA) that were already common in the local area to inform my own practice.

Though ethical codes of conduct were usually introduced as guidelines within UK institutions, all too often they have been regarded as a set of rules and implemented without critical reflection. Taking a cross-cultural perspective can imply looking at these guidelines through new eyes and countering the tendency to regard research ethics simply as a hurdle to jump over. Stressing the importance of 'individual conscience' (Vulliamy 1990: 112) and continual personal reflection on the implications of research, Vulliamy suggests that much of the literature on the ethics of ethnographic fieldwork 'which is concerned with arguments for and against covert participant observation, misses the point' (p. 113). Referring to his own research, which was not 'covert', he discusses how sometimes he did not fully explain his aims in classroom observation to the teachers concerned as this might undermine their confidence: 'so-called "non secret research" may also involve elements of deception in order for the research to prove valid' (ibid.). The process of reflecting on what is or is not 'covert' research illustrated here by Vulliamy is, of course, not unique to cross-cultural situations. Transplanting UK-developed ethical guidelines into another cultural context can, however, force us to assess the ways in which we need to rely on 'individual conscience' and what we may lose by depending on formalized codes. As I have suggested earlier, we may need to reflect more closely on who is potentially 'vulnerable' in a different culture or who may be harmed by research, rather than accepting a predetermined list of categories given by a body concerned with ethical oversight. Similarly, producing a consent form may not be the best entry point for a researcher in the UK who wants to establish an informal relationship with a respondent, any more than in Malaysia.

Finally, concern over the ethics of interpretation – discussed by international students here particularly in relation to translating data into English – is of relevance to us all. Dilemmas about how we can share the final research product (the thesis) with participants so that they can have the right to challenge our interpretation of the data are not always regarded as ethical concerns. However, even if respondents speak English as their mother tongue, they may not be familiar with the academic genre of a thesis and be unable to access what the researcher has written about them. Though the international student faces a more obvious barrier (the English language) in collaborating on the final text with participants, the challenge is similar to that faced by a UK PhD student and may result in the decision to produce two different texts to meet the needs of the two readerships. The question of interpretation relates also to the wider issue of imposing 'our' view of the world and the cultural assumptions we bring to any piece of 'evidence'.

Endpiece

Our differing cultural perspectives on the same data became clear to us as a seminar group when a Malaysian teacher trainer shared a photograph that he had taken during his observation of a PE lesson (referred to in Chapter 1). His fellow PhD students immediately asked:

> Why did the women learning a headstand have to wear so many clothes? Why do women have to train as PE instructors in a separate group from the men? The discussion illustrated Zuber's different perspective as an 'insider' – he explained that when he looked at the same photo, what struck him was that the male instructor was supporting the female trainee in an unsafe and dangerous position because of trying to appear modest. Others in our group from similar cultures explained that they felt the women trainees would probably feel happier and more comfortable doing these physical activities in a single sex group . . . Scholastica wondered when she saw the photos of the girls doing PE fully clothed and head covered, whether they felt happy about this situation but felt that they could not state this to the researcher (as he is part of the same culture).
>
> (Seminar report: 11/3/02)

This discussion illustrates how closely ethical concerns are related to issues of methodological rigour. While Zuber (the presenter) looked at the photograph from the perspective of a PE teacher trainer (noting the unsafe position), women from our group analysed the event from the assumption that girls were forced to wear unsuitable clothing because of their culture. They were concerned that the photo conveyed a message of inequality. However, two Muslim women explained that from their point of view, a single sex group for PE training was not inferior but 'more comfortable'. We were made aware in this seminar of how people's identities shaped their interpretation of this photograph and their responses. Comparing Zuber's 'insider' perspective, we wondered about the ethical dimensions of our interpretation: Was it appropriate to interpret such data from an outsider's perspective? How does being an 'insider' affect the way that respondents relate to your questions? Would the girls really 'not state this to the researcher', or did they themselves not share Scholastica's perspective on their situation?

I may appear to have strayed far from research ethics in describing this event, though this distance is in a sense the main point of this chapter. Regarding ethical concerns as integral rather than 'bolt on' to the research can enable us to take a more holistic view of our research – questioning, as in the above event, how far our cultural assumptions and beliefs shape what we observe and how we interact. Taking a cross-cultural perspective on ethics can lead to greater understanding about the values that underpin our research approach so that we can learn to articulate how those values inform our ethical stance. This is a necessary first step before research ethics can be negotiated and agreed with research participants, colleagues and academic supervisors.

There is more to learn behind the scene

By Scholastica N. Mokake

In January 2002, I started my full-time PhD research programme. After I submitted my proposal, I was told that the school had already assigned me a supervisor. I later found myself in my supervisor's office discussing how I was going to do my research. She told me it was a good time for me to write a short research plan, as I would need to submit it to the ethics committee. She opened the Research Ethics Committee Information and Discussion Pack and read Section B:

Any proposal for research which is to be undertaken by a student as part of a course must be submitted to EDU Research Ethics Committee for consideration before the research is undertaken, if the research involves:

(c) Work with children or young adults where they are asked to reveal intimate personal information about:
– Family relationships
– Potentially distressing topics
– Information about sexual behaviour
– Information about drugs
– Information about criminal activities

And this was the type of people I was going to research: I was required to submit my research plan to the committee for approval. It took me three months to get the approval. When I first wrote my plan, I focused on what I believed would be necessary for the people I wanted to interview. However, that meant I had to rewrite my plan for the committee as they insisted it was very important to carry out certain procedures, such as requiring interviewees to sign a consent form. What I had been thinking here was that I would only explain to people by word of mouth, as some of the interviewees in the villages (in Tanzania) did not know how to write their names. In such cases I would ask them to sign using their thumb prints as a signature. To some of them, it would be like 'policing' them. Although my research was to be conducted in Tanzania, I had to follow the UEA research ethics procedures.

The experience I had when I went back to Tanzania to do my research – with all the ethical procedures in place – made me realize that the type of locality where the research is conducted matters a lot. One such factor that came out clearly was the socio-economic status of the respondents. The hard facts of life in a particular area can influence the conduct of the research and the willingness of the people to participate in the research.

I remember when I was still at the proposal stage, preparing my research plan, I wrote to the ethics committee to let them know that I would be interviewing young people from the age of 10 to 18. I was told that I needed to give them a consent form to fill in permitting me to interview them. When I came to the field in Tanzania, the respondents looked at me as if I was doing something dubious and suspicious: 'Why should we sign?' 'Is it not the reality?' 'Do you think we are lying to you?' 'Why do you want us to commit ourselves, do you want to come back and accuse us of lying?' 'We don't want to be held responsible' (Fieldnotes 2003).

In some cases, I may say this approach creates mistrust between the researcher and the respondents and can make the people being interviewed hesitant to divulge information or sign the ethics consent form. In my case, doing the research in my country made me think that the local people have the right to consider the researcher and the research topic. Knowing that I am their fellow Tanzanian and I am researching for my degree, they might like to be part of it and maybe to help me succeed. Or if the topic was of interest to them and was not boring, they sometimes look at the method you are using; if the method is tedious to them, obviously they will have no interest in your research. In this case, I felt it was my duty as a researcher to make my research process interesting to those I am researching on. If on another occasion they feel that we should only chat casually with no signing of consent forms, well and good. But what if the information they are giving could affect them later? I also ask myself, am I safe as a researcher without making them commit themselves by signing and giving their consent by writing, even though they have already given out their consent by word of mouth, or should I take other members of the group as my witnesses in case of any trouble later? These are the questions I asked myself before I proceeded. I tried to explain why I was asking for their permission, but most of them did not find it necessary for me to do so. Nevertheless, I had to insist and tell them that we were following the procedure (they still wanted to know who this person called 'procedure' was!).

After that, I was able to start my research. Next, the issue of not recording their true names also cropped up – which was again another controversial issue. Most young people nowadays like to be known so they don't want their identities to be changed. They want to be known: young people want to become celebrities. You find nowadays many are participating in things like Stars in their Eyes, Project Fame, Big Brother, Miss Tanzania. 'How come I give you my story, my real life story, and you write another name?' Probably he was thinking that I wanted to use his story to promote someone else. When it came to taking photos, they really wanted to have their photos taken and they were anxious to appear in the report. I asked myself, 'Is it necessary to make our interviewees anonymous even when they want to be known for their own interest?'

One young girl I interviewed said to me, 'It is better to photograph me while I am going about my small business so that people see how poor I am. Maybe one Samaritan may decide to help me to improve this place'. This girl is doing *Mama Ntilie*, selling food in a marketplace. If you look at where the food is sold, you will doubt the hygiene and the safety of the food she is selling, but surprisingly she is getting enough customers every day, regardless of the poor state of her utensils. I think in this matter the socio-economic status determines the way the people perceive things. If I decide to do this same type of research with the rich, well-to-do families in Tanzania, maybe educated people will ask me to show them my research permit before I talk to them and they will be willing to sign the consent forms. But the people I interviewed were from the middle and low classes. In this particular study area, a person who is considered rich is the one who owns shops, bars and small businesses that can employ comfortably five to ten people, or a salaried person who can subsist comfortably throughout a month and yet have some saving. This definition of a rich person may not fit in another area, because there are people who have more than what I have mentioned above but they can never dream of living in such an area. This is a more congested area of the city suburbs. However, many outsiders have come and conducted research there and some of them used to give them money or gifts after they had finished interviewing them, so they have that mentality of thinking that they can benefit from this research financially. If not, they take this as an opportunity to speak out about what has been worrying them, through you as a researcher, so that other people know what is going on around their normal day-to-day life.

Reflections on UK ethical procedures from the perspective of an international student

I would like to preface the discussion on the ethical procedures given to international students who go back to their own home countries to conduct research in their own communities. Sometimes they find it very difficult to apply these procedures as people accept researchers unconditionally and they feel comfortable revealing things to them, thinking that the research will bring change to them. Apart from that they feel comfortable to talk with someone who speaks their language, for then these people speak freely and with confidence. The only problem at the particular place where I worked is that a lot of researchers have conducted research there and this has made the people of that area expert in answering research questions. You can feel it when you are talking to them – that they give you the answers you want to hear and not what the reality is.

Sometimes when you want to get accurate information, you may need to use a different approach. For instance, you can go to them very informally and without even telling them that you are doing research, so that the truth you are seeking is not compromised. I remember one day I visited a friend who lives in the area and I met her son with his two friends. We were chatting together, and we started talking about AIDS and later I asked them if young people of that area are aware of the HIV infection and how they could protect themselves from contracting it. They told me that some of them are very careful with their life and that truly they are abstaining from unsafe sex; but some think having sex with different people is all right. Then from that conversation I came to know that some were trying to apply preventive measures by using condoms but still they don't use them properly. Some used used condoms – that is, they use them, wash them with petrol, and re-use them next time. Some of these condoms were on hire. Apart from learning this outside my formal research sessions, I also learnt from these boys that some young people are even practising homosexuality, thinking that when they have sexual intercourse with the same sex they will not contract the disease. They thought that you can get HIV only if you have sexual intercourse with a woman.

I got all this important information without any consent form being signed or tape recording the discussion; but I took this as very important information that I needed to work on. I decided that I would go back to the area and try to interview the youth again and see if they would reveal all these to me, though in the first place they did not. I am still asking myself how I am going to use my data that comes from outside the interviews? What methodology will I use? Should I say that I was observing what was going on by participating in informal discussion with youth of the area and that qualifies me to be a participant observer? But that is only what I heard but have not seen practised. When I think of research ethics procedures, I sometimes feel that my freedom to explore in different areas is curtailed.

In my case, I also feel the subject matter contributes a lot in stopping people from being open to speak because my research is concerned with personal matters which are top secret for an individual. Though I was able to get access to the field and meet my respondents, I feared I might not be able to get the true insight into what was going on. My research is on the sex life of young people whom the society believes have no right to start practising sex and religious beliefs do not allow them to do sex. Adults condemn young people for entering into affairs that they are not supposed to indulge in and young people feel that it is their right to choose what to do with their bodies.

I was able to enter easily in the field as a Tanzanian. They took me as one of them, but still problems arose when you asked questions which touched on people's beliefs, norms and values, especially if you were not of their tribal culture or their religious persuasion. The chance of getting information is slight, as different tribes have their different secrets within their traditions and culture which they are not allowed to tell outsiders. Since I come from a different tribe, I was looked upon as a stranger even though I am a Tanzanian.

I will give an example of data that I would not have collected through following research ethics procedures. I remember one respected traditional healer in the area who claimed to heal women. The way he healed them was by rubbing some herbs on his penis and having sexual intercourse with his female clients. Now since the women believed that the medicine they were getting in this fashion was genuine, they would never divulge this secret. In fact, they believed that if they divulged this secret the medicine would not work. There were the unfortunate ones who got pregnancies from the traditional healer; and as a result, they divorced their husbands. Others performed abortions, while others became the traditional healer's 'wives'. In fact, the traditional healer had amassed twelve 'wives'. This story came out after one girl who attends seminars and likes to pop in the youth centre for information revealed the behaviour of this old medicine man. She said that she had been to the traditional healer for treatment and the man had wanted to force her to be treated through use of his penis. The girl ran away and reported the matter to a reporter, and the story was published in the newspapers. After that the other women started telling their own stories, and steps were taken against the old medicine man. Had the secret not been divulged, the abuse would have continued. Abuse conducted by respected members of society or by close family members is difficult to report. People shy away from reporting these people (Fieldnotes 2004).

Conclusion

It is not easy to get this kind of information unless you go deep in your discussion with the interviewees. My response to all these research ethics and procedures is that we should go to the field without any format of exactly what we want to do. Rather, we should have open minds and be ready to tune in to the situations that we find in the field. We should use varied tactics that will enable us to obtain information from our clients, which under normal circumstances they might not give us. I know that it is my duty to gather as much information as possible. This is not an easy task, as you need to safeguard the interest of the people and your own interest as a researcher. Sometimes I found myself in a mixed-up situation as I had dual engagement (personal and professional as counsellor) and at this stage I started asking myself: 'What is it legitimate to collect data on, what about obligation to truth, openness and confidentiality? Why is my respondent telling me all this? Is she/he telling me the truth? Do I need to investigate that or do I need to just take what she tells me? And figure out why is she telling me all that – was this a plea for help?'

A number of guidelines for ethical research have appeared recently, emphasizing the notion that the researcher should respect the rights of the people they study. That is, what I am trying to say here, I respect the rights of the people I am researching. Therefore, I am suggesting that the researcher should be left to follow procedures which safeguard the people of the researched area. It may not make sense to conduct research in Africa following the research procedures of the United Kingdom because there is a big difference in cultural approach to some issues in Africa. In my research, I found myself adopting 'a rule of thumb' in responding with sympathy and flexibility to situations and individuals: it all depends on where you are and what is your background. The notion of a 'universal research ethics' is misleading, as I believe every researcher may draw his or her line differently from someone else. When we go to the field, we should carry ethics in our head. In this respect, whatever we do is always provisional.

Scholastica N. Mokake is a qualified social worker and counsellor with experience dealing with HIV/AIDS affected families in Tanzania. She worked with a non-governmental organization in Tanzania, specializing in working with young children of all kinds – such as children in need of special protective measures, including orphans, the abused and neglected. Scholastica is now in her third year of a PhD research programme at the University of East Anglia, focusing on communication between adolescents and their parents, trying to find out about the role of counselling services in enhancing this communication. Her special interest is around issues of sexual reproductive health and HIV/AIDS. That made her come up with this research topic: 'From not communicating to children to counselling, on bridging the gap of communication in the era of HIV/AIDS'. Email: Scholastica.mokake@uea.ac.uk

Which language?

Introduction

Decisions about which language to use when writing field notes, interviewing or analysing data are integral to the research process for most international students. As I discussed in the previous chapter, working with two or more languages during fieldwork and writing up has ethical implications. There are issues around validity and translation: How do you ensure that the way you write up in English accurately reflects what people said in another language? Established ethical procedures may also need to be revisited, since respondents may not be able to read the final product in English. The researcher can also draw more fully on his or her 'insider' status by code-switching between their mother tongue and English, which could be seen as an additional interviewing strategy or more negatively as 'tricking' the respondent into giving more information than intended. As well as these ethical and methodological issues around language choice and use, there are also considerable specific practical concerns (such as the additional burden of translating transcripts and observation data) faced by an international PhD student as compared to a researcher in the UK context.

There is some overlap between this chapter and the next, which will focus on academic writing practices in relation to the PhD, in that both are concerned with writing in English as a second language, addressing issues of representation, voice, audience and form. However, this chapter is primarily about language choice and the research process – in contrast to Chapter 6, which focuses on writing the thesis, a particular text that has to be produced in the English language. By looking in detail at the kinds of language decisions students make during their fieldwork in relation to different tasks and contexts, I intend to move the discussion away from a 'deficit' view of international students (as having 'language problems') to a consideration of how language could be fully exploited as an additional resource within their research and within educational research in general. This also implies a more complex analysis of language-related research strategies (such as code-switching and translation approaches) in certain cultural and linguistic contexts, and recognizing the dynamic relationships between a variety of languages – instead of polarizing English language and 'the other' (mother tongue).

In this chapter – as in the book as a whole – I take what has been termed a 'social practice' approach to language and literacy (Street 1993; Barton 1994) within the context of the PhD. Rejecting the idea of a 'great divide' (Goody 1968) between literacy and orality, between literate and non-literate people and between literate and oral societies, the body of research known as the 'New Literacy Studies' has developed an 'ideological' model of literacy (drawing on Street 1984). Rather than viewing literacy as a neutral technical input, these researchers see literacy as embedded in social, political and cultural contexts. We all move on a continuum between literacy and orality – the implication being that literacy practices (such as writing a thesis) involve oral practices of negotiation and discussion. In the context of higher education and its writing practices, Jones *et al.* (1999: xvi) emphasize that we should be thinking at the level of 'epistemology' rather than 'skills and effectiveness': 'what counts as knowledge and who has authority over it; of identity – what the relationship is between forms of writing and the constitution of self and agency; and of power'.

Within PhD educational research, this approach involves seeing language choice as not just a technical decision about which language is more widely understood, but taking into consideration ideological concerns around identity (of research student and their respondents) and power. Much of the literature on higher education academic practices (including Jones *et al.* 1999; see also Candlin and Hyland 1999; Lea and Stierer 2000) has focused on the written texts, often in relation to the learning and teaching practices of international students. However, in this chapter I intend to look more closely at other literacy and oral practices involved in the process of writing a thesis, such as interviewing, data analysis and discussion with research participants. By analysing language issues in relation to fieldwork, I aim to offer insight into how decisions about the oral and written texts at this stage shape and influence the form of the thesis, and interactions with the students' peers and supervisors in their UK institution. These latter two areas will be explored more fully in Chapters 6 and 7.

The fieldwork process

Interviewing: who chooses the language?

How do I handle several languages in my research: two different languages for interviewing and English for writing up? Should I translate as I transcribe? How much data will I need to translate into English? What are the implications of using one language for interviews and another for reporting? Who should decide which language to use in interviews – me or the participants?

(Seminar report)

These are some of the immediate concerns around language choice expressed by international students in our research seminars at CARE. For a student going back 'home' to conduct field research, language issues are implicit in all their decisions about their research design. In contrast to many Western researchers going to non-English-speaking countries to conduct research, these students are already aware of the relative power and status of the various languages they could draw upon in interviews, and the ideological implications, for example, of choosing to speak Bahasa Malay rather than Tamil to respondents. In this case, the choice of language may affect what people say, as well as who is included or excluded from the research activities.

During my PhD field research in Nepal, I worked with people speaking both Nepali and Newari. Initially, I had not realized that though some younger Newari women spoke Nepali, most older women did not. I had unintentionally introduced a gender and age bias into who participated in focus group discussions through relying on Nepali as the main medium of communication. As well as responding to the complex and subtle differences between indigenous languages, the international student also needs to decide how far to draw on the English language in interviews and in their own writing.

The domination of the English language over indigenous languages has been identified as a legacy of cultural imperialism (Pennycook 1994) and English is still valued as a language of economic and social power in many countries of the world. As Nair-Venugopal (2004: 90) discusses in the context of Malaysia, the 'pervasive influence' of English under colonialism is now strengthened by increasing globalization: 'Emerging from globalized workplaces in multi-transnational coroporations is the hegemonic view that English is *the* international language of global/local business practices, *the* language of international capitalism'. Choosing to conduct interviews in English rather than a national or indigenous language might therefore be associated with recognizing the higher status of research participants – or with demonstrating the researcher's superior position and differing identity, as associated with an English medium higher educational institution abroad.

In some cases, however, English may be the most familiar language to both participants and researcher: Pillay, an English language teacher from Malaysia, reflected in her thesis on the implications of being raised and educated in a former British colony. She recognized that part of her identity as an English teacher was the belief that English was 'a good thing' (Pillay 1995: 300), and commented on the 'irony' that 'it is only in the English language that I can best express my views and thoughts'. Nair-Venugopal (2004: 90) describes the creation of 'multiple Englishes' in Malaysia by indigenous speakers of English and the resulting tension between 'the press for linguistic homogeneity and normativity on the one hand, and fragmentation and variability of Englishes on the other' (p. 89). This recognition of various Englishes (see Crystal 1997) could also be related to debates about how far students should produce 'standard' English in their thesis (see next chapter).

In certain cultural contexts, English may therefore be considered as introducing less 'bias' than other local languages: though Lie (2004: 82) contends that 'the unquestioning acceptance' of the 'neutral' status of English in Malaysia is 'a manifestation of the participants' general unawareness of the historical, social, political and power-centred relations of systems of language knowledge and social practice'. In our research seminars, several students related the 'neutrality' of English to issues of access and empowerment:

> This led into a discussion of the perceptions of English as a 'neutral' language in many contexts (not being associated with one particular ethnic group) and also as a language of power, offering access to other kinds of education and employment. Halim compared the situation in Malaysia where globalization is increasing the demand for English teaching and Schola mentioned the growing number of NGOs in Tanzania where English is required to write reports for donors.
>
> (Seminar report: 10/5/02)

During this discussion, another student pointed out that he had been able to draw on his knowledge of three languages – English, Tigrigna and Amharic – to interview people in the language they preferred. Significantly, many students invited participants to decide on the language medium of interviews and were flexible about switching from one language to another during the course of their interviews or discussions. Decisions about which language to use were often made for pragmatic reasons, as Ayedh Al-Motairi explained when describing his fieldwork in Saudi Arabia:

> I did the pilot study first. I had thought to do the interviews in English

as I was working with English teachers, but when I went to the field, I changed my mind. I decided to do interviews in Arabic to encourage the teachers to speak easily. I found some teachers mixing Arabic with English too. I taped the interviews and took notes – using a mixture of English and Arabic in my notes. When I am in a hurry, I rely on Arabic.

(Interview: 24/6/04)

Al-Motairi had had experience of conducting interviews in the UK as well (in English) and commented on how the situation seemed more formal than in Saudi Arabia because he was using his second language:

In Arabic, it is more like an informal conversation, not grammatical, whereas in English interviewing would be more formal because it is not my native language. I have conducted interviews with teachers in the language centre here [at the University of East Anglia], as a practice, but I found it not that easy for me. It was like a formal conversation. But when I did it in Arabic with native speakers, it was like an informal conversation. The main issue is about the language of the interviewer and the interviewee – if it differs, then the interview will be formal.

(Interview: 24/6/04)

The formality that Al-Motairi identifies is around the relationship, which changes from being that of 'insiders' conversing to that of an 'outsider' speaking to another 'outsider'. In the context of academic literacy, Turner (1999: 150) discusses this in terms of the discourse of transparency: 'when language is working well, it is invisible. Conversely, however, when language becomes "visible", it is an object of censure, marking a deficiency in the individual using it'. Al-Motairi seemed to describe a parallel situation of the language coming between himself and the interviewees, which made the interview more formal, as compared to the 'invisibility' of language in his Arabic interviews. Linked to this 'invisibility' is the need for the researcher to adapt their behaviour to the cultural expectations of a conversation or discussion. In particular, indigenous researchers recognized that it was not always appropriate to ask direct questions or to appear to be critical. The literature on cross-cultural communication in higher education classrooms is useful in this respect. For instance, Cortazzi and Jin (1997) point out that in a Japanese context, talking in a loud voice can be misunderstood as anger and that saying 'yes' may not necessarily indicate agreement, but simply that the interviewee is listening. As I will discuss in the next section, international students from CARE found themselves in the doubly difficult situation of understanding the cultural norms in their country context, yet having to decide whether to challenge them (during fieldwork) in an attempt to encourage people to be more critical and reflect personally on their situations (the expectations of PhD research).

Translating interviews

Conducting interviews in the participant's mother tongue left the researcher with the difficult task of translating their words into English.[1] As Al-Yaseen (2000) commented in her thesis, this was not only time-consuming but intellectually challenging:

> The convenience almost all the participants felt to talk and express themselves in Arabic helped to get them involved into branched but related educational matters. However I was left with an unenvious situation as I had to translate as well from Arabic into English. That made me more conscious about getting the meaning they wanted me to see and how what I wanted to see in their words. That was very tough to accomplish.
>
> (Al-Yaseen 2000: 104)

Reflecting on the time-consuming process of translating transcripts into English, several students commented on the practical advantages of conducting interviews in English rather than their mother tongue: 'There were practical reasons to interview in English: the advantage of this was that I did not have to translate the transcript of the interviews into English language which I had to do for all interviews I conducted in Malay' (Lebar 1995: 49).

Translation was seen in 'free' or 'communicative' terms, rather than a 'literal' or 'semantic' translation (Connor 1996), as Al-Nasser (1999) commented on the data that he had collected in Arabic:

> Translation was not an easy matter. Translating word by word was impossible in most cases because if it had been done, the meaning might have changed. So I had to go after the meaning of the content rather than word by word translation. This explains why there was no place in the quotes used in the case studies for what Miles and Huberman (1994: 51) call 'uhs', 'ers', 'mispronunciation' etc.
>
> (Al-Nasser 1999: 99)

The question of when to translate the data and, crucially, how much to translate into English, is related partly to how the researcher plans to analyse and discuss findings with their supervisor. In the past, students may have felt obliged to translate all their data into English, perhaps to prove to examiners or supervisors that they had the evidence.[2] However, as Al-Motairi discusses below, there is now more recognition of the labour that such translation would involve:

I transcribed the tapes all into Arabic. In the pilot study, I transcribed all the tapes into Arabic then translated into English. But I found this time consuming so for the main fieldwork . . . it was such a huge amount of data, I just did the Arabic in full. But I did not translate all the transcripts, just the parts that I needed to quote in English.

(Interview: 24/6/04)

As the above discussion suggests, the choice as to which language to conduct interviews in can be taken on pragmatic grounds (such as it being 'quicker' to interview and transcribe straight into English) and also in response to the interviewee's views. As another Saudi Arabian student commented: 'I had no choice about which language to interview in as the participants only knew Arabic . . . So it was out of my control, I had to do it in Arabic' (Interview: July 2004). However, he had planned his questions in English first in order to gain feedback from his supervisor: 'I had to be sure the grammar is correct in English and there is no ambiguity so it will be clear to my supervisor'. As a result, he felt he had completed 'two jobs': 'when I finished constructing in English, I had to do it in Arabic'.

The language used in interviews can affect the relationship between researcher and participant (including how formal this is), and also the kind of information given. Often data will be collected in at least two languages and the researcher's own fieldnotes may also be written in English and their mother tongue. This presents the researcher with further decisions about what data to translate into English, how to compare and combine data in two or more languages, and how to analyse interviews which are translated versions of the original.

Data analysis

The researcher's decision about whether to analyse findings in English or the language of data collection very much influences how much and when translation takes place. Al-Motairi explained to me that he had only translated his data after analysing it first in Arabic:

But I did not translate all the transcripts, just the parts that I needed to quote in English. This was after doing the analysis in Arabic – I came up with common and main issues and categories, then I translated these into English. My supervisor supported this idea – I explained to him that I had to do this way. Because when I translate everything and jump to the analysis phase, I may miss important information, when jumping from one language to another language. I needed to get the appropriate information first.

(Interview: 24/6/04)

For Al-Motairi, it was important to conduct the analysis in Arabic so as to ensure continuity in meaning: he saw translation into English as transforming his data, so did not want to 'jump from one language to another'. Like other international students, he wanted to do the thinking process in Arabic and felt that translating data into English before it was necessary was going to complicate this process. He talked about language issues in relation to data analysis in terms of ensuring validity and reliability. Another student went a step further than Al-Motairi, seeing the writing up stage as integral to this process of analysis and for this reason wrote his first draft of his thesis in Bahasa Malay so that he could shape his ideas in his own language. Al-Motairi showed me the Arabic transcripts of his interviews with teachers where he had highlighted the key categories in green. He explained that he was able to communicate about the process of analysis and categories emerging with his supervisor in discussion through translating the green sections – even if the supervisor was not able to read his actual transcripts. The advantage of doing the analysis in Arabic was that he would also be able to share his analysis – as well as the actual transcripts – with the respondents.

Can you do discourse analysis in Mandarin? This was a question that came up in a research students' seminar after a presentation on discourse analysis that was based on English texts. Several students felt it would be difficult to transfer this approach to data in their own language. As Al-Nasser commented in his thesis (see above), the fact that he had not included 'uhs' and 'ums' in the translated text might mean that the presentation of discourse analysis would also have to be in Arabic. Research on 'contrastive rhetoric' (Connor 1996) has illustrated how languages vary greatly in their rhetorical constructions – for example, the apparently 'linear' arguments of English text as compared to the 'spiral' arguments of Chinese academic writing (Kaplan 1966). While such research has been criticized for ethnocentric assumptions [as Connor (1996: 163) points out: 'English writing appears linear to English speakers but not speakers of other languages whose coherence patterns differ from that of English'], this body of research does alert us to the difficulties of conducting discourse analysis on a text in one language and trying to convey the findings and analysis through English.

From fieldwork into English language text: what is lost?

Talking to international students about their experiences of 'writing up', I have been struck by their worry that something will be lost through translating their data and thought processes into English for the final thesis. Ayedh Al-Motairi made this point strongly when I asked him in an interview what difference it would make if he had been writing his thesis in Arabic instead of English:

The differences are that it would be more clear – the argument would be more clear and have more strength. Through English – this interview is an example, if it was in Arabic, it would be more clear. I feel I have something more that I need to put in, but language and cultural barriers prevent it.

(Interview: 24/6/04)

In the example Al-Motairi gives of our interview, we can identify similar issues around power and control to those raised in the previous section in the context of students conducting interviews during their fieldwork (i.e. who decides which language to use when). Al-Motairi felt that he was not able to express himself fully because we spoke in English – but also, perhaps, that he had lost the opportunity (due to 'language and cultural barriers') to shape the interview as he would have done in Arabic. As I will discuss in Chapter 6, Al-Motairi's concern that his usual voice and identity would not come through so strongly in an English conversation was a worry expressed by many students when they came to write their thesis. Scholastica Mokake reflected on similar frustrations when translating her data from Swahili to English:

sometimes it was difficult to get correct words in English. Some explanations are good when they are explained in that particular language. I feel sometimes as if when I translate, I reduce the weight of that word.

(Mokake, Annual Student Progress Report, 2004)

In the next chapter, I will look in more detail at the process of writing the English text, the thesis, but in this section I will analyse the ways in which students tried to bridge – what they saw as – the gap between English and their own language. This could be seen as how to translate the untranslatable – most obviously at the level of individual words, but also attempting to explain how discourse (including actions) might be differently interpreted in their own culture. As Magyar reflects, in relation to her comparative study of a French and a UK school, 'A good translator must be good at crossing boundaries from one linguistic context to another and at embracing the inevitability of loss' (Magyar 1996: 35). Significantly, the metaphor of translation has often been used to describe the act of interpreting empirical data; in a sense, we are all 'translating' data collected through observation and oral interviews into the written form of the research text [see Foddy (1993) for an account of how the respondent and interviewer 'encode' and 'decode' their questions and answers].

The untranslatable words

> Should the word 'intelek' (the Malay transliteration) be used for
> intelligence? But this is generally applied to adults rather than chil-
> dren and carries an academic connotation of being well read and
> reasoning in a logical and informed way. 'Kebolehan' – derived from
> 'boleh' (can) – implies an ability to do things in a general sense,
> 'kebolehan intelek' is therefore a possibility. But 'cerdas' is usually
> used to describe academically able students in schools who have a
> good grasp of academic school work and are actively engaged with it.
>
> (Lewin 1990b: 137)

This discussion about how to translate the English word 'intelligence' into
Malay for a questionnaire conveys the difficulties faced by an English
researcher working with Malaysian teachers. Although a Malaysian
researcher might understand the subtleties between the various Malay
words cited here, they may – like Lewin – have to identify the meanings
that the word 'intelligence' carries in English. Through this example, we
can see the importance of cross-cultural collaboration and discussion, as
well as hints of the ways in which language might influence thought.
Although the debates on how different languages affect thought in
different ways [see Whorf (1956) on the Sapir-Whorf hypothesis] are
beyond the scope of this book, there is a sense in which the 'untranslatable' words (and concepts) are the hardest challenge faced by an international student writing in English. The difficulty of translating certain
words into English is often presented as a linguistic issue, rather than a
disjunction between indigenous concepts or beliefs and Western research
frameworks (an exception is Tuhiwai Smith's analysis of Maori theory
discussed in Chapter 1).

Many researchers over the decades – particularly anthropologists –
have struggled to convey the meaning of words that do not have an
exact or even approximate meaning in English. The recognition that there
is no exact translation often leads to quoting the word in the original with
a gloss explaining the meaning in context. In the following extract from
her PhD thesis, Puteh gives an insight into the problems she had with
translating one such word, *bawa*:

> Problems arose when attempts were made to replace or translate the
> actual interview from Bahasa Malaysia into English. The cultural
> context posed problems in finding an exact translation. Even
> when the interview was conducted in English, some of the words
> used meant something different in a truly English context. An
> example was the word **bawa** meaning 'bring'. When one teacher
> trainee said her mathematics teacher did not know how to **bawa** the
> mathematics lesson, out of context it would mean bringing the class

in a physical sense. However, what she meant was the way the teacher teaches the lesson.

(Puteh 1998: 111)

As Puteh explains, this was an instance in which word-by-word translation would not work in English and that it was more important to get across the sense of the whole sentence. What comes across here is that Puteh recognizes that translating the Bahasa Malay word involves interpreting the data and bringing in other knowledge of the situation. This is a point discussed by Pillay in relation to the word *'kita'*, meaning 'I' or 'we':

> Another problem I encountered was in translation. The word 'I' was seldom used in the interviews. One tended to think of oneself as, of, or in a group. This is because the concept of the individual and 'individualism' as understood in Western philosophy is not part of the Malay culture. So in my interviews, interviewees used the word *'kita'* and I had to decide which sense of the word kita was being used – I or we. Also, as I was an educationist myself, sometimes the word *'kita'* was used to include me as part of the group.
>
> (Pillay 1995: 292)

Pillay shows here how her decision as to whether to translate *'kita'* as 'we' or as 'I' was based on her interpretation of the respondent's reply and her understanding of how they viewed her and their relationship within the interview situation. In other words, she already has had to analyse, rather than simply report, the teacher's response to her questions. This is an extra responsibility for the student working in another language, to make explicit – as Pillay and Puteh do above – the assumptions that inform their translation into English. This relates also to Al-Motairi's comments about 'jumping' from one language to another between analysis and translation: that something may be lost in the process. In Pillay's case, it was the ambiguity around the word *'kita'* that could not be retained in the English translation.

Understanding the discourse

While individual words can be retained in the original language and 'glossed' in English, it can be more difficult to decide how to convey the meaning of certain statements and actions in the context of a different culture and discourse. This may be around explaining how questions are asked and interviews conducted in a specific cultural context. For example, Pillay described the 'rules of politeness' that she had to follow when interviewing in Bahasa Malay, as compared to English:

> One such rule is that it is considered impolite to ask direct questions of interviewees. I had to learn how not to seem to challenge their

perceptions or to ask for views that would imply direct criticisms of their educational superiors. I had to learn to ask several leading questions before asking the question that I had really wanted to ask. It was an exercise in patience, in understanding and standing back.

(Pillay 1995: 292)

This insight into how and why certain questions were asked gives us a framework in which to interpret the respondent's replies. Pillay went on to explain how a headteacher had responded to her questions about a particular policy that made 'the state "number one" in all areas' of the curriculum:

The Headteacher initially told me that it was a good policy. Later on in the conversation, she went on to talk about the difficulties encountered by her school, that it was impossible for her school with limited resources to have so many goals. She felt that she wanted to concentrate on academic goals first as this would mean improving life chances for her students. Implied in her indirect response to me was a critique of the policy.

(Pillay 1995: 292)

Pillay was aware that this series of bland replies would not amount to strong criticism in an English-speaking UK context, and wondered how to convey the meaning of the headteacher's words once detached from the Malaysian policy discourse:

But when I translated the statements into English, this did not seem to have the same impact as it did in Bahasa Malaysia. So what then? How do I tell my readers of a Western orientation that this is a powerful critique of the policy? That the statement must be understood in a cultural context where direct criticisms of ideas are said to violate codes of language use and social conduct. One does not say an idea is unworkable up front but rather one starts by praising the speaker and the idea and then makes helpful suggestions to improve it, because 'saving face' is important.

(Pillay 1995: 292)

The analysis of this oral text could be related to the discussions in research on contrastive rhetoric, which analyses the contrasting strategies used to construct arguments within written texts in different languages (see Connor 1996). Pillay emphasizes that we need to understand the rhetorical strategies used by Bahasa Malay speakers to critique and yet not disturb the social equilibrium. She also warns that interviewees' lack of direct responses and the need to qualify their views and perceptions continually (through phrases like 'not that I disagree with . . . but') could be misinterpreted as due to their 'lack of understanding or skills': 'the interpretation of what might appear to a Westerner as mixed signals are perhaps ways of polite behaviour in a society that is not used to critiquing leaders' (Pillay 1995: 293). Having worked in similar situations in Nepal, I feel this is an area often misunderstood by Westerners – the implication being that if people were more direct in their criticism, rather than giving 'mixed signals', change would quickly be initiated. From observation of Western consultants 'shouting and banging on the table' [Nepali colleagues' words] in the Ministry of Education in Kathmandu, I would agree with Pillay that this kind of direct criticism has little impact (and can have the opposite effect) in a context where criticism is put across more subtly.

The idea of implicit rather than direct criticism is expressed differently in different contexts, yet may also be linked to the respondent's position in the institutional hierarchy. As Al-Motairi described in relation to his interviews in Saudi Arabia, while many teachers followed Pillay's example of indirect criticism, some people were willing to be more open:

> It depends on the person you are interviewing. I found some teachers criticised directly, some indirectly. They would mention the issue without saying that this is not good for us. Instead they would say, 'but if we change this situation, that will be something better. We can teach in this way, if it changes in this way'. But some teachers were more direct, saying this concept is wrong and needs to be changed, then stating the reasons why.
>
> (Interview: 24/6/04)

Al-Motairi's research involved interviewing student teachers, teachers, heads and supervisors and he became aware that their relative status greatly influenced how they responded to his questions during field research: 'the student [teacher] cannot criticise directly, whereas the supervisor can criticise directly' (Interview: 24/6/04).

As this section has illustrated, the challenge for the international student is not just to translate extracts from interviews or observation into English, but to convey in English to the reader how these statements could be interpreted in their original cultural context. This involves analysing the discourse in more explicit terms than would be required for an 'insider' to interpret the actions and speech events. I noticed that students often linked 'language and culture' when they talked about translation issues, perhaps to emphasize that this was not merely a linguistic task but that they were attempting to re-interpret data in an English text for a UK audience. Through their informal learning in the UK university, it was evident that they had gained the additional skills and experience needed to transfer their embedded knowledge (for example, the assumptions about how criticism is stated, as compared to their own culture). In the next section, I will explore the implications of the discussion on language use and choice in this chapter for the wider debates around cross-cultural perspectives on educational research raised in the book as a whole.

Implications for cross-cultural educational research

The above discussion about language choice in relation to field research and writing a thesis has implications for several key areas in this book that are useful to signal at this stage. I am interested in particular in the related issues around learning and teaching research methods in higher education institutions, the form of the thesis and other research 'products', and the question of who generates which knowledge and for whom.

Learning and teaching: the supervisory role

As a supervisor, I am very aware of the need to share in the whole PhD research process as a 'critical friend' and mentor of each student. As the students' comments quoted above suggest, translating data into English is considered by some as essential for involving their supervisor in this process: How can the supervisor comment on drafts of the thesis if he or she has only been able to access a fraction of the raw data? It relates to trust too. Will the supervisor believe that the student has valuable data if he or she has not actually been able to read it in English? As indicated earlier, I see this perspective as similar to that of UK students who feel they have to add all their original transcripts as an appendix to their dissertation – anticipating the common criticism made of qualitative research, that it is based on 'anecdotal evidence'.

The practical implications for the international student who believes that they must translate every word of their data into English are, as I have illustrated above, immense. I know of at least one student who has spent over a year translating her transcripts – at the cost of completing her PhD. In my discussions with research students, I have been interested in comparing their differing practices around how far they translate data or work with the original – an aspect of their research that (like qualitative data analysis until more recently) is often taken for granted, rather than made explicit. The strategies that they have worked out for translating orally and for discussing selected written texts with their supervisors could also be shared more widely as a basis for looking more critically at the relationship between supervisor and international student. Students' greater understanding of the subtleties between the different languages and how these are translated into English makes them the 'experts' in this respect and could present a challenge for students used to a more hierarchical relationship with their teachers. Positioning the student researcher as the key translator and interpreter of their data – through working with the original language texts and discussing these orally in English – might provide the student with a way of regaining the strength of voice that they feel they lose through writing the thesis in English.

I am also aware that the points made by students here in relation to conducting interviews in differing cultures have implications for the ways in which supervisors and supervisees interact. For example, as Hawkey and Nakornchai (1980: 78) note, that 'over-politeness' might be misinterpreted as lack of interest. This area of cross-cultural communication in the supervision context will be explored further in the concluding chapter.

Whose knowledge?

The fact that the final thesis must be submitted in English means that language choice rarely enters the discussion at the writing-up stage. Concerns around academic literacy (which are not necessarily around English language ability but about form, audience and voice) become conflated with the need to produce 'good English' for assessment purposes. However, as Bhatia (1999: 31) points out in his analysis of genre, 'in academic publications, for example, it is still the generic forms of the Western world that prevail' (in contrast to the advertising world). Part of the student's task is not only to write in English but, as I will discuss further in the next chapter, to learn the conventions of academic writing in English, as opposed to those dominant in their own language.

The assumption that the purpose of the PhD is to contribute to the body of Western theoretical knowledge can lead many students to overlook completely research written in their own language or studies that are more culturally specific. An example is a Ghanaian student looking at teacher stress who drew initially on the UK literature, since the concept of 'stress' was one that he could not easily identify within the research generated in his country. This is not just a linguistic issue, but also a question about how theoretical knowledge is generated and for whom. As I discussed in the introduction to this book, a PhD is often regarded as an entry ticket to the Western academy. Challenging the nature of research knowledge within the Academy is difficult from a relatively low position of power, but is also a matter of economics: the gatekeepers of academic journals are aware that there is a wider audience for English language publications produced for a Western audience (see Canagarajah 2002).

I would not expect an international student to be in a position to challenge the balance of power in terms of who generates knowledge and what kind of knowledge is produced. However, I am concerned that because the emphasis within a PhD course is on producing the final text (PhD thesis) in English, rarely is attention given (by supervisor or student) to writing in other languages and beginning to contribute to an alternative body of research. In discussion with Ayedh Al-Motairi, he reflected on the possibility of publishing some of his findings in Arabic, particularly as the debates around English teaching had recently become the focus in the national media in Saudi Arabia: 'I hadn't thought of it before but officials might find it useful in Arabic [as they would not read English]. Just the parts that are important, such as the five common issues arising in my research' (Interview: 24/6/04).

Al-Motairi went on to say that though he had never done any research writing in Arabic (as his university degree was in English), he would not find it difficult to write an article in his mother tongue. However, he stressed that 'ordinary people cannot understand Arabic academic writing', since 'it is difficult to understand if you are not a specialist'. He compared the two languages in relation to academic writing: 'the Arabic language is full of rich linguistic terminology – even sentence construction is very strong in meaning. In English the sentence structure is very simple and easy to understand' (Interview: 24/6/04). His comments suggest that his own research writing would draw strength from the linguistic resources of Arabic. However, he also acknowledges that academic writing is currently accessible only to an elite in Arabic, given the formalized style and register employed.

If research students were encouraged to produce articles in their mother tongue as well as English, it is possible that Arabic academic literacy might evolve in response to the demands of a wider audience. There might also be more opportunity for cross-fertilization between English and Arabic academic literacy practices – with supervisors gaining an insight into how academic arguments are constructed in another language and which kinds of knowledge are valued. All these issues relate to my earlier chapters about the research question and approach, such as whether the student sees their main audience as the UK examiner or their employer or sponsor. Through combining writing in their mother tongue, students could explore how these apparently conflicting aims could be brought closer together through focusing more explicitly on the expectations and literacy practices of a non-English-speaking audience 'back home' as well as writing for the supervisor and examiner in the UK.

Language as a resource not a barrier

Leach and Little (1999) point out that culture is often viewed as a barrier rather than a resource in the implementation of educational projects. Similarly, language tends to be talked about in terms of a 'problem' within both research and teaching contexts. As I have suggested above, the international student working with two or more languages within their field research can be seen to be at an advantage in some respects. They are constantly comparing and refining concepts between differing languages and cultures, analysing data in terms of what it means within that particular discourse. Magyar (1996: 35) points out that the task of linguistic translation is part of a wider dilemma about how to interpret and represent data through text: that 'translation is just one act which threatens the belief that there can be a constant and fundamental correspondence between language and "reality"'. Compared to the UK student (who may also be working with different cultural groups though in monolingual settings), the international student using two languages in their research may have developed greater sensitivity both about their own identity as 'insider' and 'outsider' researcher (as an international student in a UK institution) and the strategies that they can draw on in their research. As the examples in this chapter illustrate, this may mean that they code-switch in interviews or analyse more explicitly how their assumptions about language and culture shape their interpretation and translation of the data.

As a UK researcher previously based in Nepal, I shared a similar experience of working in two or more languages. Although I could not read and write in Nepali as fluently as the average international student does in English, I shared the frustration that I could not get my point across as forcefully as in my own culture and language. However, I found working in a second language and switching between languages an exhilarating experience in that I was constantly reflecting on nuances in meaning and interpretation that I rarely noticed in English-speaking contexts in the UK. In the context of international research students, the challenge for teaching staff is how to support the use of two languages within writing up and data analysis as well as in fieldwork – alongside the more visible task of improving teaching and learning situations in the UK university so that international students do not feel that their lack of confidence in English is a major frustration.

Looking at language issues in relation to the PhD educational research process can make a contribution in two ways. The first is around improving support and understanding of international students' needs, through finding ways in which research students and supervisors could work collaboratively to negotiate texts in a second language or students share translation strategies with their peers. The second aspect concerns the contribution that these accounts of bilingual and trilingual research activities and processes can offer to researchers working in monolingual contexts in terms of theory-building and developing research methodology. In particular, we can gain insight into how to develop a more reflexive approach to knowledge creation: 'to neglect the processes involved in translating research data is to miss fruitful parallels between the problematics of reading and interpreting social situations, and those of reading and translating actual texts' (Magyar 1996: 37).

Translation experience

By Huda Al-Yousef

My purpose in writing this piece is to share with the reader my experience in translating part of my research data from my native language of Arabic to English. I used Arabic language during the focus group interview I facilitated with young Saudi women. This is part of my thesis in Education that I am working on at the University of East Anglia in the UK. The purpose of the interview was to explore the factors influencing young women's higher education choice.

I preferred to do the translation of my work by myself, as I thought that I was more capable of understanding these young women's words than any other translator who would only read their words from the transcript.[3] As I interviewed them, I began to understand their opinions, thoughts and culture. As Crystal (1987: 344) comments: 'translators . . . must also have a thorough understanding of the field of knowledge covered by the source text, and of any social, cultural, or emotional connotations that need to be specified in the target language'. My experience in translation (my Bachelor degree was in English language where I was trained in translation from Arabic to English and vice versa) made me think that the translation task would be an easy one. Yet when I began my translation, I encountered many difficulties which I had never expected: 'it is sometimes said that there is no task more complex than translation' (Crystal 1987: 344).

When I first transcribed the tapes of the interview, I was not sure how to start my translation, since it was a new experience for me to translate a discussion between a group of participants. Thus I decided to read the transcript of my data which was in Arabic and highlight quotes that I assumed would be important and directly relevant to my topic, then translate only these quotes. By this step I started my translation task. The difficulties started to occur throughout the process of translation. First, I faced the problem of the different cultural context within the speech of the participants from the one I am translating to (i.e. Saudi/UK). The young women included in their speech some expressions that could not easily be understood by non-native speakers of the language or anyone who is not familiar with the Saudi culture. Gender separation is a good example that differentiates the Saudi culture from other cultures and was mentioned by the participants.[4] As a translator I should 'pay full attention to the cultural backgrounds of the authors and the recipients, and to take into account differences between source and target language' (Crystal 1987: 345).

Therefore, to clarify any ambiguity resulting from the cultural differences that existed in the young women's quotes, I translated their words as they were said and I included a footnote that explains briefly the issue of gender separation in Saudi Arabia as it is related to religious and cultural regulation.

The other difficulty I faced was related to times where 'the usual meaning (or literal meaning) of a word or sentence is different from the meaning it has in certain specific circumstances' (Wen-li 2002: 158). Thus, this difference puts heavy responsibility on me to comprehend the spoken words and present their purposive meaning. Therefore, I tried to focus on translating the whole meaning of the text and not to focus on the literal translation or word-for-word translation. I followed the discourse analysis/text linguistics technique. This technique 'has shifted the focus from the isolated sentence to "text", as the largest entity of language description and study. This sounds more natural since when language users communicate they produce coherent chunks of discourse; each usually consists of more than one sentence. Consequently, the prime concern of discourse analysis/text linguistics is to account for the relationships holding among sentences of a text' (Jabr 2002: 304).

A good example of the use of the discourse analysis/text linguistics technique is represented by the following expression used by a participant to describe how the government started to encourage businesswomen in Saudi Arabia. She literally said 'recently, the government turned to business women', while the point she was trying to declare is: 'recently, the government gave attention to business women'. The misuse of terms in translation may make the reader 'confused and [they] may not be able to follow the progress of the text assuming that there are different meanings. Or the text may communicate a misconception' (Saraireh 2002: 12).

Another difficulty I encountered was dealing with some 'expressions with the same reference in the source language [that] do not always find their precise counterparts in the target language' (Wen-li 2002: 162). The difficulty here is due to the fact that I am more familiar with the Arabic language terminologies, expressions and synonyms than those in English. This makes finding the equivalent to any term a complicated task for me. This demands more effort and accuracy from me due to the difficulty of finding the appropriate equivalent to the targeted word in English. Thus while translating I encountered many words that have an equivalent in English but none of them convey precisely what the participants meant. A good example of these words is the word *haram* in Arabic, which in English is often translated as 'prohibited' and associated with religious perceptions. This word is used throughout the translation in a meaning that is totally different from its English normal 'equivalent'. Therefore, I tried to make use of the method of 'compensation' (Hale and Campbell 2002). This method allows the translator to use different words that give a more accurate meaning in context. Thus, if this word was translated literally, the quote would be 'people told me it is prohibited to apply to history', whereas the meaning the participant wanted to declare was: 'people discouraged me from applying to history'. This dissimilarity between the spoken words and their literal meaning may result in 'the text becoming ambiguous and, thus, confusing to the reader, although the original one is not. When a translated text becomes ambiguous, it is not only useless but misleading as well. Therefore, the text becomes unreliable, which could be extended to the translator himself' (Saraireh 2002: 18). I tried to avoid the confusion that may occur as a result of this ambiguity through translating my understanding of the meaning behind the spoken word and avoiding word-for-word translation. Another solution I found was to put the word *haram* as it is, then write a footnote to explain its meaning in English.

The nature of my participants was of concern to me as they were adolescents. Usually adolescents have their own codes and expressions, which may not be accurate in explaining their thoughts to other cultural groups. An example of their use of their own codes throughout the interview occurred when a participant described her suggestions for improving the higher education system in Saudi Arabia. She said 'universities should put new majors for girls' higher education'. Actually, the word 'put' here is not appropriate grammatically even in the Arabic form but young people usually have their own codes and expressions. Thus, to clarify the meaning behind this statement, I preferred to translate the word as it was said and included a footnote to explain that 'put' means 'establish'.

Here, I have tried to summarize some of the difficulties I encountered while translating the data of my research, which I viewed as a difficult task. However, it enriched my educational experience. What I aimed for when translating the words of young women by myself was to reveal their aspirations, expectations and ambitions through their own voices, though many researchers think this task impossible due to the 'lack of direct equivalence across languages, cultures and personal understandings' (Hale and Campbell 2002: 17). Yet I believe that this task is not an impossible one because 'the notion of accuracy is in itself subjective' (Hale and Campbell 2002: 17). I also think that the key role of the translator is in 'rendering of the message that is as clear to the receptors as it is the original one' (Saraireh 2002:19).

Huda Al-Yousef is an English teacher from Saudi Arabia. She is in her second year of her PhD at the School of Education and Lifelong Learning, University of East Anglia. Her research is an attempt to understand factors influencing young women's higher education choices. She took her MA in Computer Education in 1999 from the Florida Institute of Technology, USA.

6

Writing the thesis

Introduction: writing between worlds

> International students from non-English speaking backgrounds are at the centre of this tension because they are between worlds: they are doubly disadvantaged in that they are not well versed in our conventional scholarly practices and they are simultaneously excluded from and subjected by the conventions of their academic discourses.
>
> (Cadman 1994: 1)

Throughout the literature and in case studies of international students writing in English as a second language (see Aspland 1999; Nagata 1999; Cadman 2000), there is a sense of loss. They have lost the possibility of expressing themselves in their own language and are 'doubly disadvantaged', as Cadman (1994: 1) emphasizes, by unfamiliar academic literacy practices in their new institutional setting. She describes how a Chinese student felt she had begun to lose the abilities valued in her own society, in particular her 'perceptive reading and her skilful memory' (p. 2).

This chapter will build on recent research into how students are introduced to and learn 'academic literacies' (Lea and Stierer 2000), as well as research on second language writing in an attempt to explore what it means for a student 'between worlds' to write a thesis. As I discussed in the previous chapter, writing up research in a second language is a challenge in itself. Here I will look in more detail at the specific conventions associated with writing a thesis, in relation to both supervisors' and students' prior experience and their expectations of the form. This investigation carries implications not just for pedagogy (see next chapter), but also for our practice as readers, particularly assumptions about the thesis as an autonomous text. As I will discuss in this chapter, the thesis is constructed

by institutional values and practices, and may need to be 'read' in relation
to these and the oral interaction during the viva examination – rather
than being regarded as 'speaking for itself'.

More than a language issue?

Writing a thesis is often regarded by both supervisors and students as a
language issue, the focus being on writing in 'good' English, rather than
on the demands of learning academic literacy.[1] In his PhD thesis, Lebar
(1995: 59) reflected on his lack of confidence in relation to writing up his
case study research in Malaysia:

'writing a portrayal demands a good command of the language, in my
case, the English language. I was not sure whether I have the ability and
talent to engage in such style of writing'.

> Like many international students, Lebar believed that qualitative
> research required more complex English writing skills than the
> quantitative tradition from which he came. In our research student
> seminars, several students went a stage further. They rejected the
> idea that good English language writing skills alone were enough,
> pointing to the values underlying the text. In particular, they identi-
> fied the need to write critically in order to fulfil their supervisors'
> expectations and to explore what this meant in a UK context. In a
> seminar on discourse analysis, the faculty member presenting had
> suggested that you should read a text, not just for its content, but to
> ask 'what is this text doing to me?' She was then asked (by two
> Malaysian students): 'What are the differences between how we as
> students think and how you as professor think? What are the
> assumptions that you make about counts as "critical"? What is
> the difference between "judgement" and "description"?'
>
> (Seminar report: 3/5/02).

Being critical

As I discussed in earlier chapters, the desire to be (or not to be) critical
relates partly to the purpose of the research and was resisted by students
who felt it inappropriate because they intended to take a 'purely technical' stance towards their subject (for example, analysing a particular
method of testing). Other students considered that being critical (in the
direct way demanded by the very idea of a 'thesis') was culturally or
politically inappropriate back home. They pointed out that if you come
from a culture where you don't argue, it is difficult to adopt the style

expected in a thesis. Somebody else pointed out that it was not just a question of whether you *can* adopt a critical stance, but whether you *want* to (Seminar report: 9/7/02).

This issue as to how far writing a good thesis is dependent on adopting certain values is tackled by Cadman (1994: 2) when she highlights the criteria for assessing a PhD thesis, such as 'ability to make critical use of published work' and 'originality'. She describes how an international student – 'whether or not their grammar and study skills are under control' – generally begins to ask questions, such as:

- You mean I am to criticize published work!
- How do I *dare* to be original!

Although Cadman's account suggests that international students bring a differing perspective to the PhD criteria, she associates their doubts with a lack of confidence, rather than a reluctance to abandon conflicting value systems.

Canagarajah's (2002) ethnographic account of academic literacy practices at the University of Jaffna in Sri Lanka provides an alternative perspective on the accepted PhD criteria for assessing what constitutes a 'good' piece of academic writing. He describes how on his return from studying for a PhD in the USA, his Sri Lankan colleagues expressed their disappointment at his 'newly learned writing skills from American graduate school' (Canagarajah 2002: 121). Though his paper succeeded on the kind of criteria discussed by Cadman above, local Sri Lankan colleagues were shocked at the 'polemical stance, the aggressive lobbying on behalf of my thesis and findings and the explicit presentation of data' (p. 141). He noted the following specific criticisms from local scholars:

- That the paper lacked the aesthetic and emotional appeal that comes from a more relaxed development of the thesis
- That the paper was unnecessarily and unproductively contentious
- That simply annihilating the views of others doesn't necessarily mean that my view is superior
- That the paper displayed an aggressive individualism that bordered on unseemly pride, attention-grabbing and self-congratulation
- That this need to pit one's own research against that of others leads to unnecessary, hair-splitting arguments that end up confusing and baffling the audience.

(Canagarajah 2002: 141)

His colleagues' comments revealed, above all, that they did not identify with the attitudes and values associated with US academic communities, in particular the tendency to 'be critical'. They saw 'the accompanying emotional aggression and unbridled individualism' as qualities 'motivated by the working conditions of center academic communities' (i.e. the US academic institution), as compared to the more relaxed academic community in Jaffna (Canagarajah 2002: 141).

Canagarajah's case study is useful to uncover some of the assumptions made by both supervisors and examiners about what makes a good thesis. The question as to whether a student *wants* to transform their beliefs and practices is often left unasked – rather like the assumption that the thesis must be written in English. The very fact that someone has signed up for a PhD in a UK institution could be taken to imply that they had already accepted the need to adjust to the more 'critical' academic practices dominant in the UK. This relates to Clark's observation (in the context of non-conventional UK students) on the 'tension that exists between the need to provide access to conventional discourse practices and the need to develop alternative practices' (Clark 1992: 137). This chapter will consider how far it is possible to transform thesis writing practices in response to alternative cultural values or political purposes.

Writing and thinking – in English

In a study of student writing, Nightingale observed that 'good writers discover what they think as they write and not before' (quoted in Cadman 1994: 3). In the context of second language writing, the relationship between the thinking process and the writing process is more complex, raising questions about whether students should write first in their mother tongue. Ayedh Al-Motairi explained to me that this was not a straightforward decision about which language to write in first, but involved moving between different languages at different stages, combining both oral and written practices:

> When I tried to write about an idea, I had the idea fully in my mind. When I put it on the paper in English, I thought I had it there but when my supervisor reads it, he only finds part of the idea – the other part was in my head. If I put it in Arabic, I would put it all in. I gradually started to put it all in – I read more, practising writing, relying on Arabic to put it all first. I write in English but when sitting and discussing with my supervisor, I find I only have half there. I rely on my Arabic to look at what I have left out.
>
> (Interview: 24/6/04)

Amir Mohammed related how he too moved constantly between English and Arabic, not just in the writing stage, but also as he read the literature and developed a theoretical framework:

> I had to read in Arabic first to understand the issues – for example, about counselling though there is not much written in Arabic. I tried

to write about the culture to give a broad framework. So I read about Saudi society in general to help me understand the texts in English. When I am reading the English books ... I photocopy the English text and write notes in Arabic to say what it is about. It is easier for me to use later.

(Interview notes, 2004)

The question as to how far a student can learn to 'think' as well as to write in English is discussed further in the next section, in relation to pedagogical practices and research exploring the ways in which second language learners can learn to create a new voice through personal writing (outside the thesis writing). However, in the context of educational doctoral research, it is particularly important to encourage reflexivity about the ways in which we construct the academic text in English, as a strategy for learning about differing educational practices. An important aim of this chapter is to shift the emphasis from the research product and how it is assessed, to consider thesis writing as part of the learning process for both supervisors and students.

Writing up educational research

Lea and Stierer (2000: 6) comment on the 'increasing recognition of fundamental differences between academic disciplines in terms of the written genres that students are expected to master at university'. Much of the literature on academic literacy has been based on this notion of individual academic disciplines as discourse communities (Swales 1990; Hoadley-Maidment 2000). Within the context of educational research (as compared to more tightly defined disciplines such as psychology), the international student faces an additional challenge, since many different genres can be found within the same discipline. As Ball points out, there is not only diversity between disciplines but within disciplines (in Baynham 2000: 20). When starting to write the thesis, the international student may be confronted with a wide range of academic practices associated with educational research – which can either be regarded as liberating or confusing!

Rather than writing between just two worlds, as is often assumed – the real world and the academic world, or the UK and their home country – the international student may thus be aware of a diversity of audiences and forms of writing within UK educational research alone. The Academy tends to be regarded as a homogeneous entity, yet as this chapter will reveal, academic discourses are constantly being redefined and transformed through the interaction of differing cultures, disciplines and institutions. The task of writing the thesis involves not just acquiring skills of academic writing in the UK context, but is also a matter of adapting to and recognizing change. Entering a new academic institution may enable the student to become more sensitive to academic practices and the differences that he or she encounters, as compared to the supervisor who may take for granted the UK conventions. The cross-fertilization of UK and 'other' academic literacies makes it increasingly difficult to distinguish the particular characteristics of, say, Arabic or Finnish academic writing – which have been the focus of past research (see Kroll 1990; Connor 1996). This chapter is based on the assumption that academic literacy practices in both the UK and elsewhere are constantly evolving – and that both student and supervisor need to participate more actively in this dynamic process, rather than regarding the thesis as a static form or goal.

Academic literacy: a question of power not just skills

> While the need to incorporate one's audience appropriately into one's writing is regarded as a crucial dimension of securing both professional and personal goals, it is also the way that acts of writing serve to reinforce existing structures of authority and professional practice.
>
> (Candlin and Hyland 1999: 10)

Writing a PhD thesis is not only about writing appropriately for a specific audience but also about recognizing and relating to the hierarchical structures within higher educational institutions. The growing body of research on 'academic literacies' has illuminated the ways in which writing practices within higher educational institutions 'construct rather than merely reflect academic knowledge' (Lea and Street 2000: 40). As Hyland (1999: 121) points out, the tendency to think of academic writing as 'neutral' or depersonalized can be misleading: 'rather than thinking of academic discourse as impersonal, we need to think of it as reflecting the different social practices of disciplinary communities in constructing knowledge. Simply, some fields permit greater authorial presence than others'.

Taking this perspective implies recognizing that 'what makes a piece of student writing "appropriate" has more to do with issues of epistemology, rather than with surface features of form to which staff often have recourse when describing their students' writing' (Lea and Street 2000: 39). This has relevance not just for how students write, but how students' texts are read and heard by different audiences. Research on academic literacy has illustrated the difficulties faced by students entering higher education and attempting to become part of this new discourse community. In UK universities, researchers found that many tutors and supervisors were unable to make explicit the specific expectations of research writing – partly because they themselves saw the texts as 'transparent' and were unaware of their own embedded assumptions and values. They were unable, for example, to explicate further the descriptive tools they used such as 'critically analyse', 'evaluate' or 'reach a synthesis' (Lea and Street 2000: 40).

Understanding academic writing as a social practice involves moving away from the traditional study skills-based perspective. Lea and Street (2000: 35) give a useful outline of three models of academic writing: the study skills (or 'fix-it') approach being the most common. The 'academic socialization' approach takes the starting point that students need to learn how to adapt to the 'new culture' of the Academy. By contrast, the academic literacies model recognizes that the student learning academic writing is not just adjusting to a new culture, but starting to understand the institutions 'in which academic practices take place as constituted in, and as sites of, discourse and power' (Jones *et al.* 1999: xxi). It views 'student writing as issues at the level of epistemology and identities rather than skill or socialisation' (ibid.).

This understanding that academic knowledge is 'not transmitted but constructed' (Lea and Street 2000: 39) through the practices of higher education institutions lies behind my analysis of international students' experiences of writing a thesis in this chapter. Rather than just discussing the ways in which students have learnt to adapt to UK academic writing practices (academic socialization approach) or learnt specific English language or academic literacy conventions (a skills model), I intend to draw on the academic literacies model to explore how adopting a cross-cultural perspective may involve developing (and/or valuing) alternative writing practices. As I discussed above, the concept of the Academy as a homogeneous, unchanging institution has been challenged by the greater diversity of students now entering UK higher education. Conventional academic practices are already being transformed by both students and lecturers – for example, many education departments now accept a more personalized style and tone within a PhD thesis. However, such changes may present additional problems for international students whose own academic cultures may then seem further apart. In his ethnographic account of academic practices at the University of Jaffna, Canagarajah (2002) describes how he negotiated these differences in academic cultures and values on his return to Sri Lanka after studying in the USA.

In the next section, I will look at the challenges identified by international students when writing up research in my own department and the wider implications for academic writing practices. The questions running throughout this chapter are not just about which language or which form to adopt in the thesis, but about the ways in which thinking leads into writing (and vice versa) and about learning through unfamiliar educational practices.

Writing the thesis: what is the challenge?

> It is in the process by which academic research turns into academic writing that second language students become most lost, confused and powerless.
>
> (Cadman 1994: 1)

Looking back to the earlier chapters in this book on choosing a research question and a research approach, we can see that concerns about conflicting aims and audiences (UK and home) come to the fore at the writing-up stage. Worries about colleagues' expectations back home and about the criteria for assessing a PhD in the UK higher education institution can mean that the student is presented with a seemingly impossible task. How do I write one thesis that meets both requirements – or as several students have commented, should I write one thesis or two? In this section, I look at how students attempted to meet these often conflicting requirements [discussed in Canagarajah (2002) in terms of the contradictions between 'peripheral' versus 'central' requirements], as well as analysing their experiences in creating their own voice in English (the process described by Cadman above).

Form and structure of the thesis: what are the possibilities?

The structure of a conventional thesis is familiar to many international students when they start a PhD in education. As part of their initial application for a PhD, I have known students submit an outline of their proposed thesis – even detailing the anticipated content of each chapter. Arriving in CARE, however, they encounter a different tradition – that of experimenting with form, perhaps through personal narrative or a bricolage of texts. In this context, the student needs to decide whether they want to adopt a conventional thesis form (which may be the expectation of their institution or employer back home) or whether to use this opportunity to create something different. As well as taking into account their intended audience, the student has to consider their own academic writing practices – both in English and their own language.

During CARE seminars, which had involved reading and critiquing theses written by past PhD UK students, international students commented that it would be difficult for them to adopt this personalized form:

> Several people felt that the dominant style of thesis here, self-reflective and more like a journal, would not be understood back home. This led to the question, should you write different texts for different audiences?
>
> (Seminar report: 10/5/01)

Several people felt the opportunity to study in the UK meant more flexibility, the chance to challenge practices of a lifetime, but others felt that they would not easily be able to write up research in a way that satisfied both their supervisor here and their colleagues or government back home.

(Seminar report: 17/5/02)

Similar to their unease about adopting qualitative approaches in a context where the quantitative paradigm was dominant, these students felt that a journal form of thesis would be misunderstood (and by implication, not valued) in their own country. This should not be seen as an experience unique to international students but is, of course, related to disciplinary cultures too: recently I was examining a thesis in a geography department, where similar questions were raised about the appropriateness of a personalized narrative form for a PhD thesis. Although CARE international students linked their wariness about form to raising awareness among former colleagues back home and concern about the appropriateness of a personalized style within a different institution, there is also the question of how far the thesis meets the *needs* (as well as the expectations) of the 'home' audience. Al-Nasser, a student from Saudi Arabia, described in his thesis how his choice of form was influenced by how teachers might use the research findings and the desire to make his research findings accessible to his audience back home:

> I first tried the narrative format favoured and used by many case study researchers ... I failed – the reason, I thought was that I wanted a clearer format: something with a structure that would fit the needs of my audiences (e.g. a teacher who would probably be interested in looking at or reading the section on 'teaching methods').
>
> (Al-Nasser 1999: 102)

An outsider perspective on academic English

The difficulties faced by international students writing in English as a second language are well documented (Kroll 1990; Sillitoe and Crosling 1999; Flowerdew and Peacock 2001) and are particularly evident at the thesis stage, given the length and complexity of the text. Yet the form of the argument and the logic behind the thesis is often taken for granted in a conventional thesis, though research on contrastive rhetoric has revealed contrasts between how academic texts are constructed in different languages. Scott (1999: 181) cites Lee, a Korean student, who points out that the Western idea of 'critical thinking' is actually 'culturally specific but presented in the literature of the field as the universal norm'. Similarly, the Western tradition of academic writing, with the emphasis on clarity of focus and a tight structure, is considered to be an undisputable value (Turner 1999: 154). Analysis of Japanese essays, by contrast, has revealed a tendency to work round to the main point: 'the argument follows an indirect cyclical pattern' (Low and Woodburn 1999: 68). In Connor's (1996) review of research on contrastive rhetoric, she discusses many features that appear problematic when seen from the perspective of English academic writing. These include the different view of self in Chinese writing, which makes it difficult to be direct or to express a point of view at the beginning of a piece of writing. Korean academic writers put the main topic at the end of a text, rather than at the beginning, as would be expected in English. Academic writers in different languages also had different expectations of their readers. Connor (1996: 51) discusses how Finnish academic prose could be considered as 'reader responsible', since the reader is expected to make more effort to work out the argument, whereas English is 'writer responsible'. From an English language perspective, however, the Finnish prose appears 'aloof and uncaring towards the reader' because of the inductive form of argument where nothing is spelt out (ibid.).

I have found this research on contrastive rhetoric useful in making explicit my own assumptions about what constitutes a good academic text in English. Until we compare academic literacy practices across cultures and languages, we cannot begin to understand the expectations of a PhD thesis in English. Even the meaning of the word 'thesis', as Cadman points out, 'fluctuates tantalisingly between the bound volume and the thought process that informs it' (Cadman 1994: 5). This moves the discussion onto the level of academic practices, rather than the common emphasis on explaining academic conventions, such as specific ways of referencing sources in the UK institution. Exploring the form of academic writing in the student's first language can also help to explain apparent 'weaknesses' such as the 'bland and unfocused' appearance of essays by Japanese students (English 1999: 18). Without this recognition, mistakes tend to be treated at surface level: Jones *et al.* (1999: 31) describe how Japanese students paid 'lip service to academic conventions, not understanding, for example, the purpose of citing sources'. Recent discussions about plagiarism in the context of international students have drawn attention to differing understandings about what it means to draw on respected academic authority in other cultures (Cadman 2004). The international student writing in English therefore faces the double challenge – first to make explicit the academic practices within their own language, and then to work out the differences and expectations within English academic writing. Within both 'home' and 'English' academic discourses, they will encounter contrasting practices – not least the experimentation with form now acceptable in theses in UK education departments.

Although there are dangers in generalizing about the characteristics of Arabic or Finnish prose as compared to English (as well as the problem of creating cultural stereotypes, academic literacies in other languages too are constantly changing), the comparison does enable us to analyse the ways in which a student may transfer strategies from one language to another or to explore the shared knowledge or resources from which they usually draw. Many students have remarked on the difficulty of understanding and using English proverbs (such as 'throwing the baby out with the bathwater') in academic prose, as well as the frustrations of not being able to use proverbs and traditional sayings from their own language – particularly when their own academic writing relies more strongly on such rhetorical devices. The hardest challenge they face, however, is how to recreate their own voice in English. Cadman discusses this in terms of the 'controlling, personal viewpoint which provides the focus for the research' and relates this to: 'The dimension of the thinking which operates beneath the text and finds its form in the voice of the writer manipulating the linguistic techniques of academic argument, is generally most elusive for the second language user whose own culture does not demand such an approach' (Cadman 1994: 5). The international student thus faces two interlinked challenges: learning to write in a second language and adopting unfamiliar academic writing practices.

Cadman's idea of the more 'controlling' voice of the English academic writer could be related to her cultural standpoint of regarding UK academics as more direct and visibly present in the text. Talking with Ayedh Al-Motairi about the differences between Arabic and English writing, I was reminded of Connor's observation that the 'linear' characteristic of English academic arguments may only appear 'linear' to the English:

> Arabic academic writing is generally the same as English – presenting an argument, defending an idea and rejecting an idea, but the difference is that the researcher gives his judgement about an idea. Arabic academic writing gives the power to give judgement in Arabic. But this is not the same in English work, they do not insist on their judgement.
>
> (Interview with Al-Motairi: 24/6/04)

Al-Motairi's ideas about the strength of Arabic prose and the more dominant voice of the writer contradict my own assumptions (and Cadman's above) about the centrality of the researcher's voice in English academic writing. The practice of 'giving judgement', however, suggests that the Arabic academic has a more explicit role within the text than the English writer whose priority is to present a balanced view of the field.

How do we read texts?

The above discussion relates to the way in which we read texts as well as write them: my reading of English academic writing is very different from

Al-Motairi's, since we both bring different assumptions about the aims and stance of the writer. Anticipating how readers will respond is central to the research student's task in writing up their research findings. In his thesis, Tsai (1996) related how his experience of presenting an academic paper in a UK conference revealed differing expectations from in his home country: 'A Taiwanese audience tends to treat knowledge as a product to be received from an outside academic authority, whereas an English audience tends to treat knowledge as a social process of understanding and reconstruction' (p. 21).

In the context of writing, rather than orally presenting work, the international student has similarly to work out the possible differing reaction of their UK audience and their understanding of 'knowledge'. In this respect, Street (1999b: 204) emphasizes, 'academic texts are not shared ways of knowing but read and heard in different ways'. As I will discuss in the next chapter, the relationship between supervisors and students is key to creating a space where possible conflicting perspectives can be discussed and where the international student can begin to understand unfamiliar writing practices. Pardoe (2000: 142) stresses the importance of researching 'students' accounts of their texts, rather than simply the texts themselves and of trying to understand the potential "rationale" behind unsuccessful aspects of their texts'. Within the context of writing a PhD thesis, it is also important to recognize that the written text does not stand alone, since oral examination forms part of the assessment. Particularly in situations where the student has felt uneasy about writing critically for an audience back home (perhaps because of possible political repercussions), he or she can present the unwritten text orally in the viva. A colleague has also described to me how, as an examiner, he adopted new 'strategies of reading' to understand the ways in which a student had coded criticism within his thesis.

Deciding which form of thesis to adopt is thus not simply about choosing a writing strategy but also relates to issues of ideology and pedagogy. Comparing and deconstructing what has been termed the 'mystery' (Jones *et al.* 1999: xxii) of academic writing in varying institutional contexts and languages should be part of the educational process of studying for a PhD. All too often however – as I will discuss in the next chapter – the student's and supervisor's focus is on the end product (and assessment of the thesis), which prevents interaction about their contrasting assumptions about academic practices. As Candlin and Plum (1999: 196) state: 'disciplines themselves are often unclear about what "analytic writing" might consist of' and 'this vagueness is of little assistance to them [students]'. Writing a PhD thesis therefore involves learning about literacy practices in a new institution and language, and also making decisions about how to situate oneself in relation to those practices. For some students, it is a question about how far to compromise to satisfy the criteria of the audience in the UK and their employer back home. Occasionally, they may decide to write research texts in different forms for the various audiences. Their dilemmas raise questions of relevance to researchers in a wider context, such as: Is there a single 'true' knowledge? How is knowledge shaped by the institution within which it is produced? As Canagarajah (2002) illustrates through his study of the University of Jaffna, academic knowledge there was shaped through the way political and religious institutions and values influenced the Academy.

Is the personal always empowering?

Whether and how to bring the personal into the thesis is an issue much discussed within our seminar group. For some students, the choice between whether to narrate in third person ('the researcher') or as first person ('I') brought them into conflict with (what they saw as) traditional cultural values. A Saudi Arabian student explained that whereas UK students found it easy to say 'I' in seminars, she had found it very difficult to take this 'risk'. She felt that within her culture, this individualistic approach or even using the first person in the thesis could be interpreted as 'self-centred'. Other students shared her dilemma, commenting that though it seemed to be the expectation in UK academic writing to bring in personal and autobiographical details, they wondered how this would be read in their own culture. They saw the decision about whether to include personal details or adopt a personalized style as related to the purpose of the research: this seemed appropriate if the thesis was about self-discovery. Looking back at Chapters 2 and 3, the research question and approach can be seen to influence the form of thesis that a student wants to adopt, or believes that they are entitled to produce (due to sponsorship or institutional constraints).

Comparing these students' comments to research conducted with non-conventional UK students, I was struck by the assumption of the majority of researchers that personalized writing is always empowering and involves more freedom for the student (Hyland 1999). For an international student who does not share the same starting values (in particular, the desire to focus on the self), writing themselves more directly into the text can be seen as threatening their identity – an attempt to conform to Western academic literacy practices, rather than a liberating process. This supports Ivanic and Weldon's (1999: 171) observation that when writing academic essays, she heard people comment, 'I don't feel this is me'. The challenge seems to be more around adopting a style and voice with which students feel comfortable, rather than assuming that a personalized style will be empowering for every individual.

Crème (2000) describes how personal journal writing can be used as an approach to help students to find their voice. In the context of international students, this pedagogical practice may be welcomed in order to encourage a reflexive approach to writing (i.e. as a learning approach), though the student may not want to incorporate this style of writing into their thesis. Similarly, Cadman (1994: 5) describes how within an ESL context, 'strategies to help the second language writer to find his or her own voice must begin within them'. As I will discuss in the next chapter, bringing the personal into written and oral texts within the supervision and seminar situation can contribute to a more interactive learning process for both supervisor and student. However, this does not necessarily mean that the student will want to reflect this process through incorporating personalized accounts into their thesis.

Writing in a personalized English style also presents linguistic challenges for second language writers:

> Several international students felt that there were language issues involved. They had never learned to write in a personalized way in English (being more used to a formal academic style) and felt they would not be able to carry off the kind of 'journal' style thesis that was included in our selection.
>
> (Report on seminar analysing different kinds of theses: 17/5/02)

A student arriving in the UK may not be familiar with an informal register of English and may lack the linguistic resources to draw upon when attempting to write in a personal style. Chang and Swales (1999) discuss how the informal elements in English academic writing can be seen as a 'threat' to non-native speakers. They analyse features of informal English, such as use of the first person, direct questions and exclamations, and discuss how international students find these elements make academic English more complicated. They conclude that 'learning the rules of formal academic English was already a considerable challenge and one that did not need to be further complicated by having to learn how to mix formal and informal language nicely' (Chang and Swales 1999: 166). My own experience suggests that some international students do view informal personalized language more positively and have commented that the 'personal' is now influencing their academic writing in their mother tongue, beginning a process of cross-fertilization:

> I started to use the first person, putting myself and my experiences in. I found it more interesting to show your effort instead of the researcher did this . . . In Arabic I would prefer to use the first person, but it would be a question of whether this is acceptable in the Arabic context, as it is not usual.
>
> (Interview with Al-Motairi, June 2004)

Personalized writing within a PhD thesis might therefore be seen as a way of transforming conventional academic practices in differing cultural contexts – a process that can also have an impact on indigenous academic writing. However, other students view the personal style of theses as an ideological and linguistic threat: the personal implies making the individual researcher visible within the text in a way that might be considered 'self-centred' in certain cultures. A Saudi Arabian student described how he had made the transition to writing in the first person, but was determined to return to his previous style of writing once back home:

> It was a new thing for me to use the first person. I started to do it in third person, the general, but my supervisor said no, who has done this work? I felt it is a bias to write in first person. In Arabic research, it's not acceptable to talk about yourself. It's not 'our' school, it's 'the' school. I transfer my thinking in Arabic research to here. But my supervisor asked me to change. When I go back to Saudi, I will follow the other way. I prefer the general way but I have to adapt here.
>
> (Interview: July 2004)

Students' decision whether or not to adopt a personalized style thus reflects their values and beliefs, and also the influence of the institution and their own supervisor. As research with UK students has illustrated, many see the task of learning academic literacies as 'a kind of game, trying to work out the rules, not only for a field of study, a particular course or particular assignment, but frequently for an individual tutor' (Lea and Street 1999: 42). In general terms, the international student has a choice about how far to conform to expectations about the style and form of the thesis (whether those of their home or of the UK institution) or how far to challenge or adapt dominant UK academic practices within their thesis.

Bridging the gap or developing an alternative?

Two broken shells and a ball of string. In a workshop where PhD students used visual objects to discuss their experiences in UEA, two 'different species' of shell were chosen to symbolize the difficulties associated with cross-cultural communication between supervisor and student. The string represented the ongoing challenge of unravelling the research question. While the latter could be seen as a problem faced by all PhD students, the 'cross-cultural' was identified as a key issue by many international students in the group. They pointed to the 'cultural differences' between the academic culture in the UK and the country where they conducted fieldwork and the danger that their bibliography would be 'Western biased' (due to the supervisor's range of sources and the practical difficulties of obtaining indigenous research that was not published in mainstream journals). Implicit in many of our seminar discussions was the question about how to bridge the gap – between cultures, expectations of differing academic institutions and, to some degree, between supervisor and student. In the context of writing the thesis, these differences come to the fore, since students are aware of being judged by certain criteria and the need to present their research to a UK examiner.

'Unsuccessful texts are often the result of students drawing on familiar ways of learning and writing that served them well elsewhere, in their previous education or in other areas of their lives' (Pardoe 2000: 125). As I have illustrated in this chapter, there are many differences in academic practices – around language and the construction of argument, around the identity of the researcher and how his or her voice shapes the text. While international students may be inclined to rely on writing strategies they have used in the past, this is based on an assumption of similar ways of reading in the new academic context. Understanding the differences between English academic writing and the student's previous experience is their first step towards writing for a new audience. However, there is also the danger that the student will hold up English academic writing practices as the ideal.

Connor (1996: 25) stresses the need for critical pedagogy, suggesting that 'in emphasising Anglo-American patterns of writing, contrastive rhetoric may encourage students to look down on their first language writing styles'. Although in interaction with supervisors and peers, students may be able to draw on their first language strategies, it is much harder to see how the written thesis can reflect different writing practices, particularly since it has to be written in English. 'Bridging the gap' between academic cultures has tended to take the form of explanations within the methodology chapter (such as those quoted earlier from Pillay and Al-Motairi) about what is missing through writing in English – whether the untranslatable words or the indirect ways in which criticism is expressed. There is perhaps less about how the writer's identity and voice has changed through writing in English, or even how the structure or argument might be different within another academic discourse.

Could Arabic English be accepted in a thesis? Could metaphors take the place of models? These are the kinds of questions tackled by Canagarajah (2002: 70) in terms of the 'unequal relations between centre and periphery academic communities in publishing and knowledge production'. Looking at alternatives to the conventional thesis, rather than simply 'bridging the gap', we would have to consider the criteria for assessing a PhD. Though this varies between institutions, criteria such as 'contribution to knowledge' carry implications about whose knowledge counts, how such knowledge is communicated and to whom. Similarly, Arabic English may be considered 'clear' to Arabic speakers (as suggested by the above question posed by a Middle Eastern student), but would such a thesis satisfy 'clarity' criteria for a UK examiner? Teasdale and Teasdale (1999) discuss the 'indigenisation of academic knowledge' in relation to Maori PhD students in the Australian-Pacific region (see Chapter 1). Acknowledging that 'the doctoral thesis has prescribed parameters and deep-seated cultural expectations of its own' (Teasdale and Teasdale 1999: 255), they describe the ways in which students have attempted to 'fuse together' the two bodies of knowledge, indigenous and Western. They refuse to 'separate out the spiritual, cultural and intellectual' (p. 245), suggesting, for instance, that a coconut palm can be a theoretical model not just a metaphor. Teasdale and Teasdale argue that 'allowing Indigenous cultures of knowledge and learning to play a significant role in contemporary academic discourse may well be the key to our long-term survival' (p. 259). The situation that Teasdale and Teasdale describe seems very different from that of the international student in the UK struggling to find a voice in their English thesis – not least because of the social movement associated with promoting Aboriginal indigenous knowledge. A student who finds him or herself the only person from Kenya in the department, faces a more isolated challenge of how to develop an 'alternative' thesis drawing on indigenous practices. In the next chapter, I look in detail at the pedagogical implications for supervisors and UK institutions in supporting students who attempt to write a thesis that draws on two or more academic traditions.

The space for writing an 'alternative' thesis, or the 'indigenisation of academic discourse' (Teasdale and Teasdale 1999), has already been created through the experimentation with genre and differing media shaping many PhD theses written in the field of education. As I have discussed above, though many international students may consider that these 'post-structuralist' theses lie outside their experience and would be inappropriate in their own institutional or cultural context, the process behind producing such theses could provide a useful model. At present, few international students in the UK reflect critically on the challenges they have faced in adjusting to Western academia and producing a text that meets the PhD criteria. However, such reflections are often limited to the chapter on methodology, rather than running through and shaping the thesis as a whole. Like the first experimental post-structuralist theses, the challenge is how to develop an alternative kind of thesis, which could be assessed by the conventional criteria. In our group discussions, this point arose in relation to 'being critical' and what this might mean in differing cultural contexts: 'Some of the group felt we needed to be explicit about what we intended to do – it was easier to be critical about what *we* intended, rather than to be judged by someone else's criteria' (Seminar report: 17/5/02). This idea of anticipating the examiner's perspective and presenting an alternative interpretation of the PhD criteria suggests a practical way of both bridging the gap (through having two audiences in mind) and developing an alternative approach throughout the thesis.

My discussion about differing writing practices in relation to the PhD thesis has to some degree centred on issues of assessment. Unlike other forms of writing, the end goal of the PhD process involves evaluation of the thesis. Within this context, the concept of diversity and difference is problematic – though we recognize differing academic literacy practices in different parts of the world, we also have to accept that they are not all equal in status or power. As this chapter has illustrated, the PhD thesis is shaped by the practices of English academic literacy – whether conventional or 'experimental' in terms of personalized narrative or post-structuralist approaches. The international student can feel a pressure to conform to whatever are the dominant academic literacy practices in his or her UK department. How far a student feels liberated or oppressed by new academic literacies depends partly on the relationship they have with their supervisor and whether there is a 'dialogic space' (Lea and Street 2000) to explore the meanings behind such practices. The next chapter will look in more detail at how supervisors can begin to respond to international students' perspectives on the research process through their teaching and action research on their own practice.

As this chapter has revealed, the thesis is inevitably regarded as the end product of a PhD. The challenge for UK institutions and supervisors is to explore how the thesis could become more about learning than assessment. This question of how to learn and encourage greater reflexivity around our roles as students and teachers through the writing of the thesis is of particular importance for researchers in the field of education. We can begin to learn first-hand about intercultural communication and see teaching and learning processes as integral to the research process, not outside it.

The debates raised in this chapter in the context of writing a PhD thesis have wider implications for all those involved in academic writing and publishing. Analysing the unequal access of 'periphery' academics (the Sri Lankan scholars discussed earlier) to publishing in journals and books produced at the 'centre', Canagarajah (2002: 233) points to the influence of 'poverty and power' in knowledge production. Differing ideas about what constitutes 'good' academic writing mean that periphery academics are often excluded from mainstream journals, since the gatekeepers and judges of 'quality' are the 'centre' academics. Canagarajah (2002) discusses the 'exploitation' of periphery scholars' knowledge about their own communities: 'whatever realities periphery subjects may live, center scholars are needed to theorize them and give them a perspective in order for work to achieve the status of established knowledge' (p. 236). The unequal relationships in academic publishing can thus lead to a situation where periphery academics are the consumers rather than producers of knowledge: 'Due to the one-sided nature of publishing, we are forced into a position of understanding ourselves through center eyes' (p. 237). The increased understanding about differing writing practices which students and supervisors can gain through the PhD supervision relationship can be seen as one step towards democratizing academic publishing.

7

Reflections on the doctoral research process: exploring the pedagogical implications of this book

Why this chapter? Teaching and learning as integral to educational research

It is a big shock for us. We have extended family and grow up in the extended family. You can get everything, you can stay after marriage with your parents and it affects our lives. My mother washes my clothes, my father will buy my pens and papers. My parents tell us what we should do or not do. Teachers are just sending us information, there is no way to discuss it. Just sending information and no chance to express ourselves. We come here and we expect the supervisor to say 'read this book'. We think they should assign certain books. But we have to be completely independent. Your responsibility. It is a big change for us. After a while, you recognize this.

(Student describing his experiences of coming from Saudi Arabia to study at the University of East Anglia, July 2004)

At first glance, this chapter on the teaching and learning practices of PhD students and their supervisors may appear out of place in a book on research methodology. However, the reflective pieces written by international students in this book and interview data (as above) reveal the extent to which the experience of being a student in a differing educational system and living in another culture influences the assumptions and approaches they bring to their research. Talking to international students while writing this book, I have been struck by how readily they relate accounts of their own learning as 'outsiders' in an unfamiliar higher education system (such as the student in the opening of this chapter) with changing assumptions about their roles as educational researchers and the process of responding to new research practices. Our experiences and beliefs about teaching and learning shape our approach to educational research – which is what perhaps distinguishes this book from an account of cross-cultural perspectives on research in general. As a supervisor, I am only now beginning to realize that my tendency to teach research methods in a fairly conventional way (with sessions on 'case study' or 'action research') has perhaps prevented me from seeing how students' ways of learning often differ from my own and the implications of this for my own research. I am not alone in this, since much of the literature on teaching international students takes the starting point that 'they' need to learn to integrate and adapt to Western academic practices. This stance could be related to the debates within multicultural education and the changing rationale from providing compensatory education for a minority, to recognizing that responding to diversity could bring benefits for all children [see May (2001: 109) on the 'new pluralism' of the Swann Report].

The deficit approach – that international students are at an automatic disadvantage and need to 'catch up' in UK universities – puts the focus on integration and finding better support strategies, thus avoiding discussion about how UK institutions and supervisors could reflect on and critique their established academic practices. The literature on international students has also tended to put boundaries around the issues discussed; for example, cross-cultural approaches to teaching and learning are introduced to analyse the student's classroom or supervision experiences in a UK higher education institution (McNamara and Harris 1997), but not to bring into question 'whose knowledge' a research degree builds upon and contributes to. In other words, the scope of the discussion on cross-cultural perspectives is tightly circumscribed.

As this book has revealed, cross-cultural perspectives on education can enable us to critique established research practices and assumptions (such as those around ethics). As the multicultural debate highlighted in school contexts, this is not just an issue affecting international research students or those conducting comparative educational research. The aim of this book is to begin a dialogue about differing research assumptions, and to suggest how such challenges could lead to transformations in the way that we all conduct educational research. For instance, finding ways to support a student to work in two or more languages – rather than English alone – can present an educational challenge to the supervisor as 'teacher'. However, the supervisor who gains experience around code-switching (including between academic and vernacular registers of English) and greater sensitivity to issues around language choice may also decide to change how they conduct their own research, particularly in multilingual settings. Recognizing that the student needs to work out how to contribute to and develop the academic literature of another culture through their PhD research (an 'alternative knowledge') may mean that the supervisor also begins to question concepts and theories that he or she had taken for granted. This will involve sharing ideas about academic teaching practices in the home institution (as compared to research practices) in order to find out how 'notions of higher education translate to the home culture of the overseas students' (Terrell and Brown 2000: 43).

The aims of this chapter are in part to discuss teaching and learning in relation to international research students and to explore strategies for improving educational support and the dialogue with their supervisors. However, I see the benefits of taking a cross-cultural perspective on teaching and learning as two-way and will be looking at how the research methods and approaches of UK supervisors and students might change as a result of this interaction. In other words, I will be asking, what can be learned from international research students' experiences, not just in terms of teaching and learning support, but also in terms of developing alternative research approaches and practices?

Cross-cultural perspectives on learning and teaching in higher education

> Although some of the participants were familiar with quantitative inquiry and attending the course to learn about the qualitative aspect, others were not ready to do so as their context is not quite familiar with it and a change would be a risk. As for me, both types of research inquiry were completely new to me as this is the first time for me to do research. That brought more confusion to me as I felt I was behind. That made me feel the necessity to apply myself, maybe more than the others and concentrate on the course and discussion to get a good grasp of what qualitative research is.
>
> (Al Yaseen 2000: 76)

Al Yaseen expressed the feeling that she 'was behind' compared with the other students, who were already familiar with research methodology when they started the PhD course. As I discussed in Chapter 3, students from research cultures dominated by quantitative approaches felt at a particular disadvantage when joining CARE, believing that they came from a different tradition. Al-Nasser (1999: 68) described how the participants on his course were mostly Europeans who were already familiar with approaches like case study. This emphasis on what knowledge the UK students had (as compared to what Al Yaseen and Al-Nasser felt that they did not have) reflects the discourse within the literature on international students, which excludes consideration of the knowledge and skills that international students do have (which home students may not). Concerned to highlight the fact that few courses or supervisors recognize the international student's differing starting point, Elsey and

Kinnell (1990), for example, emphasize the need for students to 'catch up' on certain skills and be introduced gradually to new learning styles. Elsey (1990: 56) notes that 'the tendency for many supervisors to take things for granted in an unfamiliar academic culture for many overseas students was said to cloud the relationship from the outset'. However, such accounts of differing educational systems, more hierarchical teacher/ student relationships and learning practices that centred on memorization or apparently reproducing knowledge (see Ryan 2000: 8), did much to increase the understanding of university teaching staff about why inter-national students appeared to be dependent, passive and uncritical – the 'cultural stereotypes' unpacked by Biggs (2003) (see Chapter 1). Ballard and Clancy (1997) present detailed case studies of individual students, such as the Burmese student who feels that 'by asking questions in class we might be taking the risk of offending the teacher in front of the whole class' (p. 16). As Cosh (2000: 68) observes, it is now widely accepted that it was often a 'mismatch between expectations, learning paradigms and previous learning behaviours' that exacerbated international students' difficulties.

Within this discourse, the problems faced by international students have been analysed in terms of the wider failure of higher educational institutions to respond to their increasingly diverse research student popu-lation. Geake and Maingard (1999: 48), for instance, argue that to address the needs of NESB[1] students would be to better address the needs of all postgraduate students. Similarly, Biggs (2003: 121) takes the view that 'language problems aside, the problems presented by the cultural gap between school and university are different from those experienced by non-Anglo-Celtic ISs [international students] only in extent, not in kind'.

The discourse on international students in higher education has thus tended to be around 'needs' and 'problems', rather than 'opportunities'. As Elsey and Kinnell (1990: 6) noted, their research started with a prob-lem-centred focus, as the project arose in the context of criticisms being 'levelled at institutional practices: could universities provide education for their customers in ways that met their needs?' In particular, discussion about English language support and, to some extent, academic literacy from a skills perspective, has dominated much of the last decade's litera-ture on international students. Consequently (in contrast to Chapter 5 of this book), language issues are more often addressed as a 'problem' than a resource within the international research student context.

More recently, researchers have moved away from a problem-based approach to look critically at the implications of 'other' cultural practices and assumptions about education for HE institutions and UK lecturers' teaching and learning. Terrell and Brown (2000: 48) note that: 'the richness and delight of teaching overseas students . . . can really help the

168 Cross-cultural perspectives

tutor to see our own assumptions from a different cultural perspective'. The experience of learning from international students (as opposed to simply teaching them) may, however, bring ideological challenges – as I noted in Chapter 4 in relation to differing ethical principles and at what point the researcher working in another culture will decide to impose his or her moral view. Terrell and Brown go on to suggest that 'in academic terms it can be quite challenging since there is a fine line between a local widespread cultural assumption and being simply wrong' (ibid.). Discussing a distance education programme, Evans (2000: 112) raises questions about how far supervisors should impose 'Western views of critical enquiry' and asks, 'How does a supervisor in a Western university facilitate or allow for the development of indigenous methodologies and methods?' Though his article is concerned with what he terms 'post(al) colonialism' (a distance learning course), the issues he raises about imposing 'uncritically the practices and principles of Western research to research training in non-Western contexts' (p. 116) are equally relevant to conventional modes of course delivery. The question is no longer about how we teach students from other countries, but about whose knowledge and methods are to be drawn upon during the research process. This links directly to Canagarajah's (2002) discussion about how to promote 'periphery' academic writing, particularly in the vernacular, given the global hierarchies of knowledge where 'periphery' scholars are obliged to conform to dominant (Western) practices in order to be published.

Evans (2000: 116) is unusual in questioning the 'politics of research' in differing cultural contexts, and in particular 'the notion of critique'. The starting assumption in much of the literature (and this is reflected in many international students' own accounts in their theses) is that students lack the skills or confidence to 'be critical' and that supervisors should develop suitable teaching approaches to encourage critique. Although researchers have looked at how criticism may be expressed in different ways, both in oral and written form (see previous chapter on the conventions of constructing an argument in different languages), supervisors may begin from the assumption that the student will want to take a critical position because that is the requirement of the PhD. As accounts in this book have shown, some students feel that 'being critical' will jeopardize their position at home, or that they will adopt this approach temporarily for their thesis, then return to conducting research which can contribute to their home academic culture. As Ryan (2000: 20) reflects from the supervisor's perspective: 'am I helping them to master the discipline or training them to master the discipline in the British way?'

In the literature reviewed above, I have traced a significant change in the stance of educators – from a deficit view of the student with 'problems' to be integrated and supported more fully in the UK (or

Australian) higher education system, to a consideration of the challenges that such students bring to accepted teaching methods, values and knowledge. For instance, Reynolds and Trehan (2001: 360) discuss how to incorporate a 'pedagogy of difference' into higher education practices, suggesting that 'critical pedagogies should attend more to learning from the differences that are brought into the classroom'. In the context of adult education, Shore (2004: 117) hints at the wider implications of responding to different ways of knowing: 'Adult educators are rarely advised that the aim is "knowing differently", an outcome that could potentially destabilise every existing premise currently held about adult education policy and practice'.

Changing relationship of supervisor and student

Although there is now more consideration of the implicit hierarchies of power between supervisors and students, or between UK institutions and their home establishments, the emphasis is still on the supervisor as specialist who can determine the relevance that 'our' methods have (or do not have) for differing cultural contexts. The concept of the student as 'expert' in certain areas, as compared to the supervisor, is rarely explored – with the result that issues around 'participation' and more equal power relations are limited to a discussion of relationships at the micro level of the classroom, as opposed to a wider consideration of research methodology and knowledge production.

Another major change is that the current literature is now more cautious about creating cultural stereotypes (such as 'Iranian' learning styles or assumptions about the 'Chinese learner') with regard to teaching approaches and labelling students. The basis for developing improved strategies is the alternative starting point that 'cultures do not talk to each other, individuals do' (Scollon quoted in Killick 2000: 152). However, on the level of research methodologies, we still face the challenge of how to avoid polarizing 'Western' and the 'other'. The implication of continuing to create these stereotypes is that we too readily adopt a fixed concept of culture and fail to recognize the ways in which cultures fuse and change: in Chapter 3, I discussed how the so-called 'traditional' Malaysian values could also be labelled as 'Western' because of their colonial origins. When considering how research approaches might evolve in response to cross-cultural perspectives on teaching and learning, it thus seems particularly limiting to attempt to label methodologies as Western or non-Western. There is also the danger of assuming that all 'non-Western' approaches are similar, thereby excluding the possibility of sharing perspectives within international students as a group.

Before going on to look at the possibilities for two-way learning and how to develop a more equal research partnership between the student and UK supervisor, I will briefly review some strategies developed to enhance the supervision of international research students.

Improving the learning experiences of international research students

As more teachers in higher education begin to conduct action research into their own teaching (see Wisker and Sutcliffe 1999; Wisker 2000), practical suggestions for improving research student supervision have emerged. Case studies written by international students with their supervisors have also given insight into the differing ways in which supervisors supervise and students learn. For instance, the detailed account of two contrasting supervisors (Aspland 1999) allows us to enter the perspective of Mei, a Chinese woman coming to study in Australia. After encountering problems with her first supervisor, who was never explicit about what she should do ('I was to keep guessing all the time what it was that I had to do'; Aspland 1999: 31), Mei transferred to a second supervisor who suggested that 'certain adjustments had to be made to Mei's existing orientations to learning':

> You learn round and I learn square – I need to learn how to think round! He [supervisor] told me that critical thinking was the most important thing for me to develop and I agree with him. I think it is very good to be in Australia and learn new ways of thinking.
>
> (Aspland 1999: 34)

From such case studies, we learn that successful supervision relationships involve openness and reflexivity from both parties.

In Mei's case, the supervisor had experience of Chinese culture, but as Geake and Maingard (1999: 48) ask: 'Is it feasible for all our supervisors to change to suit another culture?' It is not necessary for a supervisor to recognize an 'Iranian' learning style [though as Sandeman-Gay (1999: 40) comments, this knowledge makes it easier to adapt teaching strategies] or to have worked in the student's home country, but they should be able to create a dialogic space where differences can be discussed. The starting point that 'learning is not an individual act but a social practice' (Jones *et al.* 1999: 9) shifts the focus from the individual international student to their relationship and interaction with their supervisor and peers. Mei's case illustrates the importance of making differences explicit and building on prior experience, through a shift in emphasis rather than a radical change in learning and teaching practices. Kiley (2000: 98) stresses the importance of the student 'gradually moving in a carefully structured manner from more dependent to more independent relationship'.

Whose teaching and learning practices are best?

The idea of building on previous learning strategies can imply valuing educational practices that we may regard as outdated or even oppressive in the UK context, such as 'rote learning'. As Ballard and Clanchy (1997: 17) note, 'there is now a developing body of research that suggests that many students come from cultures in which close memorisation is recognised as the path to a deeper understanding of the material being learned (Kember 1996, Marton *et al.* 1993)'. This challenges previous assumptions about repetitious learning and suggests that some Japanese students, for instance, may need to find ways of bringing this kind of learning into their PhD study. Ryan (2000: 3) stresses the value of reflexivity on the part of the supervisor and that the 'first step is to review our own cultural values and practices'. She provides a checklist of questions such as 'are you prepared to explore ways of changing your teaching and learning practices?' Supervising international students is recognized to be more time-consuming – yet this issue is often tackled at the individual rather than the institutional level. Knight (1999: 94) argues that the 'role of the supervisor needs to be extended but that limits should also be considered'. He discusses the 'extent of the supervisory responsibility' (ibid.), in relation to practical constraints as well as issues around ownership of the text (hence the suggestion to 'edit students' work lightly' rather than to undertake major corrections).

Research training now generally includes classroom or group teaching as well as individual supervision. The literature on how to develop inclusive teaching practices in a multicultural undergraduate context has much that is relevant to research methods classrooms too. For instance, Ryan (2000) discusses the importance of giving feedback in a way that avoids 'loss of face' for the individual student and the need to recognize how talking is used in different cultures. Whereas in Western cultures it is usual to try to assert oneself in groups, in Eastern cultures, Ryan suggests, a greater priority is to create harmony. Ryan usefully lists some of the common characteristics of learning environments in different cultures (such as respect for authority figures, importance of the right answer, expectation that student will listen quietly, personal opinions appearing arrogant, in order to encourage supervisors to consider 'how the student can be "scaffolded" into local academic requirements' (Ryan 2000: 16). In the group teaching context, English language problems also came to the fore. An Indonesian student discussed his frustration in group discussions: 'I think slowly because I have to translate to English and when I want to speak . . . by the time I work out the idea in English the topic has changed' (Kiley 2000: 89). Teaching strategies included lecturers asking international students to speak first, encouraging more small group interaction and 'native tongue discussion groups' (Ryan 2000: 19).

Adapting to life and learning back home

Adopting a more holistic view of supervision involves taking into account not only the learning environment that a student has come from, but also the context to which they will return. As Chapters 2 and 3 illustrated, many students develop their research questions and approaches with a view to meeting the demands of their home institution, as well as those of their UK higher education institution. A non-threatening supervision environment can enable students to discuss differing ethical practices or research priorities in their home context. The student's reason for doing a PhD will influence what they learn in the process and the supervisor needs to engage with their personal and professional, as well as their academic, agenda. As several of the reflective pieces in this book reveal (see Madini, Chapter 1 and Castaneda-Mayo, Chapter 3), a pressing question for many students is 'how do we deal with the change in ourselves as a result of doing a PhD?' As Karim Sadeghi poignantly illustrates from his perspective in Iran (Chapter 2), the student may return to an institution where their newly gained knowledge and research experience is not valued.

In Chapter 6, I discussed the body of research on academic literacies in relation to the writing and reading practices of international students. Research on contrastive rhetoric can help supervisors to read and interpret their students' written work through providing understanding of differing writing conventions; for instance, Sillitoe and Crosling (1999: 169) describe how 'in contrast to Western writers, Japanese writers like to give "dark hints" to leave behind "nuances"'. Lea and Street's findings on how undergraduate students read their tutors' feedback also has implications for international students who may be completely unfamiliar with these writing conventions. From their research, Lea and Street (1999: 64) observed that 'guidelines only address the presuppositions about writing embedded in the tutor's field and do not address the assumptions and practices around writing that the students themselves may bring with them'. The concept of the student becoming part of a new 'community of practice' can enable academics to be more explicit in explaining about their own practices and assumptions. As I explored in the previous chapter, adopting a personalized style and finding a voice in a second language pose particular challenges for the international student. Moodie (1995) discusses the use of personal journals as a way for the student to learn a new writing style and to develop a reflexive stance on their research.

This section has highlighted some of the strategies developed by research supervisors to enable both students and academics to reflect on and adapt their teaching and learning approaches. These strategies imply taking a more holistic perspective on the PhD: considering the interplay of relationships that shape the PhD as a learning process, rather than simply looking at the thesis, a text produced according to certain conventions. In the second half of this chapter, I will look beyond the PhD to consider how the engagement between supervisors and international students can contribute new perspectives on educational research.

What can we learn from cross-cultural interaction between supervisors and students?

The ideal of 'two-way learning' between supervisor and student sounds straightforward from the perspective of improving cross-cultural under- standing. However, 'cultural' differences in academic practices also involve issues of power and inequality: English academic writing is not only different from Japanese, but in the context of an assessed course of study in a UK university, is better. The question posed by Evans (2000: 112) about how far a supervisor can allow for the development of indigenous methods, suggests that he or she also has the authority to decide which approaches can be validated within their educational system. When we move from a skills-based perspective on academic literacy to a consideration of the academic discourse within higher educa- tion, we have to decide whether to challenge the implicit power hierarch- ies shaping those practices or to use a greater understanding of cultural 'difference' as a force for change. As I discussed in Chapter 1, the term 'culture' is often used as an excuse for avoiding discussion or advocating change: we may be hesitant to challenge 'cultural practices' which we do not agree with. However, this chapter is based on the premise that aca- demic cultures can be transformed and that within the UK higher educa- tion system, we need to acknowledge that the cultural challenge can be multi-dimensional. The balance of power (between supervisor and stu- dent, and between UK/overseas institution) has often meant that the stu- dents' previous academic practices were devalued in the UK context. In the next section, I look at how a more egalitarian teaching environment (such as the ideal described in the literature reviewed above) can enable students and supervisors to compare and critique their differing cultural practices. I will make a distinction here between academic practices – those associated with the Academy and the specific higher education institution – and research practices (though these are also often shaped by the higher education institution's values).

Academic practices

Reading, writing and talking take on a certain meaning within the context of the PhD. As I explored in the previous chapter, 'writing up' is a stage within the PhD course centred on the production of the thesis with associated expectations around form, style and voice. Though the genre of the PhD thesis has to some extent been transformed through experimentation with multi-media material and bricolage, I argue here that the academic practices associated with undertaking a PhD have rarely been challenged.

Taking what has been termed a 'social practice' approach – as compared to a skills perspective – on academic literacy enables us to analyse various ways of reading and writing text in differing cultural contexts. We also move away from the idea of innate ability to one of learned practices. Smith (1999: 147) points out that 'many supervisors believe critical thinking is more an innate capacity than a variety of learned practices, and it is thus often left to the individual student's own initiative'. Considering 'being critical' as a learned practice puts an emphasis on exploring what being critical means in differing contexts. The issue is how to teach an international student to 'be critical' in the British way or to educate British readers to understand 'being critical' in another culture (as Puteh did in her thesis – see Chapter 2).

I have already discussed differing academic writing practices in languages such as Finnish, Japanese and Arabic (see Chapter 5). Within the PhD context, problems have arisen when a student quotes extensively from other texts, giving rise to accusations of plagiarism, or that they have failed to construct an argument in the way required within a thesis. Equally important is to recognize that we also read texts in different ways. Smith gives an insight into reading practices within Confucian cultures, where there is greater emphasis on gaining moral understanding from a text. The reader within the Chinese tradition will be asking: 'What are the effects of this study or reading in terms of an ethical outcome or how does it enable the knower to know how to act properly?' (Munro in Smith 1999: 150). Though Smith's article explains the differing assumptions that a Chinese reader brings to a text, he runs the risk of generalizing about a culture and does not bring in the idea of 'Confucian' reading practices changing over time, partly due to the impact of academics returning from study overseas. Looking at these differing writing and reading practices from the perspective of 'two-way learning', the important point is not simply for the supervisor to understand where the student is coming from and make allowances or provide appropriate training (as suggested in Wisker 2000). Understanding how texts are read and written in differing cultures can also help us all to look critically at our own academic texts and how we construct them, as well as learning how to interpret work produced in other academic cultures. In the context of the PhD, it is worth noting however that it is unlikely that assessment criteria could ever change to recognize these differences in writing and reading practices.

Linked to this increased understanding, is students' frustration that though they may succeed in adopting English academic writing practices, they will find difficulty in transferring these practices to their home academic institution. Ayedh Al-Motairi said, for instance, that he would like to adopt the first person in Arabic writing, but he felt that this would be misunderstood back home. This aim of contributing to 'another' academic culture – particularly through bringing new writing and reading practices – often remains unfulfilled by international students whose main priority is to obtain the PhD. Once supervisors have an understanding of these differences in academic practices, it may be possible to work collaboratively to enable the student to publish their work in a form which can be acceptable in their home institution, yet also begin to push the boundaries. When I asked a Saudi Arabian student whether he would publish his thesis in his home country, he suggested that the issue was also about translating English academic texts into Arabic: 'Most researchers don't think of translating English books to Arabic so it is not just about my paper. I would like to translate counselling books into Arabic. It would provide the best opportunity for myself and others, just to do a summary' (Interview: 30/7/04).

Interaction between supervisors and students about their differing academic practices could therefore have implications far beyond the individual PhD and lead to ways of challenging the dominant balance of power in knowledge production. Developing indigenous academic practices through finding ways of integrating new knowledge and research practices learnt in the UK could mean that indigenous cultures are reinvigorated (rather than assuming, for instance, that 'Confucian' reading practices remain unchanged). At present, international students assume that their research should contribute primarily to the Western Academy, given the higher status of English language journals. However, this cross-cultural interaction about academic practices at a micro level might lead us to find ways of contributing to 'other' bodies of knowledge and transforming both UK and Arabic academic practices as a result. Researchers in both UK and home institutions need to become more reflexive about their academic practices, in order to understand both the constraints and the opportunities presented by their differences.

Completing a PhD is not just about writing a thesis – the oral practices associated with seminars and supervisions are also shaped by cultural practices specific to the institution (see first part of this chapter). In Chapter 5, I also discussed how decisions about which language to work with in supervision and analysis of data can begin to shift the power from the supervisor to the student. Analysing data in a language that is unfamiliar to the supervisor encourages the student to take the lead in determining which methods to adopt or which concepts to prioritize. An academic practice peculiar to the PhD is that of the viva and the oral 'defence' of the thesis. Denicolo and Pope reflect on the differing metaphors used within a Thai context:

The war metaphor which prevails when we require our students to defend their thesis could be replaced by the metaphor of the dance. The viva should be seen as an opportunity for the candidates to display their interests and engage in a conversation which enables all participants to benefit from the engagement of minds rather than adopting an adversarial stance.

(Denicolo and Pope 1999: 69)

They suggest that this would not result in 'any diminution of standards' (p. 70) but would facilitate a more supportive atmosphere (similar to the 'dialogic space' proposed for supervision meetings). Reflecting on how Western concepts of argument and debate have shaped our academic practices can thus enable us to identify constraining factors, not just for international students, but for all those participating in an event such as the viva.

Research practices

Although I have made a distinction between academic practices and research practices in this chapter, the two overlap to a great extent since educational research practices are largely informed by PhD research experience. Practitioners in schools and other educational institutions engaged in action research could be regarded as working outside the Academy, though their 'mentors' are often university-based researchers. I am looking here at the implications of the cross-cultural critique of academic practices above for the way we conduct educational research.

Greater understanding of cross-cultural communication in oral and written forms has benefits not just for teaching situations (such as those discussed above) but also for how we as researchers interact with participants. For instance, realizing that a student may be more subtle in their criticism in a seminar can increase the researcher's sensitivity to comments in research interviews or discussion groups. Similarly, we learn to interpret events in fieldwork and read texts differently if we have become aware of differing meanings attached to behaviour within multicultural classrooms. This heightened cultural sensitivity – becoming aware of double meanings – enables us to reflect differently on the questions we research, the boundaries we set and our own role as researchers (both within our own culture and outside). Looking back at the situation of the international student faced with two audiences and conflicting aims, we can see that the issues discussed in Chapters 2 and 3 apply equally to the UK researcher who locates his or her research within a wider global context. New questions – such as whose knowledge do I contribute to and how? – arise once a researcher steps outside the research conventions with which he or she is familiar. In a culture used to quantitative research, how do we go about using qualitative approaches and what can we learn from the ways that 'insiders' negotiate new methods with their academic communities?

As I discussed in Chapter 4, cross-cultural perspectives on established ethical procedures can lead us to recognize the limitations in accepted research practices, such as anonymizing participants or handing out consent forms. In addition, looking at any research from a differing ethical viewpoint can illuminate values that we take for granted and help us to recognize the ethics of interpretation: which interpretation do we put greater value on and why? The 'outsider' view on our ethical procedures – such as that of Scholastica Mokake (Chapter 4) – points to the importance of integrating ethical concerns throughout the research process, rather than taking a 'bolt on' approach, like that now prevalent in much UK educational research.

As well as critiquing our accepted practices from an unusual angle [as Ryan (2000: 3) suggests, to 'learn to step outside your culture like an anthropologist'], adopting a cross-cultural perspective can lead us to recognize and prioritize new issues within our research methodology. In Chapter 5, I described the experiences of researchers working with two or more languages in the fieldwork situation and the writing of the text. This raised teaching concerns about how to support students to use multiple languages in their research, and also introduced the idea of language as a resource rather than a problem. Accounts of research in bilingual situations reveal how researchers can employ additional strategies, such as code-switching, to draw on the differing identities of both participant and researcher. Huda Al-Yousef's discussion (Chapter 5) of how she translated young Saudi women's words into English addresses not simply a technical issue of how best to convey their meaning, but also the question of how to recreate their identity and spoken discourse in English. Although UK researchers may be working in monolingual situations, we can gain similar insight into the importance of conveying differing registers of the various groups within a community. Taking the concept of code-switching a step further, we can also begin to anticipate the differing audiences of our research texts – as many international students already do through writing simultaneously for their supervisor and their employer. As Canagarajah (2002: 295) points out, this is a strength that 'periphery' scholars can draw upon: 'the codeswitching that many writers perform as they communicate in different languages to different audiences shows that they have the rhetorical competence to negotiate the terms of communication in diverse contexts'. The code-switching strategies used by periphery scholars to construct a 'multivocal text' (ibid.) within the same text can also be learned by academics at the 'centre' in order to address more diverse audiences and as a strategy for 'democratizing' academic knowledge construction.

This book has aimed to analyse the ways in which a cross-cultural perspective on educational research can help to illuminate assumptions behind our accepted research practices (both here and there) and contribute new research approaches. In the context of globalization, we would be foolish to assume that UK research is only conducted for a UK audience – and this recognition needs to inform our research process from the formulating of research questions to the writing up of the findings. I have focused in the previous chapters on what could be considered on one level as a case study of cross-cultural understanding and 'misunderstandings' between UEA students and their supervisors. The aim of this case study is not simply to suggest ways of tackling these misunderstandings through increased dialogue or improved supervision, but also to use the student's outsider perspective on dominant research practices to analyse educational research practices more generally. Through this lens, we can reflect critically on issues such as interaction within fieldwork situations, construction of the research text, role of the researcher, ethical procedures and language strategies, with the aim of recognizing and responding to differing cultural values and practices.

Conclusion: changing research cultures

The nature of working towards a PhD degree, which is ultimately based on research, has its own merits and demerits. Based on my personal experience, I believe it has helped me to develop a high self-esteem through being independent and taking responsibility to handle my work and be responsible for it. I developed a critical ability to think about my work, choose relevant material to read . . . in addition to being critical to what to include and what not to include. It has helped me to establish a strong contact with my supervisor . . . However the demerits of such an approach, research-based degree, can be presented in the word 'isolation'. It is a hard feeling to experience. For the years I spent doing the degree, I always felt that I was all by myself. That made me realise if I was on the track, especially that we PhD students rarely met. Although we first met as one group during the five week course, yet after that everyone of us went to his/her own world as each one of us dealt with a different topic and followed maybe a different methodology.

(Al-Yaseen 2000: 94)

While writing this book, I have been aware of the danger of suggesting that change in research approaches will come about on an individual basis – whether in Riyadh or Norwich, it is not simply a matter of an individual choosing to adapt his or her approach. As Al-Yaseen comments above, the isolation of working for a PhD in that each student is absorbed in their own study, means that there are few opportunities for interacting about their research. In particular, it is unusual for international students to tackle the challenges posed by unfamiliar methodology and approaches collaboratively as a group, rather than as individuals. Where several students have come from one country to study in our department, they have however sometimes considered ways of working together when they return home to change the dominant research culture. A case in point is the qualitative research network set up by ex-CARE students in Malaysia. Whereas the isolated PhD student may not have the opportunity to challenge research practices in his or her institution, once they return home the support of other like-minded researchers can help to sustain the momentum and make changes on an institutional level.

We commonly refer to 'research culture' in relation to institutions rather than to countries, as shorthand for the research practices and beliefs associated with a certain context. Since coming to work at CARE, I have become aware that the assumptions that both international students and other researchers bring to this institution – in terms of what they believe CARE stands for – are shaped by experiences in the past and established research traditions. Just as stereotypes of 'Arabic' culture can be promoted, it is possible to generalize about an institution's research 'culture' based on past practices. This can mean that the research culture becomes 'fixed' in the eyes of the outside world, rather than seen as evolving and responding to change. With the constant flow of international students moving through CARE's graduate research programmes, the 'research culture' has been influenced by new ideas, experiences and collaborations arriving from afar. Wisker (2000: 121) comments, 'the key issue when working with postgraduates from different cultural contexts is whether the approaches we have to learning and research . . . are themselves culture and value free or a product of a certain set of ideologies born of our own culture'. Rather than search for 'culture and value free' research approaches, the cross-cultural perspectives described in this book can enable us to identify our (both students' and supervisors') biases. This process involves standing outside our familiar research culture, so that the question 'how do you teach people to be critical?' changes to 'how do you teach people to be critical in UK academic discourse?' It is important to create a research culture that can embrace change – not just to improve cross-cultural learning and communication between researchers, but also to recognize and take an institutional position on conflicting beliefs and practices within differing research traditions.

The role of increasing cultural understanding has been highlighted in particular in the context of teaching and learning (Cortazzi and Jin 1997; Ryan 2000). Within a research context, there has been less attention to the ways in which our cultural background influences fieldwork (how we interact and ask questions), our differing interpretations of qualitative data, and the methods we choose to adopt. International students writing in this book have suggested the importance of seeing learning in a wider context than the higher education classroom: Manal Madini (Chapter 1), for instance, reflects on how the understanding she has gained from living in another culture and her children going to school in the UK has affected her research in Saudi Arabia. Howida Mostafa (this chapter) describes how her perspective on teacher education in Egypt changed after becoming a student in the UK and experiencing different approaches to teaching and learning, as well as observing a UK teacher education course. In particular, she reflects on how cultural values (specifically the hierarchical social relationships valued in Egyptian society and families) shape educational structures and practices.

Change for now or forever?

In my previous role as aid worker in Nepal, I was often expected to evaluate change in human behaviour as a result of development intervention (such as the impact of adult literacy programmes on whether parents sent their children to school). I soon realized that such changes in attitudes and behaviour usually came about in a roundabout way and could not be attributed to any one event. Similarly, the international students writing in this book suggest that the whole experience of living and studying in the UK – rather than a certain course or supervisor – contributed to their changing perspective on educational research. I also see a parallel with the development context described above in how sustainable these changes are: a Saudi student returning to an unsupportive research culture may feel that her experience of another kind of research is temporary and cannot be followed in her own country. This relates to how far the individual feels empowered to question accepted cultural values once back home.

Several chapters in this book have analysed the tension experienced by international students in attempting to respond to two audiences with differing agendas, assumptions and values. They see a choice between adapting to the dominant form (in this case, the UK higher education requirements) and bridging the gap through acting as mediator to try to compromise conflicting expectations. As I have suggested in this book, there is also the possibility of developing an alternative approach and using the tension between two audiences as a positive force for change. This involves addressing questions around power and identity, asking what counts as knowledge and who has authority over it. Learning to become a member of the UK higher education 'community of practice' through undertaking a PhD course of study need not necessarily mean that an international student loses their identity as a Malaysian academic researcher who abandons 'indigenous' academic and research practices. Within the UK higher education community, we should also recognize that our research can be enhanced through learning about the practices of other academic communities. Though Barnett (1997) argues that the point of higher education programmes is 'critical engagement with theory and practice', we are often hesitant to question our own academic practices. Developing more inclusive teaching approaches in our multicultural university classrooms [Biggs' (2003) third level of 'teaching as educating'] can be the first step towards adopting a cross-cultural perspective on educational research.

The influence of culture on education in two different contexts

By Howida Mostafa

A personal perspective on learning

I entered the Faculty of Education (FoE) and majored in English because I wanted to be an English language teacher. But throughout my years of study, I became more ambitious and managed to join the faculty staff. Then the Egyptian government awarded me a scholarship to study for a PhD in England. So, as a researcher I experienced studying in two different cultures, which has influenced how I approach the learning–teaching process and teacher education.

My epistemological perspective on knowledge and learning, throughout my years of schooling in Egypt, featured basically a transmissive and exam-oriented mode of learning and teaching. Textbooks and the teacher were the main sources of gaining knowledge. The audio-lingual or the grammar-translation approaches were mainly applied as language teaching methods in my learning institute. Learning EFL was conducted through memorizing, repeating and drilling the grammatical patterns and vocabulary that aimed to prepare us for examinations. My prior schooling indicated that teaching a foreign language is basically through mastery of grammar structures rather than the development of communicative strategies. The English lessons taught had been largely teacher-centred in which acquiring grammatical patterns and structures were the main concern of the teacher.

I was dissatisfied with the bridge between theory and practice. My perception of what I learnt at the faculty seemed difficult to reconcile with the practical experience in the classroom. My epistemological stance had not changed until I came to England. But, coming to England, observing and following the PGCE[2] course as part of the field-work, helped me to get a deeper understanding of the processes of learning to teach EFL and to rethink my own professional practice. Joining the Centre for Applied Research in Education (CARE) and attending its five-week course, I also had direct experience of the communicative approach that was based largely on our interaction, involvement and communication with the tutors. The experiences I gained from attending these courses differed substantially from my prior knowledge and experiences about seminars and university-based sessions. This widened my conceptualization of teaching and learning through communicative language teaching (CLT).

So, I began to question my previous beliefs about language teaching and learning: what it meant to learn to become an EFL teacher and to learn to teach EFL in Egypt, and to think how to provide an effective professional preparation for the Egyptian students in my university. I experienced a shift in my own epistemological position from a Behaviourist to a Constructivist view. Instead of being passive, receiving knowledge from fixed sources outside myself, I constructed the knowledge presented in this PhD study through my own interpretations of the situations I observed and through my interaction with the research participants. This has led me to gain insights about the effectiveness of learning and teaching through communication, collaboration, involvement and interaction between teachers and learners by using the CLT approach, rather than the audio-lingual approach, which does not give any room for developing communicative competency.

The impact of culture on educational practices and teacher education

From my experiences, it is clear that culture has an influential impact on educational practices and teacher education. Culture influences the way people look at each other, the workplace community, teacher status, gender relationships, and ways of bringing up children, epistemology and even ways of dressing up. Teaching and learning cultures in schools are socially constructed. So, the professional preparation of the PGCE students is culturally distinctive from the Egyptian one. The Egyptian cultural values and beliefs determine the students' ways of thinking and behaving.

Egypt, like all other societies, has its distinguishing culture. This is one of the oldest cultures in the world. As an Arabic, Muslim society, Islam dominates Egyptian society and affects people's behaviour, trends, values and their way of life. It also has an effect on education, as there are separate schools for boys and girls at both preparatory and secondary stages. The curriculum, in all stages, includes some verses from the Qur'an for all students to study and know the main principles of Islam. There are also Al-Azher institutes, which are established only for Muslims at all stages of education, in which boys and girls have completely separate institutes even at the university stage. Islam as a subject is not however included in the curriculum of the universities unless it is the student's own subject of speciality.

Islam specifies what is permitted or prohibited for both women and men and is indirectly responsible for there being many more female teachers than male ones. That is because Islam puts particular boundaries on the relationship between men and women in society. So, how they are to communicate and treat each other at work or the university is subject to traditional and cultural views. This can be seen in the following two reasons for this phenomenon. Firstly, some conservative parents, especially in southern parts of Egypt, do not wish to enrol their daughters in faculties other than the Faculty of Education. They see that this is the only way to ensure that their daughters will be appointed to a job where they do not have to mingle with men. This deprives females of their right to choose which faculty they would prefer to attend. In general, parents tend to consider the teaching profession as more suitable for females and unsuitable for males, as females are considered to have more patience, more experience and more tenderness. Secondly, males are unwilling to enter the teaching profession because of the low status of teachers in our society.

Understanding power hierarchies

There are many other issues, which are clearly influenced by culture. The nature of how much freedom human agents have to act will influence how structure is constructed. Understanding how much freedom individuals have might help to interpret why they act in particular ways. The powerful impact of the government on education is visible in the centralized system of allocating students to the different faculties. The central coordination bureau located in the capital is responsible for assigning the students to the faculties according to their marks and not taking into account their actual choice. Some students who are unable to gain a high enough grade to enter courses of their first choice end up following a teacher-training course. This means that students are following the course unwillingly because they have no other higher education opportunity. Therefore, the social structure and human agency framework can give an insight into why most of the student teachers in the Egyptian context unwillingly enter the Faculty of Education. This also enables us to understand how their counterparts in the English context are able to choose to become teachers and join the PGCE course.

In a hierarchical structure, there are dominating discourses within both the local communities of the university and the schools and the wider society. These discourses say that the university is seen to be more powerful than the school and, in turn, the university members are perceived as more powerful than schoolteachers. So when they come to work together, everyone has in mind that permeating discourse which makes people 'higher' up in the hierarchy look down at people in 'lower' positions. This situation is very complex because schoolteachers do not seem to be willing to participate in in-service training in the Faculty of Education in order to develop professionally and better understand their supervisor role. They seem to feel that faculty members do not treat schoolteachers as peers. Furthermore, they think that if they receive in-service training and student teachers find out about it, this will make them seem incompetent as supervisors.

So, even within the school community, that hierarchical view exists. For schoolteachers to achieve that status, they exercise internal power (power relationships within schools) at the expense of their colleagues who are lower down the hierarchy within the school community. The director of the school exercises power over the headteacher, the headteacher exercises power over newly graduated teachers and those teachers exercise power over the pupils. Another part of achieving that status and power is that some schoolteachers tend to make student teachers' time in schools stressful. By doing so, they believe that student teachers will perceive them as powerful and having authority. The case in the university is not much different, although the university is perceived by the wider society to be more powerful than schools. The university is not an independent organization but also has to follow the instructions and regulations issued by the Ministry of Higher Education.

Another area where control is exerted relates to parents and children. Most of the female students enter the Faculty of Education because conservative parents consider teaching as the best profession for them. Also some male students are forced to enter the Faculty of Education because their parents want them to find a job immediately after graduation. This is a result of the poor financial status of the majority of people in Egypt. But this has a negative impact on the teaching profession. Teachers who enter the profession in this way are reluctant and poorly motivated. They are likely to be 'conscripts' and not change agents.

My account has illustrated how different cultures influence the way people behave, learn and teach. Society is structured on bases of economics, status, power and cultural traits. All people in schools and universities work within that hierarchical chain which shapes the social relationships and interactions among them.

Howida Mostafa is a lecturer in the Faculty of Education in El-Minia University, which is located in the central part of Egypt. Her field of specialization is Methods of Teaching English and she gained her PhD from the University of East Anglia in 2003. She has been working for many years as an English language teacher trainer, supervising student teachers on their school practice. Howida comments: 'I found it a very valuable opportunity to write down my reflections about my experiences of studying in two countries. It helped me to realize the great differences between them in all aspects of life'.

Notes

Chapter 1

1 I have chosen to use the term 'international student' in preference to 'overseas student' in this book, partly as a reflection of the most common label now used to refer to those students who are not in the 'home' student category. As this chapter will argue, both terms lack meaning except in so far as they serve to denote the 'other' (in this context, students who originate from outside the UK). As Barker (1997: 112) points out: 'The issue of ethnocentrism is still tied to language instead of to the fundamental values and beliefs, which may, for instance, be revealed even in the use of the term "overseas students"'. Ryan and Zuber-Skerritt (1999) distinguish this group of students as 'NESB' (non-English-speaking backgrounds) – however, this label could appear to exclude those students who originate from countries (often former colonies) where English is the main medium of instruction in schools and colleges and spoken at home, alongside indigenous languages.

2 For a more detailed account of CARE's history as a research institution, see Chapter 3. As a relative newcomer to CARE (in 2000), I am also aware that my historical perspective is limited to oral accounts from colleagues and a few written documents, so is quite different from those colleagues involved in the early days of the Centre.

3 I discuss this research on teaching international students in higher education in more depth in Chapter 7.

4 MacLure (2003: 175) usefully summarizes Gee's distinction as 'Discourse with a capital "D" to distinguish such broader sociocultural conceptualisations from the more localised meanings of discourse (with a small "d") within linguistic approaches, where it is often synonymous with text, communication of "language in use"'.

5 See Robinson-Pant (1996) for a discussion about the relationship between PRA and indigenous numeracy and literacy practices.

6 Judith Castaneda-Mayo, Manal Madini, Scholastica Mokake, Howida Mostafa, Asmahan Abd. Razak, Karim Sadeghi and Huda Al-Yousef.

7 My decision to 'allow' participants to rewrite their words may be criticized by some researchers. However, as the seminar summaries (which are posted on our department student intranet) are to some extent negotiated texts in the first place (rather than transcripts of discussions), it seemed appropriate for students to rewrite some comments in recognition of the even more public space of the book.

8 In Chapter 6, I will look in more detail at the specific practices associated with writing a thesis, drawing upon Teasdale and Teasdale's (1999) analysis.

Chapter 2

1 An additional perspective on this chapter is usefully provided by my colleague, John Elliott, who conducted an e-mail conversation with his doctoral students. The resulting conference paper, 'Doing applied educational research for a PhD: a conversation between a group of doctoral students and their supervisor' (September 2004), includes a section on 'Defining a focus for a PhD in applied educational research: intentions, influencing factors and issues'. While the paper brings out similar points around the tension faced by students responding to their supervisor's interests and advice, as compared to their institutions, the students participating in the e-mail conversation all appeared to be subject to fewer political and institutional restrictions than many people quoted in this chapter.

2 It should also be noted that though I had intended to use pseudonyms for all the students quoted in these extracts, nearly everyone said they would prefer that I use their 'real names' because 'what I said was real' (comment in response to the first draft of this book). In these cases, I have responded to their request and removed the pseudonym.

3 See the section following this chapter, 'Challenges facing a PhD graduate from the UK: an Iranian context', for Karim Sadeghi's own account of this process of defining a research area in Iran, as well as his experiences on returning home and attempting to share his research with colleagues.

4 See 'The insider/outsider dilemmas in educational research – a Mexican experience' for Judith Castaneda-Mayo's account of how she made this transition (section following Chapter 3).

5 This touches on the concept of 'circular borrowing' (introduced to me by John Elliott), which has been used to describe the ways that ideas are sometimes borrowed from the West, reconstructed by indigenous cultures and then borrowed back by the West. The dangers of Western 'exploitation' of this knowledge creation process are discussed in Canagarajah (2002).

6 Karim Sadeghi's reflective piece (following this chapter) illustrates this well.

7 This observation is based partly on personal experience in Nepal. I remember a particular instance in the immigration office when after days of standing waiting for papers to be processed, my husband (a Nepali national) challenged the official about their bureaucratic procedures. The Deputy Director of Immigration immediately issued my visa but with a warning to my husband that he was not 'acting like a Nepali' and had become impatient and critical like a foreigner because of his education in the UK!

8   See also 'There is more to learn behind the scene' (Chapter 4) for Scholastica Mokake's critical reflections on UK research ethics procedures in the Tanzanian context.

Chapter 3

1   I am not attempting to suggest that certain research tools (such as case studies or questionnaires) belong exclusively to a qualitative or quantitative methodology, but a difficulty arises in this chapter since the terms 'case study' or 'action research' had come to symbolize qualitative research for many people arriving at CARE.

2   Othman Lebar, an academic visitor from Malaysia, commented in a seminar that 'nowadays, qualitative research approaches are more accepted and less "alien" in Malaysia than when he did his PhD (in the nineties)' (Seminar report: 28/10/03).

3   See Asmahan Abd Razak's account at the end of this chapter about how as researcher she had to take account of how hierarchical relationships shaped her interview encounters during fieldwork in Malaysia ('Behind the scene: the "culture" of interviewing in Malaysia').

4   See Robinson-Pant (2001b) for a more detailed analysis of this research project.

5   The concern with whether research methods are 'indigenous' has also been much debated by development practitioners using PRA (Participatory Rural Appraisal), an approach using visual methods such as mapping and ranking. In 'PRA: a new literacy' (1996), I traced the origins of these methods, to analyse how far research activities such as ranking drew on indigenous counting practices.

6   Participatory Rural Appraisal (PRA) is a development planning approach promoted by many non-governmental organizations that enables poorer communities to reflect on their situations in order to initiate change. PRA draws on the philosophy and methods of Participatory Action Research (PAR), an approach directly influenced by Freire's work and widespread in South America (see Fals-Borda and Rahman 1991).

7   See Judith Castaneda-Mayo's section in this chapter ('The insider/outsider dilemmas in educational research – a Mexican experience') for a reflexive account of the dilemmas she faced when conducting fieldwork with her former colleagues.

8   This tension has been explored much in relation to PRA by PhD students who use participatory approaches within their thesis: see 'Participatory research: ideas on the use of participatory approaches by postgraduate students and others in formal learning and research institutes' (IDS Topic Pack 1997). However, PRA practitioners have the additional dilemma about the scope of their intended action as they work with a less clearly defined group of participants.

9   See Howida Mostafa's reflections on her cross-cultural learning ('The influence of culture on education in two different contexts') in Chapter 7.

10 This term, contributed by my colleague Rob Walker, helps to describe the 'mirage' followed by students like Al-Nasser in his thesis. My analysis here has

also drawn from Rob's conceptualization of students' learning and their shift from quantitative to qualitative approaches in terms of a movement from 'bureaucratic' to 'democratic' values, as well as from literacy-based to oral communicative practices (R. Walker, personal communication, 2004). However, I have avoided using 'bureaucratic' and 'democratic' as they tend to be value-laden terms in my own cultural context.

11 The term I would use in reference to those with autonomy (P) and lack control (p) in this context.

12 A Cantonese word that literally means 'bowing'; figuratively it means 'cannot go against someone of high status or position or someone with power or authority'.

13 Maintaining a person's dignity by not humiliating, ridiculing or mocking one, especially in front of others.

Chapter 4

1 See Scholastica Mokake's reflections on UEA ethical procedures in the context of her Tanzanian fieldwork in the last section of this chapter, 'There is more to learn behind the scene'.

2 I am using the terms 'North' and 'South' here to refer to the political and economic inequalities within the world, as a less value-laden alternative to 'first' versus 'third' world (or developed versus developing countries). In other parts of the book, I have adopted the terms used by the writers whose ideas I am drawing upon: for instance, 'Western' (from Tuhiwai Smith, Chapter 1) and, later in Chapters 6 and 7, 'centre'/'periphery' (from Canagarajah).

3 The questions that follow are extracted from Warwick's and Lewin's discussions.

4 Participatory Learning and Action (PLA) was proposed in the 1990s as a more appropriate term to describe these visual research activities than 'PRA' (Participatory Rural Appraisal). But development workers in the South were reluctant to change the name as the term 'PRA' carried the weight of a social movement in many rural contexts.

5 I am not trying to essentialize here about what constitutes a 'UK' or 'Malaysian' approach to research ethics, but use the terms as shorthand to refer to the differing ethical guidelines I have described above. There are, of course, many other approaches to research ethics in both Malaysia and the UK.

6 I am grateful to Terry Phillips for indirectly providing me with much of this background on the history of our research ethics committee, through his briefing seminars and his 'mentoring' role as Chair of the Research Ethics Committee. Terry also read and commented on this chapter shortly before his death on 26 October 2004.

7 A recent opinion column in the UK press headed 'Getting permission for social research is now a nightmare' described the paperwork involved in a health research project – the standardized form for seeking ethical approval 'runs to 68 pages, has 174 separate fields to complete, requires up to eight signatures of authorisation and . . . can take more than 44 hours to complete' (Brindle, *The Guardian*, 5/01/05, p. 5).

Chapter 5

1   See Huda Al-Yousef's account at the end of this chapter ('Translation experience'), describing the issues she encountered when translating young women's discussion from Arabic into English.

2   This could also be related to the more general dilemma about how much 'evidence' to include with a research text to prove that the analysis arose from the data collected. Many students attach their actual transcripts as an appendix and samples of their analysis of raw data.

3   I taped the discussion then I transcribed it.

4   'Old people aren't satisfied with a girl when she attends Medicine College. They start to ask how could she leave her house for long hours? How could she sleep at the hospital? How could she work with men at the same place?' (an example of a participant's reflection on gender separation in Saudi Arabia).

Chapter 6

1   This discussion could be extended further through considering the many 'Englishes' that students bring from their home context (see previous chapter on 'Malaysian' English).

Chapter 7

1   Non-English speaking background: the term used for 'international student' in Ryan and Zuber-Skerritt's (1999) book.

2   Post Graduate Certificate in Education: I observed the UK teacher-training course in modern foreign languages during my first year at UEA, as a comparison with the teacher education programme at my institute in Egypt.

References

Akeroyd, A.V. (1984) Ethics in relation to informants, the profession and governments, in R. Ellen (ed.), *Ethnographic Research: A Guide to General Conduct*. London: Academic Press.

Al-Nasser, S.A.S. (1999) The teaching of English as a foreign language in private elementary schools in Riyadh City, Saudi Arabia: a diagnostic study. PhD thesis, School of Education and Professional Development, University of East Anglia, Norwich.

Altbach, P.G. (2003) *The Decline of the Guru: The Academic Profession in Developing and Middle-income Countries*. New York: Palgrave Macmillan.

Al-Yaseen, W.S. (2000) Developing listening–speaking skills interactively in the primary foreign language classroom. Possibilities and hindrances: a case study in Kuwaiti primary schools. PhD thesis, Centre for Applied Research in Education, School of Education and Professional Development, University of East Anglia, Norwich.

Andrews, R. (2003) *Research Questions*. London: Continuum.

Aspland, T. (1999) 'You learn round and I learn square': Mei's story, in Y. Ryan and O. Zuber-Skerritt (eds.), *Supervising Postgraduates from Non-English Speaking Backgrounds*. Buckingham: SRHE/Open University Press

Ballard, B. and Clanchy, J. (1984) *Study Abroad: A Manual for Asian Students*, 2nd edn. Kuala Lumpur: Longman.

Ballard, B. and Clanchy, J. (1988) Literacy in the university: an 'anthropological' approach, in G. Taylor (ed.) *Literacy by Degrees*. Milton Keynes: SRHE/Open University Press.

Ballard, B. and Clanchy, J. (1997) *Teaching International Students: A Brief Guide for Lecturers and Supervisors*. Burwood, VIC: IDP Education Australia.

Barker, J. (1997) The purpose of study, attitudes to study and staff–student relationships, in D. McNamara and R. Harris (eds.), *Overseas Students in Higher Education: Issues in Teaching and Learning*. London: Routledge.

Barnett, R. (1997) *Higher Education: A Critical Business*. Buckingham: SRHE/Open University Press.

Barrett, R.J. (1999) The writing–talking cure: an ethnography of record-speech events in a psychiatric hospital, in C.N. Candlin and K. Hyland (eds.), *Writing: Texts, Processes and Practices*. Harlow: Addison Wesley Longman.

Barton, D. (1994) *Literacy: An Introduction to the Ecology of Written Language*. Oxford: Blackwell.

Baynham, M. (2000) Academic writing in new and emergent discipline areas, in M.R. Lea and B. Stierer (eds.), *Student Writing in Higher Education: New Contexts*. Buckingham: SRHE/Open University Press.

Bhabha, H.K. (1990) Introduction: narrating the nation, in H.K. Bhabha, *Nation and Narration*. London: Routledge.

Bhabha, H.K. (1994) *The Location of Culture*. London: Routledge.

Bhatia, V.K. (1999) Integrating products, processes, purposes and participants in professional writing, in C.N. Candlin and K. Hyland (eds.), *Writing: Texts, Processes and Practices*. Harlow: Addison Wesley Longman.

Biggs, J. (2003) *Teaching for Quality Learning at University*, 2nd edn. Buckingham: SRHE/Open University Press.

Bowles, S. (1977) Unequal education and the reproduction of the social division of labour, in J. Karabel and A.H. Halsey (eds.), *Power and Ideology in Education*. New York: Oxford University Press.

Bridges, D. (2003) *Fiction Under Oath? Essays in Philosophy and Educational Research*. Amsterdam: Kluwer Academic.

Cadman, K. (1994) Constructing a thesis: a question of identity? Quality in Post-graduate Research: Making it Happen Conference, 7–8 April, University of Adelaide, SA, Australia (available at: www.canberra.edu.au/QPR).

Cadman, K. (2000) 'Voices in the air': evaluations of the learning experiences of international postgraduates and their supervisors, *Teaching in Higher Education*, 5(4): 475–492.

Cadman, K. (2004) On not naming plagiarism: rethinking possibilities for writing practices among research students, supervisors and examiners. Report of Symposium on Research Writing or How did you write your thesis, what writing support did you get and who said you plagiarised?: Quality in Postgraduate Research 2004 (available at: www.canberra.edu.au/QPR2004).

Canagarajah, A.S. (2002) *A Geopolitics of Academic Writing*. Pittsburgh, PA: University of Pittsburgh Press.

Candlin, C.N. and Hyland, K. (eds.) (1999) *Writing: Texts, Processes and Practices*. Applied Linguistics and Language Study. Harlow: Addison Wesley Longman.

Candlin, C.N. and Plum, G.A. (1999) Engaging with challenges of interdiscursivity in academic writing: researchers, students and tutors, in C.N. Candlin and K. Hyland (eds.), *Writing: Texts, Processes and Practices*. Harlow: Addison Wesley Longman.

CARE (1994) *Coming to Terms with Research: An Introduction to the Language for Research Degree Students*. Norwich: Centre for Applied Research in Education, School of Education and Professional Development, University of East Anglia.

Chambers, R. (1997) *Whose Reality Counts? Putting the Last First*. London: Intermediate Technology Publications.

Chambers, R. (1998) Foreword, in J. Holland and J. Blackburn, *Whose Voice? Participatory Research and Policy Change*. London: Intermediate Technology Publications.

Chan, D. and Drover, G. (1997) Teaching and learning for overseas students: the

Hong Kong connection, in D. McNamara and R. Harris (eds.), *Overseas Students in Higher Education: Issues in Teaching and Learning*. London: Routledge.

Chang, Y. and Swales, J. (1999) Informal elements in English academic writing: threats or opportunities for advanced non-native speakers?, in C.N. Candlin and K. Hyland (eds.), *Writing: Texts, Processes and Practices*. Harlow: Addison Wesley Longman.

Clark, R. (1992) Principles and practice in the CLA classroom, in N. Fairclough (ed.), *Critical Language Awareness*. New York: Longman.

Connor, U. (1996) *Contrastive Rhetoric: Cross-cultural Aspects of Second-language Writing*. Cambridge: Cambridge University Press.

Cortazzi, M. and Jin, L. (1997) Communication for learning across cultures, in D. McNamara and R. Harris (eds.), *Overseas Students in Higher Education: Issues in Teaching and Learning*. London: Routledge.

Cosh, J. (2000) Supporting the learning of international students in large group teaching, in G. Wisker (ed.), *Good Practice Working with International Students*. Birmingham: Staff and Educational Development Association.

Crème, P. (2000) The 'personal' in university writing: uses of reflective learning journals, in M.R. Lea and B. Stierer (eds.), *Student Writing in Higher Education*. Buckingham: SRHE/Open University Press.

Crossley, M. and Vulliamy, G. (eds.) (1997) *Qualitative Educational Research in Developing Countries: Current Perspectives*. London: Garland.

Crossley, M. and Watson, K. (2003) *Comparative and International Research in Education*. London: Routledge Falmer.

Crystal, D. (1987) *The Cambridge Encyclopaedia of Language*. Cambridge: Cambridge University Press.

Crystal, D. (1997) *English as a Global Language*. Cambridge: Cambridge University Press.

Denicolo, P. and Pope, M. (1999) Supervision and the overseas student, in Y. Ryan and O. Zuber-Skerritt (eds.), *Supervising Postgraduates from Non-English Speaking Backgrounds*. Buckingham: SRHE/Open University Press.

Devereux, S. and Hoddinott, J. (1992a) The context of fieldwork, in S. Devereux and J. Hoddinott (eds.), *Fieldwork in Developing Countries*. Hemel Hempstead: Harvester Wheatsheaf.

Devereux, S. and Hoddinott, J. (eds.) (1992b) *Fieldwork in Developing Countries*. Hemel Hempstead: Harvester Wheatsheaf.

Dore, R. (1976) *The Diploma Disease*. London: George Allen & Unwin.

Dudley-Evans, A. and Swales, J. (1980) Study modes and students from the Middle East, in British Council (ed.), *Study Modes and Academic Development of Overseas Students*. London: British Council.

Ellen, R. (1984) *Ethnographic Research: A Guide to General Conduct*. London: Academic Press.

Elliott, J. (1978) What is action research in schools?, *Journal of Curriculum Studies*, 10(4): 355–357.

Elliott, J. (1983) A curriculum for the study of human affairs: the contribution of Lawrence Stenhouse, *Journal of Curriculum Studies*, 15(2): 105–123.

Elliott, J., Lam, J., Rau, G. *et al.* (2004) Doing applied educational research for a PhD: a conversation between a group of doctoral students and their supervisor, Paper presented at ECER, September.

Elsey, B. (1990) Teaching and learning, in M. Kinnell (ed.), *The Learning Experiences of Overseas Students*. Buckingham: SRHE/Open University Press.

Elsey, B. and Kinnell, M. (1990) Introduction, in M. Kinnell (ed.), *The Learning Experiences of Overseas Students*. Buckingham: SRHE/Open University Press.

English, F. (1999) What do students really say in their essays? Towards a descriptive framework for analysing student writing, in C. Jones, J. Turner and B.V. Street (eds.), *Students Writing in the University: Cultural and Epistemological Issues*. Amsterdam: John Benjamins.

Escobar, A. (1995) *Encountering Development: The Making and Unmaking of the Third World*. Princeton, NJ: Princeton University Press.

Evans, T. (2000) Post(al) colonialism and liberation methodology: international off-campus postgraduate research in education, in G. Wisker (ed.), *Good Practice Working with International Students*. Birmingham: Staff and Educational Development Association.

Fals-Borda, O. and Rahman, M.A. (eds.) (1991) *Action and Knowledge: Recent Views of Participatory Action-research*. New York: Apex/New Horizons Press.

Firth, R. (1966) *Housekeeping Among Malay Peasants*. London: Athlone Press.

Flowerdew, J. and Peacock, M. (2001) *Research Perspectives on English for Academic Purposes*. Cambridge: Cambridge University Press.

Foddy, W. (1993) *Constructing Questions for Interviews and Questionnaire Survey: Theory and Practice in Social Research*. Cambridge: Cambridge University Press.

Geake, J. and Maingard, C. (1999) NESB postgraduate students at a new university: plus ca change, plus c'est la meme chose, in Y. Ryan and O. Zuber-Skerritt (eds.), *Supervising Postgraduates from Non-English Speaking Backgrounds*. Buckingham: SRHE/Open University Press.

Gee, J. (1990) *Social Linguistics and Literacies: Ideology in Discourses*. London: Taylor & Francis.

Gil-Anton, M. (2003) Big city love: the academic workplace in Mexico, in P. Albach (ed.), *The Decline of the Guru. The Academic Profession in Developing and Middle-income Countries*. New York: Palgrave Macmillan.

Glaser, B. and Strauss, A. (1967) *The Discovery of Grounded Theory*. Chicago, IL: Aldine.

Goody, J. (1968) *Literacy in Traditional Societies*. Cambridge: Cambridge University Press.

Goody, J. (1977) *The Domestication of the Savage Mind*. Cambridge: Cambridge University Press.

Hale, S. and Campbell, S. (2002) The interaction between text difficulty and translation accuracy, *Federation Internationale des Traducteurs (FIT) Revue Babel Arab Translators' Babel*, 48(1): 14–33.

Hassan, Z. (2003) *PE Teacher Education in Malaysia: A Case Study*. Norwich: Centre for Applied Research in Education, School of Education and Professional Development, University of East Anglia.

Hawkey, R. and Nakornchai, C. (1980) Thai students studying, in British Council (ed.), *109-Study Modes and Academic Development for Overseas Students*. London: British Council.

Hoadley-Maidment, E. (2000) From personal experience to reflective practitioner: academic literacies and professional education, in M.R. Lea and B. Stierer (eds.),

Student Writing in Higher Education: New Contexts. Buckingham: SRHE/Open University Press.

Hyland, K. (1999) Disciplinary discourses: writer stance in research articles, in C.N. Candlin and K. Hyland (eds.), *Writing: Texts, Processes and Practices.* Harlow: Addison Wesley Longman.

IDS (1997) Participatory research: ideas on the use of participatory approaches by postgraduate students and others in formal learning and research institutes. IDS Sussex: IDS PRA Topic Pack (available from participation@ids.ac.uk).

Ivanic, R. and Weldon, S. (1999) Researching the writer–reader relationship, in C.N. Candlin and K. Hyland (eds.), *Writing: Texts, Processes and Practices.* Harlow: Addison Wesley Longman.

Ivanic, R., Clark, R. and Rimmershaw, R. (2000) What am I supposed to make of this? The messages conveyed to students by tutors' written comments, in M.R. Lea and B. Stierer (eds.), *Student Writing in Higher Education: New Contexts.* Buckingham: SRHE/Open University Press.

Jabr, A. (2002) Arab translators' problems at the discourse level, *Federation Internationale des Traducteurs (FIT) Revue Babel Arab Translators' Babel,* 47(4): 304–322.

James, K. (1980) Seminar overview, in British Council (ed.), *109-Study Modes and Academic Development of Overseas Students.* London: British Council.

Jones, C., Turner, J. and Street, B.V. (eds.) (1999) Introduction, in C. Jones, J. Turner and B.V. Street (eds.), *Students Writing in the University: Cultural and Epistemological Issues.* Amsterdam: John Benjamins.

Kaplan, R.B. (1966) Cultural thought patterns in intercultural education, *Language Learning,* 16: 1–20.

Kember, D. (1996) The intention to both memorise and understand: another approach to learning, *Higher Education,* 31: 341–354.

Kemmis, S. (1981) Action research in retrospect and prospect, in C. Henry and R. McTaggart (eds.), *The Action Research Reader.* Burwood, VIC: Deakin University Press.

Kiley, M. (2000) Providing timely and appropriate support for international postgraduate students, in G. Wisker (ed.), *Good Practice Working with International Students.* Birmingham: Staff and Educational Development Association.

Kirby, P. (2001) Participatory research in schools, *Forum,* 43(2): 74–77.

Knight, N. (1999) Responsibilities and limits in the supervision of NESB research students in the social sciences and humanities, in Y. Ryan and O. Zuber-Skerritt (eds.), *Supervising Postgraduates from Non-English Speaking Backgrounds.* Buckingham: SRHE/Open University Press.

Korten, D. (1980) Community organisation and rural development, *Public Administration Review,* 40(5): 480–511.

Kroll, B. (1990) *Second Language Writing: Research Insights for the Classroom.* Cambridge: Cambridge University Press.

Kuhn, A. and Wolpe, A.M. (1978) *Feminism and Materialism: Women and Modes of Production.* London: Routledge Kegan Paul.

Kumar, S. (1996) *ABC of PRA: A South–South Workshop Report.* Bangalore: ActionAid India/SPEECH.

Lather, P. (1994) Textuality as praxis. Paper presented to the *Annual Meeting of the American Educational Research Association,* New Orleans, April.

Lave, J. and Wenger, E. (1991) *Situated Learning: Legitimate Peripheral Participation.* Cambridge: Cambridge University Press.

Lea, M.R. and Stierer, B. (eds.) (2000) *Student Writing in Higher Education: New Contexts.* Buckingham: SRHE/Open University Press.

Lea, M.R. and Street, B.V. (1999) Writing as academic literacies: understanding textual practices in higher education, in C.N. Candlin and K. Hyland (eds.), *Writing: Texts, Processes and Practices.* Harlow: Addison Wesley Longman.

Lea, M.R. and Street, B.V. (2000) Student writing and staff feedback in higher education: an academic literacies approach, in M.R. Lea and B. Stierer (eds.), *Student Writing in Higher Education: New Contexts.* Buckingham: SRHE/Open University Press.

Leach, F.E. and Little, A.W. (eds.) (1999) *Education, Cultures and Economics: Dilemmas for Development.* London: Falmer Press.

Lebar, O. (1995) *Evaluating Initial Teacher Education in Malaysia: A Case Study.* Norwich: Centre for Applied Research in Education, School of Education and Professional Development, University of East Anglia.

Lewin, K. (1990a) Beyond the fieldwork: reflections on research in Malaysia and Sri Lanka, in G. Vulliamy, K. Lewin and D. Stephens (eds.), *Doing Educational Research in Developing Countries: Qualitative Strategies.* Basingstoke: Falmer Press.

Lewin, K. (1990b) Data collection and analysis in Malaysia and Sri Lanka, in G. Vulliamy, K. Lewin and D. Stephens (eds.), *Doing Educational Research in Developing Countries: Qualitative Strategies.* Basingstoke: Falmer Press.

Lie, K.Y. (2004) Multicultural meaning makers: Malaysian ways with words and the world, in P. Kell, S. Shore and M. Singh (eds.), *Adult Education @ 21st. Century.* New York: Peter Lang.

Low, G. and Woodburn, L. (1999) On not disturbing 'our group peace': the plight of the visiting researcher, in C. Jones, J. Turner and B.V. Street (eds.), *Students Writing in the University: Cultural and Epistemological Issues.* Amsterdam: John Benjamins.

MacLure, M. (1993) Mundane autobiography: some thoughts on self-talk in research contexts, *British Journal of Sociology of Education,* 14(4): 373–384.

MacLure, M. (2003) *Discourse in Educational and Social Research.* Maidenhead: Open University Press.

Magyar, A. (1996) Deconstructing the boundaries of culture: studies in a French and English rural primary school. PhD thesis, Centre for Applied Research in Education, School of Education and Lifelong Learning, University of East Anglia, Norwich.

Malaysian Government (1999) *General Circular No. 3 Year 1999: Regulations for the Conduct of Research in Malaysia.* Kuala Lumpur: Malaysian Government.

Marton, F., Dall'Alba, G. and Tse, L.K. (1993) *The Paradox of the Chinese Learner,* Occasional Paper 93.1. Melbourne, VIC: Educational Research and Development Unit, Royal Melbourne Institute of Technology.

Mason, J. (2002) *Qualitative Researching.* London: Sage.

May, S. (2001) *Language and Minority Rights.* Harlow: Pearson Education.

McNamara, D. and Harris, R. (eds.) (1997) *Overseas Students in Higher Education: Issues in Teaching and Learning.* London: Routledge.

Miles, M. and Hiberman, A. (1994) *Qualitative Data Analysis*. Thousand Oaks, CA: Sage.

Moodie, J. (1995) The development of a critical voice in the writing of international postgraduate students, in *Changing Identities*. Clayton, VIC: Monash University Press.

Nagata, Y. (1999) 'Once I couldn't even spell "PhD student", but now I *are* one!' Personal experiences of an NESB student, in Y. Ryan and O. Zuber-Skerritt (eds.), *Supervising Postgraduates from Non-English Speaking Backgrounds*. Buckingham: SRHE/Open University Press.

Nair-Venugopal, S. (2004) Adult educators' talk: responding to the challenges of linguistic normativity, in P. Kell, S. Shore and M. Singh (eds.), *Adult Education @ 21st. Century*. New York: Peter Lang.

Pardoe, S. (2000) A question of attribution: the indeterminacy of 'learning from experience', in M.R. Lea and B. Stierer (eds.), *Student Writing in Higher Education: New Contexts*. Buckingham: SRHE/Open University Press.

Paz, O. (1961) *The Labyrinth of Solitude* (translated from Spanish by L. Kemp, Y. Milos and B. Phillips). New York: Grove Press.

Pillay, H.D. (1995) Fragments of a vision: a case study of the implementation of an English language curriculum programme in five Malaysian secondary schools. PhD thesis, Centre for Applied Research in Education, School of Education and Professional Development, University of East Anglia, Norwich.

Puteh, M. (1998) Factors associated with mathematics anxiety and its impact on primary teacher trainees in Malaysia. PhD thesis, Centre for Applied Research in Education, School of Education and Professional Development, University of East Anglia, Norwich.

Rabinow, P. (1977) *Reflections on Fieldwork in Morocco*. Berkley, CA: University of California Press.

Razavi, S. (1992) Fieldwork in a familiar setting: the role of politics at the national, community and household levels, in S. Devereux and J. Hoddinott (eds.), *Fieldwork in Developing Countries*. Hemel Hempstead: Harvester Wheatsheaf.

Reynolds, M. and Trehan, K. (2001) Classroom as real world: propositions for a pedagogy of difference, *Gender and Education*, 13(4): 357–372.

Robinson-Pant, A. (1996) PRA: a new literacy?, *Journal of International Development*, 8(4): 531–551.

Robinson-Pant, A. (2001a) Development as discourse: what relevance to education?, *Compare*, 31(3): 311–328.

Robinson-Pant, A. (2001b) Women's literacy and health: can an ethnographic researcher find the links?, in B.V. Street (ed.), *Literacy and Development: Ethnographic Perspectives*. London Routledge.

Ryan, J. (2000) *A Guide to Teaching International Students*. Oxford: Oxford Centre for Staff and Learning Development, Oxford Brookes University.

Ryan, Y. and Zuber-Skerritt, O. (eds.) (1999) *Supervising Postgraduates from Non-English Speaking Backgrounds*. Buckingham: SRHE/Open University Press.

Sadeghi, K. (2003) An investigation of cloze procedure as a measure of EFL reading comprehension with reference to educational context in Iran. PhD thesis, Centre for Applied Research in Education, School of Education and Professional Development, University of East Anglia, Norwich.

Sandeman-Gay, E. (1999) Supervising Iranian students: a case study, in Y. Ryan and O. Zuber-Skerritt (eds.), *Supervising Postgraduates from Non-English Speaking Backgrounds*. Buckingham: SRHE/Open University Press.

Sanjek, R. (1990) *Fieldnotes: The Makings of Anthropology*. New York: Cornell University Press.

Saraireh, M. (2002) Inconsistency in technical terminology: a problem for standardisation in Arabic, *Federation Internationale des Traducteurs (FIT) Revue Babel Arab Translators' Babel*, 47(1): 10–21.

Scott, M. (1999) Agency and subjectivity in student writing, in C. Jones, J. Turner and B.V. Street (eds.), *Student Writing in the University: Cultural and Epistemological Issues*. Amsterdam: John Benjamins.

Shore, S. (2004) Reflexive theory building 'after' colonialism: challenges for adult education, in P. Kell, S. Shore and M. Singh (eds.), *Adult Education @ 21st. Century*. New York: Peter Lang.

Sillitoe, J. and Crosling, G. (1999) Thesis planning and writing: a structured approach, in Y. Ryan and O. Zuber-Skerritt (eds.), *Supervising Postgraduates from Non-English Speaking Backgrounds*. Buckingham: SRHE/Open University Press.

Smith, D. (1999) Supervising NESB students from Confucian educational cultures, in Y. Ryan and O. Zuber-Skerritt (eds.), *Supervising Postgraduates from Non-English Speaking Backgrounds*. Buckingham: SRHE/Open University Press.

Stierer, B. (2000) Schoolteachers as students: academic literacy and the construction of professional knowledge within Master's courses in education, in M.R. Lea and B. Stierer (eds.), *Student Writing in Higher Education: New Contexts*. Buckingham: SRHE/Open University Press.

Street, B.V. (1984) *Literacy in Theory and Practice*. Cambridge: Cambridge University Press.

Street, B.V. (1993) *Cross-cultural Approaches to Literacy*. Cambridge: Cambridge University Press.

Street, B.V. (1999a) Meanings of culture in development: a case study from literacy, in F.E. Leach and A.W. Little (eds.), *Education, Cultures and Economics: Dilemmas for Development*. London: Falmer Press.

Street, B.V. (1999b) Academic literacies, in C. Jones, J. Turner and B.V. Street (eds.), *Students Writing in the University: Cultural and Epistemological Issues*. Amsterdam: John Benjamins.

Swales, J. (1990) *Genre Analysis: English in Academic and Research Settings*. Cambridge: Cambridge University Press.

Tan, K.S. (1989) The uses of television in primary schools: case studies in Malaysia and England. PhD thesis, Centre for Applied Research in Education, School of Education and Professional Development, University of East Anglia, Norwich.

Teasdale, J.I. and Teasdale, G.R. (1999) Alternative cultures of knowledge in higher education in the Australian-Pacific region, in F.E. Leach and A.W. Little (eds.), *Education, Cultures and Economics: Dilemmas for Development*. London: Falmer Press.

Terrell, I. and Brown, S. (2000) A practical guide to delivering higher education programmes to overseas students: ten things I should have known before I started, in G. Wisker (ed.), *Good Practice Working with International Students*. Birmingham: Staff and Educational Development Association.

Tickle, L. (2001) Opening windows, closing doors: ethical dilemmas in educational action research, *Journal of Philosophy of Education*, 35(3): 345–359.

Tikly, L. (1999) Postcolonialism and comparative education, International Review of Education, 45(5/6): 603–621.

Todd, E.S. (1997) Supervising overseas students: problem or opportunity?, in D. McNamara and R. Harris (eds.), *Overseas Students in Higher Education: Issues in Teaching and Learning*. London: Routledge.

Trahar, S. (2003) Conversations across cultures: the impact of multiculturalism on postgraduate teaching and learning practices in the higher education learning environment. Paper presented to the *7th Oxford International Conference on Education and Development*, Oxford.

Tsai, C.T. (1996) Approaches to curriculum development: case studies of innovation in the social studies curriculum in the UK and Taiwan. PhD thesis, Centre for Applied Research in Education, School of Education and Professional Development, University of East Anglia, Norwich.

Tsegay, T.S. (2001) Needs analysis and course design for adult civil servants: a case study of English for Legal Purposes at the Ethiopian Civil Service College. Unpublished seminar paper, Centre for Applied Research in Education, School of Education and Professional Development, University of East Anglia, Norwich.

Tsegay, T.S. (2002) A report on the methodological implications of a fieldwork process. Unpublished seminar paper, Centre for Applied Research in Education, School of Education and Professional Development, University of East Anglia, Norwich.

Tuhiwai Smith, L. (1999) *Decolonizing Methodologies. Research and Indigenous Peoples*. London/Dunedin: Zed Books/University of Otago Press.

Turner, J. (1999) Academic literacy and the discourse of transparency, in C. Jones, J. Turner and B.V. Street (eds.), *Students Writing in the University: Cultural and Epistemological Issues*. Amsterdam: John Benjamins.

UEA (2003) *Research Ethics Pack*. Norwich: School of Education and Professional Development, University of East Anglia.

Vulliamy, G. (1990) The conduct of case-study research in schools in Papua New Guinea, in G. Vulliamy, K. Lewin and D. Stephens (eds.), *Doing Educational Research in Developing Countries*. Basingstoke: Falmer Press.

Vulliamy, G. (2004) The impact of globalisation on qualitative research in comparative and international education, *Compare*, 34(3): 261–284.

Vulliamy, G., Lewin, K. and Stephens, D. (eds.) (1990) *Doing Educational Research in Developing Countries: Qualitative Strategies*. Basingstoke: Falmer Press.

Walker, R. (1980) The conduct of educational case studies, in W.B. Dockrell and D. Hamilton (eds.), *Rethinking Educational Research*. London: Hodder & Stoughton.

Walker, R. (2003) Unpublished briefing paper, April. Centre for Applied Research in Education, School of Education and Professional Development, University of East Anglia, Norwich.

Warwick, D.P. (1983) The politics and ethics of field research, in M. Bulmer and D.P. Warwick (eds.), *Social Research in Developing Countries*. London: Wiley.

Watt, J.C. (1980) Performance of overseas postgraduate students: a management teacher's view, in British Council (ed.), *109-Study Modes and Academic Development of Overseas Students*. London: British Council.

Wenger, E. (1998) *Communities of Practice: Learning, Meaning and Identity*. Cambridge: Cambridge University Press.

Wen-li, K. (2002) How can semantic work to help translation, *Federation Interna-tionale des Traducteurs (FIT) Revue Babel Arab Translators' Babel*, 47(2): 158–174.

Whorf, B.L. (1956) *Language, Thought and Reality*. Cambridge, MA: MIT Press.

Wilson, K. (1992) Thinking about the ethics of fieldwork, in S. Devereux and J. Hoddinott (eds.), *Fieldwork in Developing Countries*. Hemel Hemstead: Harvester Wheatsheaf.

Wisker, G. (ed.) (2000) *Good Practice Working with International Students*. Birming-ham: Staff and Educational Development Association.

Wisker, G. and Sutcliffe, N. (eds.) (1999) *Good Practice in Postgraduate Supervision*. SEDA Paper 106. Birmingham: Staff and Educational Development Association.

Index